The Economics of
Child Labour in the
Era of Globalization

Policy issues

Sarbajit Chaudhuri
and Jayanta Kumar Dwibedi

Routledge
Taylor & Francis Group

LONDON AND NEW YORK

First published 2017 by Routledge

2 Park Square, Milton Park, Abingdon, Oxfordshire OX14 4RN
52 Vanderbilt Avenue, New York, NY 10017

Routledge is an imprint of the Taylor & Francis Group, an informa business

First issued in paperback 2019

British Library Cataloguing in Publication Data
A catalogue record for this book is available from the British Library

Library of Congress Cataloging-in-Publication Data
Names: Chaudhuri, Sarbajit, 1965– author. | Dwibedi, Jayanta
  Kumar, author.
Title: The economics of child labour in the era of globalization :
  policy issues / by Sarbajit Chaudhuri and Jayanta Kumar Dwibedi.
Description: First Edition. | New York : Routledge, 2017. | Series:
  Routledge studies in development economics ; 131 | Includes
  bibliographical references and index.
Identifiers: LCCN 2016025042 | ISBN 9781138647855 (hardback) |
  ISBN 9781315397504 (ebook)
Subjects: LCSH: Child labor—History. | Child labor—Developing
  countries. | Fertility, Human—Economic aspects—Developing
  countries. | Developing countries—Economic policy. | Human
  capital—Developing countries.
Classification: LCC HD6231 .C443 2017 | DDC 331.3/
  1091724—dc23
LC record available at https://lccn.loc.gov/2016025042

ISBN: 978-1-138-64785-5 (hbk)
ISBN: 978-0-367-37465-5 (pbk)

Typeset in Galliard
by Apex CoVantage, LLC

The Economics of Child Labour in the Era of Globalization

Children in poor countries are subjected to exploitation characterized by low wages and long hours of work, as well as by unclean, unhygienic and unsafe working and living conditions, and, more importantly, by deprivation from education, all of which hampers their physical and mental development. Child labour is a complex issue, and clearly it has no simple solution. This book sheds some understanding of its root causes.

The book attempts to delve into many of the important theoretical aspects of child labour and suggests policies that could indeed be useful in dealing with the problem under diverse situations using alternative multisector general equilibrium models.

Sarbajit Chaudhuri is Professor with the Department of Economics, University of Calcutta, Kolkata, India. He received his PhD in 1995 from the Jadavpur University, Kolkata, working under the supervision of Professor Manash Ranjan Gupta. He has published more than 75 research papers in journals of international repute, such as *Journal of Development Economics, Economica, International Review of Economics and Finance, Metroeconomica, Review of International Economics, Review of Development Economics, Economic Modelling, Research in Economics, Japan and the World Economy, Pacific Economic Review, The Japanese Economic Review, The Manchester School, Bulletin of Economic Research, Journal of International Trade and Economic Development, Review of Urban and Regional Development Studie*s and *The Economics of Transition*, among others.

He has also authored books titled *Foreign Direct Investment in Developing Countries: A Theoretical Evaluation* (2014), *Revisiting the Informal Sector: A General Equilibrium Approach* (2010) and *Some Aspects of Agricultural Credit in a Developing Economy* (2004). He has served on the editorial boards of many journals. For his work, he was made an honorary member of the Canadian Economic Association in 2006. His areas of interest include development economics, international trade, labour economics, agricultural economics and applied microeconomics.

Jayanta Kumar Dwibedi is Associate Professor of Economics at Brahmananda Keshab Chandra College, Kolkata, India. He obtained his PhD from the University of Calcutta, India, in 2008, working under the supervision of Professor Sarbajit Chaudhuri. With his specialization in trade and development and labour economics, he has published a number of research articles in many renowned international and national journals such as *International Review of Economics and Finance, The Manchester School, Bulletin of Economic Research, Research in Economics, Review of Development Economics* and *Economic and Political Weekly*. His current research interests include development economics, labour economics and issues related to public finance and public policy. Recently, he has completed two collaborative studies (with CTRPFP, CSSSC) for the Central Finance Commission, India, and the State Finance Commission of West Bengal, India.

Routledge Studies in Development Economics

For a complete list of titles in this series, please visit www.routledge.com/series/SE0266.

This book is dedicated to our mentors

Professors Sugata Marjit, Manash Ranjan Gupta and Sajal Lahiri

Contents

Foreword

Although the incidence of child labour has been going down, it still remains a dominant reason why poor families on the whole continue to remain poor through generations. The intergenerational persistence of poverty – which many empirical studies on child labour have found – is possibly due to the fact that children from poor families do not accumulate vital human capital by working and not going to schools. Furthermore, although in India the overall incidence of child labour is about 10 per cent, if one restricts to poor families alone, the percentage of children in nearly full-time employment – often hazardous employment – is significantly higher.

Even forgetting about the ethical issues, the main economic reasons for arguing for the elimination of child labour is the fact that, by working, most of those children are being denied schooling, and this stops them from breaking down the vicious cycle of poverty, high fertility, poor health and low human capital.

The issues facing policy makers in the emerging countries in this respect have been analyzed in this book by two prominent and prolific economists in a rather unified theoretical framework. The authors of the present book have been working and publishing on policy-oriented theoretical work on the economics of child labour, and in this book they have weaved their existing and some new works in a systematic fashion.

The empirical literature on child labour is really vast, and household micro data sets from almost all corners of the world have been analyzed extensively, testing numerous hypotheses on the cause and remedy of this unfortunate phenomenon. Surprisingly, the theoretical literature is relatively sparse. Thus, this book is a very welcome addition to the literature. Furthermore, theoretical analysis of the problem in general equilibrium frameworks is even rarer. Given the magnitude of the problem, any serious policy initiative has to be taken on a large scale, influencing almost every market in the economy and affecting prices, wages and other conditions. Because of these consequences, often a very well intended policy initiative has counterintuitive consequences, as the present book shows again and again. Thus, a general equilibrium analysis of the problem in the present book is very welcome indeed.

In order to set up meaningful and appropriate theoretical models, the first step has to be an attempt to understand why poor families send their children to work and not to schools. That is, a proper analysis of the determinants of the supply of child labour has to be the starting point, and this is precisely what the present book does very effectively. It does so after a very extensive initial chapter looking at the empirical situation from a historical perspective. It also discusses the empirical literature so that the theoretical analyses are properly informed by the empirical reality and not just theoretical finger exercises.

We learn a number of important points from the present book. For example, just relying on growth or even focusing on poverty reduction is not likely to solve the problem, even in the long run. For both the short run and the long run, interventions need to be made in many different areas: in the field of education, in the labour market, in the output market and so on. It is not only that poor families should be encouraged to send their kids to school by means of carrots and sticks; the education system itself needs reform to make returns on education worthwhile. However, the authors are also right to throw some caution to the wind. They show that using many policies simultaneously can sometimes yield conflicting outcomes in general equilibrium frameworks, dampening the aggregate effect.

Both authors are experts on two subdisciplines of economics, namely international trade and development economics. It is therefore not surprising that they put globalization at the heart of their analysis. Also, this brings to the forefront the role of the international community, which so far has taken a rather negative role. Perhaps encouraged by the protectionist forces in the developed countries, many segments of the population who consider the issue to be mainly one of ethics have resorted to informal trade sanctions in the form of boycott against sweatshop products. Attempts are being made to incorporate international labour standards in the WTO agreements. Sweatshops are often the worst form of child labour, which is completely unacceptable for ethical endeavour and economic reasons. Health hazards in such workplaces seriously damage the long-term health of those children, and every effort should be made to make such workplaces safer. However, is boycotting products produced in sweatshops the right policy? The authors argue that such policies can be counterproductive.

To summarize, Professor Sarbajit Chaudhuri and Professor Jayanta Kumar Dwibedi have written a policy-oriented theoretical book on a very important and topical subject. They examine the consequences of a large number of policy options individually and jointly. I appreciate this endeavour by the authors and wish the book the very best.

SajalLahiri
Vanvedeer Chair Professor of Economics
Southern Illinois University Carbondale

Preface

The problem of child labour is considered a slur on the fair face of the globalized world both on humanitarian and economic grounds. On the one hand, working at a very early age, often under hazardous work conditions instead of schooling, deprives the children probably of the most beautiful phase of their life that significantly retards their physical and mental development and prevents them from growing up as normal human beings. On the other, it affects their earnings opportunities in the future and adversely affects human capital formation and future growth prospects of the economy although it raises the present consumption of the poor families that supply child labour. On the contrary, it may be argued that nonhazardous child labour is not at least bad given the widespread unemployment problem in the developing economies, because working at a relatively early age leads to some on-the-job training that enhances a child worker's probability of getting a relatively decent job when he becomes adult in the future. It would be wise not to enter into such a theoretical debate because if we look around the developing world we find that different measures are being undertaken to eradicate child labour, suggesting that child labour is indeed bad.

Because child labour is a multi-dimensional problem, one cannot readily identify a single policy that can indeed mitigate the problem under all situations. Although several policy-oriented theoretical articles relating to child labour have been published in different journals, we do not come across a single book that comprehensively addresses most of the issues and dimensions of the problem in a simple theoretical and formal framework. This book makes an attempt to fill in this vacuum using a wide set of simple general equilibrium models that capture many of the salient features of the developing countries and to recommend a composite policy that is expected to be successful in tackling the problem under different situations.

The major part of the book is based on Chaudhuri's own and collaborative research with Dwibedi, carried out in Kolkata, India, prevailing over adverse circumstances arising out of both internal and external factors, and published in different international journals over the last decade and a half.[1,2] Throughout the book we have used the simple 'hat calculus' as developed and popularized by R.W. Jones in his two seminal articles, Jones (1965) and Jones (1971). We have not felt the necessity to discuss in detail on extensions of the simple two-sector general equilibrium models, inclusion of non-traded goods and factor market imperfections and the techniques of measuring social welfare in a small open economy because these are already available in Chaudhuri and Mukhopadyay (2014, Chapter 2). The contents of the book can indeed be a part of a course on labour economics at the postgraduate level in universities in the developing countries. Although the book is primarily targeted towards postgraduate students and researchers who are pursuing policy-based theoretical research on labour economics including child labour and trade and development, it is also aimed at suggesting the appropriate composite policy to policy makers in the developing nations for combating the problem of child labour in the society.

We wish to express our intellectual indebtedness to Professors Sugata Marjit, Manash Ranjan Gupta, Sajal Lahiri and Shigemi Yabuuchi. Our interactions with them either face-to-face or through email have helped us immensely in understanding the pros and cons of applications of the simple general equilibrium models to trade and development. We would also like to thank Professors Kausik Gupta, Saibal Kar, Krishnendu Ghosh Dastidar, Indrajit Ray and Dr. Biswajit Mandal for their continuous academic help over the last several years. Chaudhuri wishes to express his sincere gratitude to his teachers, Professors Ajit Choudhury and Asis Kumar Banerjee and his senior colleague Professor Sankar Kumar Bhaumik for their mental support and continuous encouragement to move forward despite adversities.

Finally, Chaudhuri wishes to thank his wife, Pampa and daughter, Salonkara for their continuous inspiration and help during the entire period of writing this book and helping him immensely at the stage correction of page proofs. He is grateful to his parents for their spiritual support. Dwibedi would like to thank his parents and his father-in-law for their blessings and encouragement. He also thanks his wife, Aishika for her continuous encouragement and support. Finally, from Dwibedi's part a word of thanks for his son, Bhramar, for being a productive diversion.

Sarbajit Chaudhuri
Jayanta Kumar Dwibedi
Kolkata, India
September 17, 2016

Notes

1 An extremely unfortunate internal challenge that the young scholars face is the restriction at entry point in many of the universities and research institutes. Despite having a commendable list of publications in highly internationally reputed journals, one often finds it extremely difficult, if not impossible, to get absorbed in such a place only on merit although, in a society with rampant corruption and nepotism, it is not completely unexpected. Even if one clears the hurdle luckily, in many cases, scholars do not find congenial environment to work peacefully due to stiff resistance from many of the other people simply because he/she wants not to resort to unproductive practices. A hapless researcher-cum-teacher often gets the impression that he/she is working in a corporate office, where one has to satisfy the boss, and carry out his/her orders. He/she is often heavily scolded by the boss even publicly because of his/her effort to swim against the tide. However, of late the situation is changing for the better at least in India, thanks to the recent policies adopted by the national

regulatory authority in academics. Although these policies do not talk about the quality of publications, the dedicated scholars having quality publications to their credit firmly believe this loophole in the rules would be taken care of in the near future and the other people would begin to understand that teaching is not their only duty to discharge at the university level.

2 Of all the challenges academic scholars face today, carrying out quality research and publishing papers in reputable international journals of big multinational publishing companies is an uphill task. For researchers in developing countries such as Chaudhuri and Dwibedi, the mandatory high submission fees required to do so do not make the situation any easier. Marjit and Kar (2011) have also talked about such academic hardships in their book *The Outsiders* ....

There should be equal opportunity for all scholars endeavouring to publish their scholarly work, regardless of where they reside, whether in a developed or a developing region. Scholarly work in its ideal state aims to fulfil the mandate of disseminating knowledge to a wide audience. Yet scholars at times encounter setbacks. Setbacks may come in the form of the subject matter being too specific to garner much interest, but these scholars never lose heart.

Hopefully, the dedication and passion of these scholars will one day be duly rewarded.

References

Chaudhuri, S. and Mukhopadhyay, U. (2014): *Foreign Direct Investment in Developing Countries: A Theoretical Evaluation*, Springer, New Delhi.

Jones, R.W. (1965): 'The structure of simple general equilibrium models', *Journal of Political Economy*, 73(5):57–572.

Jones, R.W. (1971): 'A three-factor model in theory, trade and history', In *Bhagwati, J et al (Eds), Trade, Balance of Payments and Growth*, North-Holland, Amsterdam, pp. 3–21.

Marjit, S. and Kar, S. (2011): *The Outsiders: Economic Reform and Informal Labour in a Developing Economy*, Oxford University Press, New Delhi.

1 A survey of literature on child labour

1.1 Introduction

Although the incidence of child labour worldwide has decreased over the last two decades or so, both in absolute and percentage terms, the use of children at work is still one of the most disconcerting problems in the transitional societies of the developing economies. Working children in these countries in general are subjected to a process of implacable exploitation characterized by low wages, long hours of work, unclean, unhygienic and unsafe working and living conditions and, more importantly, deprivation of education, all of which hamper their proper physical and mental development. Apart from its short-term ill effects on health and welfare, child labour impedes children's human capital accumulation and prevents them from becoming natural productive adults in the future. Low human capital formation adversely affects future economic development, which, in turn, reinforces the child labour problem itself. Trapped in a vicious circle of underdevelopment, child labour reproduces generations of less educated and less skilled workers.

In the last two and a half decades, the issue of children at work has increasingly attracted the attention of different social, national and international organizations throughout the world. Particularly after the initiation of globalization, the issue of child labour has assumed central importance in social policy discussions. Consequently, statutory provisions and efforts have been concerted towards its eradication and prevention. Unfortunately, despite all efforts and statutory provisions, child labour continues to be a problem of enormous dimension, especially in developing and low-income countries. A large number of studies conducted so far point out the extremely deplorable and inhuman exploitation of child labour in developing countries, including India. According to ILO (2012), 168 million children (in the 5 to 17 age group) worldwide are child labourers, accounting for almost 11 per cent of the child population. More than half of them, about 85 million children, were found in different hazardous activities. Some of them were caught in the worst forms of child labour, including slavery, trafficking, debt bondage and other forms of forced labour, forced recruitment for armed conflict, prostitution, pornography and other illicit activities. Though the incidence of child labour at an aggregate level shows a declining trend, the absolute size of the child labour force is still large enough to be a matter of serious concern.

1.2 Historical perspective

Though the awareness about and concern for working children has increased after the initiation of globalization, the problem itself is not new. It has been in existence from immemorial time. It had existed in earlier ages in agricultural societies, but during the Industrial Revolution of the eighteenth century in Great Britain, it was especially prominent and began to be opposed.[1,2] In the preindustrialization period, children primarily worked alongside their parents, learning to gather food, hunt, collect firewood, tend the cattle, cultivate crops, planting seeds, pulling weeds, picking the ripe crops and helping in the households. The incidence of child labour was significantly widespread, though the children did not work in factories at that time. Since the experience of working in farms, alongside their parents, is less harmful than working in factories, according to some researchers, child labour did not appear as an issue before industrialization. With industrialization, as more and more children were hired in factories and mines, the connotation of 'child labour' began to change. Children were forced to work long hours under hazardous conditions for minimal pay.[3] During this period, children aged 5 or more were seen working especially in the textile industry. Child labour also was found in coal mining, where children used to work long hours in dark, damp mines, carrying coal on their backs up to the surface. Social reformers began to condemn child labour because of its detrimental effect on the health and welfare of the children. There were, however, disagreements. Those who opposed the use of child labour criticized child employment for strict discipline, harsh punishment, unhealthy working conditions, low wages and inflexible work hours. On the other side, those who supported employment of children in factories argued that industry needed low wage labour, that the education provided by schools was ill-suited to the needs of the poor and that child labour relieved the state of caring for the poor. They further argued that the employment of children in these factories was beneficial to these child workers, their family and country and that the conditions were no worse than they had been on the household farms. Many factory owners also used the threat of international competition as an excuse for employing children in their factories. However, as the prevalence of child labour increased through the early nineteenth century, opposition also intensified. In fact, child labour was more prevalent in nineteenth-century industrial economies than it is in the present-day developing countries.[4] It was particularly extensive in the earliest industrialization period. It was not until the nineteenth century that government began to regulate the conditions of the employment of children and to restrict the age at which children could be employed. England, in 1802, passed the first child labour legislation, but it applied only to those children who had no parents and who were not enforced to work. Several Factory Acts, gradually strengthening inspection, shortening hours and raising ages at which children could work, followed the initial legislation. The three most important of them were (1) the Cotton Factories Regulation Act of 1819 (which set the minimum working age at 9 and maximum working hours at 12), (2) the Regulation of Child Labour Law of 1833 (which established paid inspectors to enforce the laws), and (3) the Ten Hours Bill of 1847 (which brought down the working hours to 10 for children and women).

With increasing prosperity in terms of the substantial increase in per-capita income and the introduction of a series of legislative interventions, today's developed world is rid of the problem of child labour. Nonetheless, whether growth of the economy was behind this or the legislative interventions acted effectively has yet remained a debatable question. Social historians believe that the transformation in social values, particularly the attitude towards children, was the most important factor behind the decline in child labour in these countries (Zelizer 1985). They argue that it was the rise of the family ideology of the father as the breadwinner and the mother as housewife that transformed children from valuable wage earners to emotionally priceless objects. Economic historians maintain that it was the rise in the standard of living that allowed parents to keep their children at home. Some of them also further held that families had started showing interest in education and began sending their children to school. Advances in technology and the use of new heavier and more complicated machinery, which required the strength of skilled adult males, also contributed to the decline in child labour in Great Britain and other industrialized countries. Some economic historians also laid emphasis on legislative interventions, particularly the implementation of compulsory education, as the most important contributing factor behind the decline in child labour in these developed countries.

The issue of which factor played the key role in eradicating the problem in developed nations is important because it is expected to play a crucial role in designing appropriate policies to fight against the menace prevailing in today's developing countries. Nardinelli (1990) and Cunningham and Viazzo (1996) have argued that compulsory education or a direct ban on child labour cannot be as effective as economic growth and that the right policy would be to wait for economic progress. Moehling (1998) has investigated the historical role of law in the decline of child labour in the United States during 1880 to 1910. Although her study points out that legislative intervention in terms of minimum age restriction had little impact on child employment in the U.S., the issue has so far remained inconclusive.

1.3 Data on child labour

Child labour reemerged as an issue of public concern during the last two decades with the increasing integration of the world economy. It has assumed central importance in social policy discussions and statutory provisions, and efforts have been intensified towards its avoidance and eradication. Child labour is a sensitive subject, and numbers on its magnitude play an important role in global policy making. Unfortunately, an accurate measure of working children is difficult to obtain because there is no single, clear-cut definition of child labour under international law.[5] Countries have not only different minimum age work restrictions but also varying regulations based on the type of labour. The ILO's Convention No. 138 (Minimum Age Convention, 1973) specifies 15 years as the minimum age for admission to any type of employment or work in normal circumstances.[6] Taking a clue from that, most of the empirical surveys usually classify children under 15 years of age, who work on a regular basis for which they are paid or that results in output destined for the market, as 'child labour'.

Clearly, household works performed at parental homes are not counted as child labour.[7] Even with this definition, it is difficult to estimate the extent of child labour correctly because there are problems related to official underreporting. Ashagrie (1998) commented, "It is common knowledge that data on child labour are extremely scarce. The reason for this is the absence of an appropriate survey methodology for probing into the work of children which, for the most part, is a 'hidden' phenomenon". Ashagrie (1993) made the first attempt to put together an international dataset on child labour. His estimates show that, in 1990, there were about 79 million working children worldwide and that 55 million of them were in Asia. Subsequently, experimental child labour surveys were carried out in selected urban and rural areas of Ghana, India, Indonesia and Senegal during 1992–1993, under the auspices of the ILO Interdepartmental (INTERDEP) Project and the International Programme on the Elimination of Child Labour (IPEC). Their primary objective was to collect and disseminate comprehensive and up-to-date statistics on working school-age children at the national, regional and global levels. Based on the findings of these experiments, as well as the results of national surveys carried out since then using the newly developed methodologies and also taking into account other demographic and socio-economic factors, the ILO produced estimates on the size of working children at the regional and global levels that have been internationally accepted and quoted as ILO figures. According to ILO (1996) estimates, in 1995 there were about 250 million working children (5–14 years old) worldwide, and at least 120 million of them did full-time paid work. Being the most populous region of the world, Asia carried about three-quarters of the world's child labourers. About one-fifth of the world's child labour lived in Africa. Though in absolute terms this problem seems more severe in Asia vis-à-vis Africa, in terms of participation rate, the picture is different. Figures compiled by ILO (1996) have shown that in Asia about 12.77 per cent of the children in the 10–14 age group were economically active, while the corresponding figure for Africa was 26.23 per cent.

In January 1998, ILO took a step further by launching its Statistical Information and Monitoring Program on Child Labour (SIMPOC) as an interdepartmental program to help member countries generate comprehensive, reliable and comparable quantitative and qualitative gender-sensitive data on child labour. Based on the compilation of data from SIMPOC and other sources, ILO (2002) estimated about 211 million 'economically active children' in the 5–14 age group in the year 2000. This accounts for nearly one-fifth of all children in this age group. Out of 211 million, 186 million were termed as child labour, and about 114 million of them were found in various forms of hazardous work.

With SIMPOC, ILO has been measuring global progress on child labour by publishing comparable child labour data from the year 2000 (ILO 2002). A more recent set of global data on child labour is now available (ILO 2012) that tracks the global child labour trends for the period 2000 to 2012. According to this report, about 144 million children in the 5–14 age group were 'economically active' in 2012 (120 million of them were child labourers), of whom 38 million were engaged in various forms of hazardous work.[8] In terms of participation rate, around 11.8 per cent of the world's child population was economically active in 2012, as against 17.6 per cent in the year 2000. When compared with ILO (2002) figures, the number of economically active children fell by 32 per cent and the decline was much sharper in the hazardous work category (66 per cent) during 2000–2012. Although ILO's estimates of economically active children show a declining trend, the absolute size of the child labour force is still large enough to be a matter of deep concern.

1.4   A brief review of contemporary literature

The growing awareness about and concern for child labour in recent years has led to an enormous literature on the issue.[9] Researchers and policy makers have been trying to identify the root causes and suggest appropriate remedial measures. In the conventional literature, it is commonly believed that the root cause of the widespread existence of child labour in the developing world is abject poverty, which compels people to have large families and make children go out in the job market so as to earn and support their families. However, another view is that poverty in itself is not a sufficient explanation for child labour. In the literature, apart from poverty, the supply of child labour has also been attributed to factors such as binding credit constraints, failure of the educational system, the objectives of households to maximize present income, a dualistic economy characteristic of the developing countries with the coexistence of formal and informal sectors, etc. In the next section, we review the existing literature on child labour to discuss these factors in detail.

1.4.1   Poverty

It is commonly believed that child labour is fundamentally a by-product of abject poverty and that, therefore, policies should focus on economic development and increasing income. A good deal of research has already focused on the inextricable connection between poverty and child labour. Unitary models of parental decision making (Becker 1964) are usually based on the assumption that parents are moved by purely altruistic motivations (Becker-Barro approach). Those who maintain that poverty is the main driving force behind child labour and that children are the family's only means of survival start with the assumption of parental altruism. A distinctive paper in this regard is that of Basu and Van (1998). They have shown that if child labour and adult labour are substitutes (*substitution axiom*) and if child leisure is a luxury commodity to the poor households (*luxury axiom*), unfavourable adult labour markets, responsible for low adult wage rates, constitute the main factor behind the incidence of child labour.[10] According to the luxury axiom, there exists a critical level of adult wage rate, and adult workers earning below this wage rate consider themselves as poor and do not have the luxury to keep their offspring at home or send them to school. They are forced, out of sheer poverty, to send at least some of their children to the job market in order to supplement low family income. The substitution axiom implies that children's entry into the workforce leads to a decrease in the demand for adult labour, thereby causing adult wages to fall. These assumptions lead to the possibility of multiple equilibria in the labour market. One of the possible outcomes is a 'good' one in which adult wages are high and children do not work. Another outcome is a 'bad' one in which all households send their children to work. Swinnerton and Rogers (1999) extended the Basu-Van model by incorporating a *distribution axiom*. They have shown that, in addition to the "*luxury*" and "*substitution*" axioms, for the results of Basu and Van (1998) model to hold, there is the need for an additional assumption (*distribution axiom*), which states that income or wealth from nonlabour sources must be sufficiently concentrated within a few of the economic agents. Swinnerton and Rogers (1999) have demonstrated that with sufficient equality in the distribution of nonlabour income, market equilibrium with child labour cannot exist in the Basu-Van model.[11] This is a valuable theoretical contribution to the literature that formalizes why distribution considerations are also important.[12] Ranjan (2001) has analyzed the relationship between distribution of income and investment in human capital in the presence of imperfect capital markets. Using an overlapping generations general equilibrium model, he shows that greater equality in the initial distribution of income is associated with lower incidence of child labour.

The parental altruism assumption, however, is not universally acceptable. Burra (1997) has reported evidence of parental selfishness. Gupta (2000) also supports this view. His analysis shows how the child wage and its allocation between child workers' consumption and his guardian's consumption are determined from a Nash bargaining game between the employer of the child worker and his selfish guardian. In Gupta (2000), the child worker has negligible bargaining power in the household, and the child's welfare is not a matter of concern to the parent. To the guardian, the child is like an asset that can be leased out for rental income. The model shows that an increase in the adult wage income raises the child wage rate but the child's consumption remains unaffected. This result has important policy implications. If with agricultural development, the adult wage rate rises, the cost of employing child labour increases as well. But the child labour does not get any benefit from it. The guardian derives the entire benefit. Therefore, with an increase in adult wage, the guardian will be interested in increasing the supply of child labour. This will increase not only the birth rate but also the drop-out of children from school at a very early age. Nevertheless, if the luxury axiom is correct, one can expect that the incidence of child labour will fall if the level of the minimum wage is raised. Basu (2000) shows that the effect of minimum wage legislation on the incidence of child labour could be counterproductive. He argued that the children of employed adults would indeed be less likely to work. However, if wage legislation causes adult unemployment to increase, the children of the newly unemployed adults would be more likely to work.

Empirical evidence given by Bonnet (1993), Krueger (1996), Grootaert (1999), Grootaert and Patrinos (2002) and Edmonds (2005) support the poverty hypothesis, which states that children are sent out to work to supplement low family income. Bhalotra (2004) tested the parental altruism assumption using Pakistan Integrated Household Survey (PIHS 1991) data. She investigated whether parents increase their consumption without caring for their children. The main finding is that the within-household allocation of resources is consistent with parental altruism. Analyzing National Sample Survey data from India, Kambhampati and Rajan (2005) confirm the luxury axiom. They have shown that an increase in parents' wages reduces child labour. However, they find that mothers' work actually increases the probability of girls' work. World Development Report (1995) also recognized poverty as the greatest single force, which creates the flow of children to the job market. It called for a multifaceted approach with programs that increase income security, reduce education costs and improve the quality of schooling. It concluded that "as the incidence of poverty falls and education improves, child labour will decline". Bhalotra (2000) investigated why children work by studying the wage elasticity of child labour supply. If poverty were compelling, then children would appear to work towards a target income. Incorporating a subsistence constraint into a model of labour supply, she argues that a negative wage elasticity favours the hypothesis that poverty compels work, while a positive wage elasticity would favour the alternative view that children work because the relative return to school is low. Using household survey data from Pakistan, she finds a negative wage elasticity for boys, supporting the view that boys work due to poverty compulsions and a wage elasticity of zero for girls. Using aggregated data from Sub-Saharan Africa, Admassie (2002) finds that poverty is indeed one of the most important factors behind the high child labour incidence in Africa. The study highlights poorly developed agriculture and high fertility rate as other important factors behind participation of children in economic activities. Fallon and Tzannatos (1998) provide cross-country evidence, showing that the incidence of child labour declines with the rise in per-capita GDP. Krueger (1996) has found a steep cross-country negative correlation between GDP per capita and the participation rate of children between 10 and 14 years in 1995. A study by Nagaraj (2002) on the *beedi* industry in Tamil Nadu and Karnataka, India, shows that the number of children in the 5–14 years age group attending school rises strictly monotonically as the household monthly per-capita expenditure rises. Cartwright and Patrinos (1999) find somewhat similar results in Bolivia, showing how poverty plays a central role in driving children to the job market. According to their estimates, a 1 per cent increase in household expenditure reduces the likelihood of child labour by 5 per cent. Using data from 1990 Encuesta de Hogares, conducted by the Direction general de Estadistica Censos, Patrinos and Psacharopoulos (1995) show that in Paraguay, total monthly family income is sufficiently negatively associated with child labour. Blunch and Verner (2001) reinstate the positive relationship between poverty and child labour. Using data originated from the Core Welfare Indicators Questionnaire (CWIQ) 1997 for Ghana, they have shown that children from poorer households are almost four times as likely to be engaged in harmful child labour compared to children from wealthy households. Edmonds (2005), using rural household survey data from Vietnam, has shown that between 1992–1993 and 1997–1998, Vietnam's GNP per capita grew at the rate of 6.5 per cent per annum, and child labour fell by 26 per cent over the same period. He finds strong corroboration of the hypothesis that rising living standards cause a decline in child labour. In particular, he finds that an increase in household income can explain 94 per cent of the decline in child labour for households that are at the poverty line. Wahba (2000) has analyzed the 1988 Labour Force Sample Survey of Egypt, which involves a nationally representative sample of 10,000 households. She finds a strong negative relationship between adult market wage rate and child participation rate in the labour market. Canagarajah and Nielsen (1999) have conducted empirical studies on Côte d'Ivoire, Ghana and Zambia. They have found some support for the poverty hypothesis. They have argued that other determinants like school costs, transportation costs, imperfect capital markets and household composition have a significant effect on child labour and school attendance. Cartwright's (1999) study, using 1993 survey data for rural and urban children in Colombia, also confirms the role of poverty behind child work.

However, the findings of some micro level empirical studies, based on household survey data, are not always supportive of the poverty hypothesis. Some of these studies have failed to demonstrate a strong positive relationship between household poverty and child labour. Patrinos and Psacharopoulos (1997) in their study on Peru have found that none of the potential measures of household assets or income appears to play a significant role. Ray (2000a, 2000b) finds a similar result for Peru. Ray (2000b) tested the luxury axiom of Basu and Van (1998), which states that adults send children to work only if income from their own labour falls to very low levels. He extended this idea to the context of children's education to imply that there is a negative association between years of children's schooling and household poverty. In other words, parents will reduce the schooling of their children if the household's adult earnings fall below the poverty line. Ray's (2009b) work on Pakistan confirms the hypothesized relationships between child labour and household poverty and between child schooling and household poverty. He finds, when a Pakistani household falls into poverty, it increases each child's paid employment by approximately 500 hours annually, just as the luxury axiom predicts. Such a household also reduces the schooling of its children. In contrast, the Peruvian data fail to detect any significant association between household poverty and child labour or between household poverty and child schooling. Nevertheless, as pointed out by Basu and Tzannatos (2003), "income that a household targets as minimum acceptable may not coincide with the nation's or region's official poverty line. Hence, using a poverty head-count ratio based on the official poverty line may not explain the incidence of child labor". Canagarajah and Coulombe (1997) analyzed 1991–1992 data on child labour in Ghana. Their findings contradict the conventional claim of poverty being the main determinant of child labour. However, they found a strong negative relationship between poverty and schooling. Sasaki and Temesgen (1999) analyzed child labour in Peru. No significant relationship between household income per capita and the schooling/ work decision was found.

Another critique of poverty-based explanations of child labour has come from Bhalotra and Heady (2003). They have argued, using data from Pakistan and Ghana, that children in land-rich households are often more likely to be in work vis-à-vis the children of land-poor households. Because a larger land holding typically means greater wealth, this seems to suggest that greater poverty does not lead to more child labour. In the absence of a properly functioning labour market, more land leads to more productive use of the household's labour, including child labour. Children are used as complementary inputs to other capital, particularly land (Sharif 1994). Hence, if two households are equally disinclined to send their children to work, one with more land may find child labour more rewarding. Jensen and Nielsen (1997), Cartwright (1999) and Edmonds and Turk (2002) also found similar evidence in Zambia, Vietnam and Colombia, respectively.

Edmonds and Turk (2002) found that households in new businesses appear to rely on family labour and are therefore more likely to engage their children in both traditional and household work. Cartwright (1999) found children in rural Colombia, whose family operates a household enterprise, are nearly 8 per cent more likely to work than other rural children. However, both studies found a strong correlation between improvements in the standard of living and decline in the incidence of child labour in general. These findings can be explained by what is known as the 'wealth paradox'. As explained in Basu et al. (2010), in developing economies, poor households want to send their children to work to supplement their low family income but are unable to do so because they have no access to labour markets (imperfect labour markets) close to their homes. In this situation, household with some wealth, in the form of land or a small business, will be able to engage their children in work more because they can now do what they had earlier wished to do.

Other findings, however, cannot be explained in terms of the so called wealth paradox. For example, Duryea and Arends-Kuenning (2003) found that child labour was higher when average wages increased in Brazil. Kruger (2007) finds that temporary improvement in economic conditions due to a coffee boom in Brazil resulted in an increased incidence of child labour. They have argued that in the case of temporary fluctuations in income, the substitution effects of temporary income changes are greater than income effects and that therefore temporary improvements in economic conditions may increase children's employment. The empirical finding of a study conducted by Swaminathan (1998) in a city in Gujarat, India, reveals some counterintuitive results in this regard. She has found that the incidence of child labour has increased significantly in the city of Bhavnagar, Gujarat, India, despite high economic growth. Similarly, Barros et al. (1994) found that the incidence of child labour was much higher in wealthier states relative to that in the poorer states of Brazil. Using data from a nationally representative household survey (NSSO), Nandi (2015) finds that a household's work in an employment scheme reduces the probability of school attendance of 14- to 17-year-old boys by 14 per cent. The study clearly suggests that school attendance can fall even with an increase in income opportunities. Some of these findings cannot be explained in terms of the wealth paradox or strength of substitution effect over income effect in the event of temporary improvement in economic conditions.

Empirical evidence available so far indicates that. although there is a very strong cross-country negative correlation between child labour and per-capita GNP (Krueger 1996; Fallon and Tzannatos 1998; Grimsrud 1999), some micro studies failed to demonstrate poverty as the primary factor behind child labour. This could be due to genuine country variations or may be a result of methodological problems. Chaudhuri and Dwibedi (2007) have provided an explanation of why growth with inflows of foreign capital is not sufficient to solve the problem of child labour. They have shown that higher economic growth may sufficiently raise the demand for commodities/services that use child labour, thereby worsening the problem of child labour. Dwibedi and Marjit (2015) explain this apparent paradox in terms of the relative income concern of the households. They argue that people in general are not just concerned about their own consumption; they are very much affected by the consumption of their peers in their society. While taking decisions regarding the time allocation of their children between work and leisure, parents do keep an eye on their relative position in the society. Using a simple theoretical model of household decision making, the researchers show that the child labour supply from a poor family can increase even with improvements in its economic condition, if the family's relative position in the society deteriorates and if the relative status effect is sufficiently strong.

Bhalotra and Tzannatos (2003) have surveyed the empirical literature on child labour in order to understand the variety of results that it has produced. They argue that measurement errors, inappropriately controlled endogeneity, arbitrary functional forms used in the estimations and failure to take into account the role of wealth (especially land) are the possible reasons why some studies have not found poverty as the primary factor behind the child labour incidence. Even then, it would be appropriate to recognize that poverty is not the only reason behind child labour and that other important factors are responsible for this problem as well.

1.4.2 Credit market failure and quality of education

Some researchers focused on the poor quality of education and capital market failure behind child labour. Ranjan (1999, 2001), Baland and Robinson (2000) and Jafarey and Lahiri (2002, 2005) emphasize the importance of capital market imperfection as a contributing factor to inefficient child labour. If the present discounted value of return from education is greater than the child wage in the current period, it is clearly optimal for a family to borrow against the child's future income to finance the child's education. To be more specific, it is in the interest of the child to make any requisite contribution to household income by borrowing against future income, thus freeing the child to attend school rather than work. However, the explanation of child labour incidence in terms of credit market imperfection crucially hinges on the presupposition that the return to education is sufficiently high, which in turn assumes that the quality of schooling is also satisfactory. Nevertheless, a few important empirical studies[13] have reported the abysmal state of the existing primary education system in the developing countries. Besides, this theory of child labour is based on the notion of a mutually altruistic household. It is implicitly assumed that when parents borrow against the future incomes of their children, the repayment of the loan is a shared burden. However, Baland and Robinson (2000) have argued that in the absence of mutual altruism, the provision of credit at a reasonable rate might not be enough to rectify the occurrence of excessive levels of child labour. Prevailing laws and attitudes in most societies do not allow parents to undertake debts that can be passed on by them as the responsibility of their children in future.

In the developing economies, agriculture is primarily primitive and dependent on weather conditions. Rural households, most of which are dependent on agriculture, directly or indirectly, are vulnerable to income fluctuations. Credit constraint plays a crucial role behind the labouring decision of these poor households. Given their limited access to credit and insurance markets, rural households use their children to buffer their consumption against income shocks. Jacoby and Skoufias (1997) have used panel data from rural India to examine the response of human capital investment in children to income shocks. They find evidence of children being taken out of school and sent out to work in response to negative income shocks. They concluded that "child labour, and thereby school attendance, appears to play a significant role in the self-insurance strategy of poor households in rural India". Analyzing Living Standards Measurement Study (LSMS) panel data for Peru, Ilahi (2001) has shown that external shocks such as sickness of family members or job loss by an adult affected children's school attendance, and the impact was even greater on girls. Dehejia and Gatti (2002) have examined the relationship between child labour and access to credit using cross-country data. Their study indicates a strong negative relationship between credit availability and child labour. This relationship has been found to be strong for low-income countries. Dessy (2000) has shown that in an economy where the benefits of having children are outweighed by rearing costs, a policy of free education with no compulsory education laws may lead the economy to an underdevelopment trap with a high fertility rate and higher incidence of child labour. On the contrary, a compulsory education policy is expected to mitigate the problem.

1.4.3   *Fertility decision and child labour*

Another strand of literature focuses on the fertility decision and its implication for child labour incidence.[14] If the number of children in the household determines the potential supply of child workers, one can expect that children from larger households are more likely to work. Becker and Lewis (1973) argue that, in the quality–quantity trade-off, parents with large number of children are less likely to invest in schooling.[15] Parents may also choose to have large families to diversify income risk. Lloyd (1994) reviews empirical evidence from developing countries to analyze fertility decision and their implications for investment in young people. His review finds that larger household size reduces children's educational participation and increases the probability that a child will work. Knodel et al. (1990) and Knodel and Wongsith (1991) show that family size exerts a significant negative impact on child schooling in Thailand. Analyzing Peru Living Standards Survey (PLSS) data, Patrions and Psacharopoulos (1997) have shown that household size reduces children's educational participation and increases the probability that a child would be sent to the job market. They have argued that age structure and activities of siblings are also important in determining the relationship between family size and child labour.

The notion that larger household size increases the probability that children will work is, however, not without question. Some researchers argue that larger families may facilitate schooling, at least for some children. If it is assumed that poverty is the only factor behind child labour and children are sent to work to compensate the shortfall between subsistence needs and current income, the presence of older siblings may decrease the likelihood of market work by younger siblings. Montegomery et al. (1995) have examined the determinants of fertility and child schooling in Cote d'Ivoire and Ghana to assess the evidence of a trade-off between the number of children born and levels of child schooling. In Cote d'Ivoire, they find evidence of such a trade-off in urban areas but not in rural areas. Female schooling, higher income and improved child survival are associated with lower fertility and higher child schooling. Chernichovsky (1985) finds that family size raises the educational attainments of children in rural Botswana. He argues that this could be due to diminishing returns to labour in a household (with given amount of assets), which reduces the indirect costs of schooling and may lead to role assignment within the household, with some children being reserved for household and farm activities, while others are permitted to attend school. Patrinos and Psacharopoulos (1995) have observed that the number of siblings does not have much of an effect on school enrollment, although it does have a significant impact on the probability of child labour. De Graff et al. (1993) have found that the relationship between household size and child work is not the same for market since it is for domestic work, and it depends on the sex and birth order of the child. The extent to which child work is affected by household size is also determined by household composition and social norms.

A good deal of research in this area has pointed out that child labour is not an outcome of higher fertility; rather, it is encouraged by prospects of child work. The argument is that parental decision is not always guided by altruistic consider-ations; parents see children as a kind of capital asset, expected to provide a stream of payments and personal services in old age. The need for the old-age security of parents, in the absence of proper insurance and pension facilities, and the prospect of sending children to work can encourage fertility decisions (Dasgupta 1995; Rosenzweig and Everson 1977). Using data from India, Rosenzweig and Everson (1977) have analyzed the joint household decision regarding fertility and children's time allocated between schooling and work. They find that the motivation for having large families was due to the higher return on child labour relative to the return from investment on skills acquisition. Eswaran (1996) has found an explanation in the need for old-age security of the parents behind the incidence of high fertility rate and lower investment in the education of their off-spring (hence a high incidence of child labour) in a backward society where the child mortality rate is quite high. He has suggested improvement in health care services and legislation of compulsory education to eradicate child labour from the system. Jensen (1990) has found evidence that pension coverage reduces fertility in developing countries, which supports the old-age security hypothesis. Cigno et al. (2001) also observe that provision for schooling and public health improvements discourage fertility and reduce child labour. There is, of course, an important weakness in this line of argument. If the economic cost of having children is sufficiently high, the income from child labour may not be sufficient to justify this endogenous fertility hypothesis.[16]

1.4.4   Social norms

Cultural factors and social norms do affect decisions like fertility and child's activ-ity. The connection between social influence and child labour has been discussed extensively by Rodgers and Standing (1981). Social historians believe that the main force behind the elimination of child labour from today's developed world was the rise of the domestic ideology, which transformed children from valuable wage earners to emotionally invaluable objects (Zelizer 1985). Basu and Van (1998) also recognized the importance of social norms behind parental decisions regarding child labour and analyzed its policy implications. They have argued that social norms in certain societies are such that child labour is considered natural and nothing to protest against. In certain other societies, the acquired morality may lead to aversion to child labour. Hence, one way to remove child labour is to try to make it customary for children not to work. They pointed out, " If for instance, child labour is banned for some time, then it is conceivable that our judgment in that matter will change so that after some time, even if the law is revoked, we would not want to send our children to work regardless of household income". Policy intervention in a model like this has the potential to solve coordination problems between households and switch the economy from an equilibrium with low social stigma attached to work and the existence of child labour to an equilibrium with high social stigma in which children do not work. Lopez-Calva (2002) has constructed a model to internalize social norms and explained how 'stigmatization' affects the child labour decision. The paper assumes that a parent who sends a child to the labour market faces a social stigma that reduces her own utility and that the stigma cost falls with an increase in the proportion of the population that violates the norm. The model predicts multiple equilibria as described by Basu and Van (1998). Andvig (2001) has explored the relationship between children's labour and their socialization. It concludes that it is almost impossible to explain the great difference in tasks and in total working hours between girls and boys in many African communities without invoking social norms as behavioural guidance. Weiner (1991) also explained child labour in the context of the socio-economic and caste hierarchy in India.

1.4.5 *Intrahousehold bargaining*

A strand of literature on child labour focuses on intrahousehold heterogeneity of preference and its implication on decisions regarding household consumption, fertility, schooling and child labour. Normally, household models characterize the household as a single unit of decision making (unitary model) where the intra household heterogeneity of preferences is ignored. Nonetheless, one can argue that household behaviour is an outcome of internal bargains and is not determined by any single representative unit (collective model).[17] Browning et al. (1994) argue that one cannot treat many-person households as a single decision maker. Factors such as the relative incomes of the household members may affect the final allocation decisions made by the household. Using survey data from Brazil, Thomas (1990) shows that unearned income in the hands of a mother has a bigger effect on her family's health than income under the control of a father, such that for child survival probabilities, the effect is almost 20 times higher. Basu (2006) points out that the husband and the wife may have different preferences, and depending on the balance of power between them, the household may choose differently. He used the collective model of household to show that as the source of income in a household becomes more diverse, the household is less likely to send its children to work. Galasso (1999) examined the connection between child's work and the intrahousehold balance of power between the father and mother. Her study finds some support for the view that children work less and study more in households where the mother has greater weight in decision making. Some argue that intrahousehold bargaining can also take the form of bargaining between the parent and the child. According to this line of thinking, child workers are independent bargainers and can influence the allocation of resources within the household. Baland and Robinson (2000) noted that as a child cannot precommit to compensate the parents from future income, the only option parents have for increasing current household consumption is to put the child to work.[18] Children may leave the family after receiving education, making it difficult for parents to internalize the future benefits of investing in their children's education. Thus, child labour arises due to this type of bargaining failure. Governments can use legislations that can solve this type of intrahousehold bargaining problem. Moehling (2005) examined the impact of child's work on the intrahousehold resources allocation using data from the Bureau of Labor Statistics Cost of Living Survey 1917–1919 (U.S.). Her study points out that working gave children greater influence in household decision making and larger share of household resources (specifically clothing). Andvig (2000) investigated how the exit possibilities of a child (migration) are likely to have an impact on the distribution of goods and labour efforts inside the family unit where the children already stay.

1.4.6   *Human capital formation and the poverty trap*

It is axiomatic, indeed, that children's working affects their physical and moral well-being and social development. The consequences are far-reaching. On the one hand, working lowers schooling and adversely affects human capital accumulation and hence future earning ability as an adult.[19] On the other, as an adult, it also affects the attitude towards education of his children. Dynamic analysis of child labour by Basu (1999), Dessy (2000), Ranjan (2001) and Emerson and Souza (2003) assumes that a person who receives more education as a child grows up having higher human capital and therefore higher labour income. A person who works more and receives less education as a child will naturally grow up as a poor adult. If poverty pushes children to the workplace, it will tend to perpetuate across generations. Basu and Tzannatos (2003) have described this as a "dynastic trap" and noted, "A child laborer tends to grow up to have children who are child laborers by virtue of their family history". Dessy (2000) has noted that an economy that starts with very low levels of per-capita human capital (below a particular threshold level) may slip into an underdevelopment trap corresponding to a child labour regime with low levels of human capital and high fertility. In contrast, an economy that starts with per-capita human capital above this threshold level will move to a steady-state equilibrium corresponding to low fertility, high human capital and no child labour. Baland and Robinson (2000) demonstrate how inefficiently high levels of child labour may persist in equilibrium if credit markets are imperfect or if bequests are zero (even if parents are altruistic towards their children). Ranjan (2001) has also analyzed the dynamic implication of capital market failure and has argued that a concerted effort to educate one generation will be self-sustaining and will bring the economy to a new steady-state equilibrium with no child labour.

   Empirical studies in this area also reveal that the parent's education plays a crucial role in children's schooling decision. Parent's education influences child schooling not just through income effect (more educated parents probably earn more and hence spend more on child schooling), it imparts some informational externality that affects the decision that parents make for their children. The higher the number of years both of the parents spent in school, the more likely that they will choose higher schooling time for their children. Less educated parents are likely to send their children to work, and consequently these children would grow up to be less educated parents, who will subsequently send their children to work. In rural Colombia, one additional year of schooling by each parent lowers the probability of their child's full-time work by 2 percentage points (Cartwright 1999). Grootaert (1999) also found something similar for Cote d'Ivoire. Each year of a father's education lowers the probability of a child's drop-out by 1.8 per cent, and one additional year of education of the mother reduces the dropout probability by 3.5 percentage points. Canagarajah and Coulombe (1997) also find that the father's education has a significant negative effect on child labour. Wahba (2000) finds that, in Egypt, parents who were child labourers themselves in the past are more likely to send their children to work. Analyzing the household survey data from Brazil, Emerson and Souza (2003) have also reached the same conclusion.

1.4.7 Policy issues

The unprecedented media and public concern for child labour, in the era of globalization, has brought a broad consensus on the need to eliminate the nuisance of child labour from society. However, there are wide disagreements on the best way to achieve that target and on whether legislative interventions are at all likely to be effective in eradicating this problem. Basu (1999) has distinguished legislative interventions in terms of intranational, extranational and supranational interventions. *Intranational* interventions may take the form of a national policy of banning child labour or policies like compulsory education and many other different types of instruments. One popular form of controlling child labour is to fine the farms if they are found to be employing children. However, as pointed out by Basu (2005), a small dose of intervention of this kind may actually aggravate the prevalence of the evil in the system. He opined that "developing countries like India, trying to legislate against child labour, has to be careful in its design of the law and in the choice of the size of the punishment. Otherwise, the law could have the effect opposite to what is intended". Nardinelli (1990) and Moehling (1998) also pointed out that historically legislative restrictions had little impact on child employment. Weiner (1991) viewed that compulsory education is more effective than simply banning child labour, as the child's presence in school is easier to monitor than a child's absence from work. Dessy (2000) has also advocated in favour of the imposition of compulsory education as a means to combat the incidence of child labour.

There is now increasing pressure from some developed countries to introduce environmental and social standards into the World Trade Organization (WTO) charter as a legitimate basis for trade intervention. The inclusion of an 'international labour standard' and a 'social clause' in the WTO charter will enable them to ban imports of products 'produced by child labour'. The use of child labour in production is one way of violating labour standards, and the imposition of sanctions on the imports of commodities produced using child labour is one such social clause. The argument in favour of the clause is that the use of child labour gives the developing countries a trading advantage in labour-intensive goods, which is illegitimate because the use of child labour in production activities is socially unethical and unacceptable. Those opposing the inclusion argue that *supranational interventions* of this kind will encourage protectionism and will hurt not only the workers in the developing countries but also the consumers in the developed nations. According to them, the international campaign against child labour, waged by protectionist forces in the developed world, is hardly guided by any ethical or humanitarian motives. On the contrary, their sole motive is to preserve the interests of the developed countries by depriving the labour-intensive export industries of the developing countries and their cost advantages in the international market.

On the other hand, *extranational* policies take the form of social labeling to completely banning imports of goods produced by child labour. Although export industries are the most visible sector in which children work, we must not lose sight of the millions of children worldwide who work in nonexport areas, often in hazardous and exploitative conditions. In fact, only a very small percentage of child workers are employed in export sector industries – probably less than 5 per cent.[20] A study in Bangladesh in 1995, for example, revealed that children were active in more than 300 different kinds of job outside the export sector. These ranged from household chores to brick making, from stone breaking to selling in shops and on streets, from bike repairing to garbage collecting and rag picking. Moreover, this estimation took into account only jobs done in cities. Most of the children in the developing countries work on farms and plantations or houses, far from the reach of labour inspectors and media scrutiny. Thus, social labelling can be applied only to a few products (mostly exported ones), so that the potential effect is limited. Besides, it is also difficult to monitor the labelling operations. Several economists, for example Bhagwati (1995), Srinivasan (1996) and others, have argued that legislative fiats to combat child labour in terms of an outright ban or social labelling of products are not the right approach to the problem. A total ban would be counterproductive in the sense that it may adversely affect the welfare of the poor households and force the children to resort to more hazardous and illegal activities. As the Bangladeshi experience has shown, the possibility of introduction of the U.S. Harkins Bill, which calls for a complete ban on imports of any goods that are manufactured wholly or partly by child workers, led to a chaotic process that left many children worse off than they were before.[21]

Child labour is a complex issue, and clearly it has no simple solution. Understanding its root causes will guide us in designing appropriate policies.[22] The recognition of the fact that poverty is the single largest force behind the widespread existence of child labour in the developing world calls for policies that will improve the living standards of the poor families. However, policy prescriptions directed towards poverty alleviation are difficult to be implemented properly due to various bottlenecks and vicious circles typical of the developing economies; even if implemented, they will take a long time to mitigate the problem. The question is are we going to wait till poverty is eliminated? Or should we think about other complementary policies?

Other policies like the betterment of educational opportunities and/or compulsory education designed for human capital formation can more effectively remove children from work. Ravallion and Wodon (2000) have shown how educational incentive policies increased school enrollment in Bangladesh. However, they found that these policies have not had much impact on reducing the incidence of child labour. Skoufias and Parker (2001) have shown that cash transfers, targeted at the very poorest households and tied to school, are fairly effective. Eswaran (1996) has suggested improvement in health care services and legislation for compulsory education to eradicate child labour from the system.

Some economists also pointed out the importance of imperfect credit markets as a contributing factor to inefficient child labour. According to this line of thinking, the provision of cheap credit to finance education can improve schooling and reduce child labour incidence. Baland and Robinson (2000) have noted that the inability of the child to access the capital market, or the inability of the child to precommit to repay education loans obtained by the parents on the child's behalf, or the absence of mutual altruism may give rise to inefficiently low educational attainment. However, a lack of mutual altruism is a questionable assumption, particularly in the context of well-known cultural norms regarding the provision of old-age support to parents in the developing world. However, it should be pointed out that this view crucially hinges on the presupposition that the return to education is sufficiently high, which in turn, assumes that the quality of schools is also reasonably high. Nevertheless, PROBE (1999) reported the very poor quality of schooling in countries like India. UNICEF (1997) also cited the low quality of schooling as the most important factor behind high dropout rates in the developing countries. Therefore, it is believed that the betterment of educational opportunities in terms of affordability and quality and a policy of compulsory education designed for human capital formation can more effectively remove children from work.

1.4.8 Globalization and child labour

For the last few decades, countries, whether developed or developing, have been resorting to revolutionary changes in their trade and investment policies. National economies are increasingly linked through international markets for products and factors, leading to increased cross-border flows of goods, capital and labour. World societies are now more connected through flows of information, technology and management know-how. The world is getting more and more integrated day by day. Consequently, the world economy has experienced a quantitative leap in the volume and value of international trade and financial transactions. The process of globalization might have significant implications on a number of social and economic aspects of the developing states. Child labour is, indeed, one of the most important of these agendas. Policy makers, NGOs and researchers are engaged in protracted debates in exploring the complex relationship between child labour and globalization.

Opponents of globalization argue that openness will induce developing countries to use more child labour to remain low-cost and competitive. They also hold that trade openness may depress the earning opportunities of poor households because exposures to foreign competition may force inefficient firms in import-competing industries to pull their shutters down and go out of business. Regardless of the long-term benefits of this reallocation of resources, in the short term, these adjustments may create difficulty for some households with children. Foreign direct investment (FDI), another facet of globalization, may tend to exploit lax labour standards prevailing in the developing world, leading to more decentralization of the production process in terms of subcontracting. There are, in fact, instances of multinational corporations subcontracting to enterprises that employ children.[23]

Proponents of globalization, on the other hand, argue that increased openness will lead to more development for all. Globalization is also assumed to increase the demand for skilled labour with a higher productivity. This, in turn, will lead to increased interest in human capital formation and thus investment in education, making child labour less attractive.

Empirical evidence available so far gives us some conflicting signals. A few of them suggest that increased openness and flow of foreign capital helped in reducing (or at least not aggravating) the problem of child labour, while others believe that it made the situation worse. Edmonds and Pavcnik (2005) provide a study of micro data from the 4000-household-panel Vietnam Living Standards Survey. Vietnam restricted its exports of rice until 1993. These quotas suppressed the domestic price of rice. Between 1993 and 1997, Vietnam gradually relaxed this exports quota so that by 1998, Vietnam was completely exposed to the international market. During this period of liberalization, the price of rice increased by 30 per cent relative to the rise in the consumer price index. Edmond and Pavcnik (2005) have examined the impact of this price rise on the child labour incidence during this period. They found that both adult wage and child wage increased owing to the hike in the price of rice. Though the price increase has made child labour more attractive, they have also found an even stronger income effect, which eventually led to a reduction in child labour incidence. Cigno et al. (2002) have analyzed the impact of trade liberalization on child work using cross-country panel data. Their study indicates that trade reduces or, at worst, has no significant effect on child labour. Using cross-country data, Edmonds and Pavcnik (2006) find that openness is negatively associated with child labour only if no other variables, particularly income, are included in the regression models. This suggests that openness reduces child labour but only through a positive income effect. Neumayer and Soysa (2005) have examined the impact of trade openness and foreign direct investment on the incidence of child labour using cross-country data. Their study suggests that countries with more liberalized trade regime and greater penetration by foreign direct investment are associated with lower child labour incidence. Unlike Edmonds and Pavcnik (2006), this study indicates that globalization reduces child labour incidence not only through income effect but also via other routes.

Studies by Loker (1999) and Lieten (2003), on the other hand, suggest that globalization has been increasing the child labour incidence. Loker (1999) has argued that many nations, including parts of Latin America, became home to millions of children who resembled "grit in the prosperity machine". Lieten (2003) has argued that openness led to higher poverty, more decentralization of production and greater sourcing of cheap labour for exports and thus more child labour. He questioned the results based on cross-country data on the grounds that one cannot draw reliable conclusion analyzing countries with dissimilar GNPs and dissimilar openness in policies.

A few theoretical analyses have examined the efficacy of trade sanction in reducing the incidence of child labour in the developing countries. Basu and Van (1998) argue that banning child labour may or may not produce the desired result. In a situation where multiple equilibria are in the labour market, a ban is a benign policy intervention and worthwhile. In such a situation, banning child labour will raise adults' wages by reducing the effective supply of labour, and that may eventually bring the economy to a 'good' equilibrium with no child labour. Once the 'good' equilibrium is achieved, the law of banning child labour is no longer needed. In this sense, Basu and Van (1998) described the intervention as "benign intervention". For an extremely poor country, however, there might exist only one equilibrium, and a ban in this case can worsen the condition of the working households. A partial ban (which is more likely because it is very difficult to implement a total ban in a developing country) is especially likely to backfire and cause the problem to deteriorate. An overlapping-generations general equilibrium model by Ranjan (2001) shows how trade sanctions against countries using child labour may fail to reduce the incidence of child labour. Jafarey and Lahiri (2002) have argued that in the presence of credit constraints, trade sanctions could be counterproductive. According to them, however, credit on its own is unlikely to eliminate child labour. Improvement in the economic condition and better quality of primary education will be more effective in controlling the problem. Gupta (2002) has also examined the efficacy of trade sanctions as a policy to curb the incidence of child labour and has reached similar conclusions. Chaudhuri and Gupta (2004) find that the consequence of trade liberalization on the incidence of child labour crucially hinges on the relative factor intensities of the different sectors of the economy.

1.5 Plan of the present book

Though there is a broad consensus on the need to eliminate child labour from the society, there is wide disagreement on how to achieve that objective. In this context, it is important to note that the efficacy of any policy on the child labour incidence should be carried out in a multisector general equilibrium framework. This is because a policy designed to mitigate the problem of child labour in a targeted sector may drive the children into other sector(s) of the economy and compel them to undertake illegal and more hazardous activities. Thus, one cannot evaluate the success of a particular policy unless one takes into account its effect on the aggregate number of child workers, spread over different sectors of an economy. However, adequate attention has not so far been paid in the existing literature in analyzing specifically the policy issues relating to the problem of child labour using the general equilibrium framework.

In the literature, we come across diverse opinions of different economists in their research articles. Some argue that legislative interventions in the form of social labeling or trade sanction should be resorted to in order to eradicate child labour in the developing world. Many of the economists have recommended poverty-alleviation programs to rid the system of the evil because it is a widely held view that abject poverty is the root cause behind child labour. Making primary education compulsory, the provision of midday meals to keep children in school and credit market reforms are the other suggested policies to fight against child labour. Liberalized economic policies are also often recommended to do away with child labour. However, it is important to note that which policies should ultimately be undertaken must depend on the specific characteristics of the economy in question. Against this backdrop, this book attempts to delve into many of the important aspects of child labour theoretically and suggest policies that could indeed be useful in dealing with the problem under diverse situations using different multisector general equilibrium models.

The ongoing process of globalization has produced considerable impact on the problem of child labour in developing countries. Globalization was expected to produce significant downward pressure on the problem through reduction in poverty. Economic liberalization is actually a policy package. It includes both inflows of foreign capital as well as the reduction of protection of domestic industries, structural reforms like deregulating the labour market and integrating the domestic market with the world market.

Although some attempts have been made in analyzing the relationship between globalization and child labour empirically, the issue has so far remained theoretically under-researched. The key question that analysts have attempted to address is whether globalization increases or helps in reducing the child labour incidence. However, it would be inappropriate to give an unambiguous answer to this question. Because globalization is a complex process with different aspects, its overall consequences on the problem of child labour is likely to be inconclusive. Some of the aspects of globalization might have created difficulties for households with children, while some others may have helped in reducing the problem. In this book, we attempt to examine the consequences of different constituents of globalization on the incidence of child labour with the help of several general equilibrium models reasonable for the developing economies. Our primary focus is the analysis of different policies that are expected to be successful from the viewpoint of both the magnitude of the problem and the welfare of the families that supply child labour.

Chapter 2 analyses the household decision-making exercise regarding the time allocation of its children. It derives the child labour supply function from the household's welfare maximization problem. We consider different types of household decision making. First, in a static framework, an altruistic representative household is assumed to choose between household consumption of different commodities and children's leisure by the process of maximizing its family welfare. Derived child labour supply function highlights the importance of adult income and the earning opportunities of children in influencing the household decision regarding its supply of child labour. It is to be noted here that in this case we consider 'poverty' to be the factor responsible for the child labour incidence. In this case, there is no room for human capital formation. Second, in a lifetime utility maximization approach, we consider the role of human capital formation in household decision making. This allows us to incorporate the schooling decision and the importance of the return to education in determining the supply of child labour by each family in the present period in a dynamic set-up. These two types of child labour supply function are used in the subsequent chapters.

Chapter 3 investigates the consequence of trade sanctions on the problem of child labour in a developing economy in terms of two general equilibrium models with child labour. The first one is a three-sector, full-employment model with two traded agricultural sectors. One of these two sectors produces an exports good, while the other produces a nontraded final good that is consumed by the poorer segment of the working households. Our analysis suggests that trade sanctions on the exported good not only accentuates the incidence of child labour but also makes the poor families worse off. Then, using a two-period, specific-factor Harris-Todaro type of general equilibrium model with endogenous skill formation, we show that, although trade sanction lowers the incidence of child labour, the policy affects both the unemployment situation of adult unskilled labour and the welfare of the child labour supplying families adversely. We therefore argue that trade sanctions are not the right approach to eradicate child labour because the policy might not only sometimes be counterproductive but also might make many unskilled workers jobless and the poor families worse off.

Chapter 4 of the book analyzes the implications of a subsidy policy on education, agricultural price subsidy and liberalized trade and investment policies on the incidence of child labour in a developing economy using a three-sector general equilibrium model with informal sector and child labour. We show that different policies, if undertaken concurrently, might produce mutually contradictory effects, thereby producing little or no impact on the incidence of child labour.

Empirical studies, available so far, have reported that trade and investment reforms have produced some favourable impact on the problem of child labour. However, there are reasons to believe that the incomes of the poorer segment of the working population have not satisfactorily increased in the developing economies during the liberalized regime. Hence, it is perplexing how the child labour situation has improved in these economies, especially when poverty has not decreased acceptably following economic reforms. Chapter 5 identifies the different channels through which economic reforms can affect the incidence of child labour in a developing nation by means of a three-sector general equilibrium model. It delves into the complex relationship between globalization and the return to education, as well as its implication for human capital formation and child labour. It shows that inflows of foreign capital might exert downward pressure on the child labour incidence by raising the return to education and lowering the earning opportunities of children and that a reduction in poverty is not a necessity in mitigating the prevalence of the evil in society.

Chapter 6 tries to give one possible explanation why child labour is in many cases found to be increasing even with an increase in the earning opportunities of the poor. It develops a three-sector, full-employment general equilibrium model with agricultural dualism and child labour. The analysis shows that a price subsidy policy to backward agriculture may raise the incidence of child labour through its demand pull effect, even though it improves the welfare of the families that supply child labour. On the contrary, a subsidy policy to benefit advanced agriculture mitigates the child labour problem only at the cost of welfare of the poor families.

We advocate in favour of subsidy policies in the form of direct cash transfer to the poor households, an approach that is found to be productive in lessening the gravity of the child labour problem and at the same time in improving the economic conditions of the poor families.

Chapter 7 examines the consequence of midday meal programs and/or cash stipend schemes on the incidence of child labour using a two-period, three-sector general equilibrium model with skill formation. The analysis finds that the policy might produce a perverse effect on the problem of child labour because it not only lowers the initial income from nonchild sources of a family but also decreases the return to education. The welfare of the working family is also likely to worsen.

Although over the last few years the incidence of child labour has decreased worldwide both in absolute and percentage terms, there has been an increase in the relative importance of child labour in services sector in recent years. More specifically, among different services rendered by children, the incidence of child labour in domestic work has increased significantly. A relevant question is therefore why child labour in services like domestic work has increased significantly both in absolute numbers as well as in terms of activity rate, especially when the child labour incidence in both counts has appreciably fallen in the world as a whole. Chapter 8 tries to explain this perplexing finding theoretically in terms of a four-sector general equilibrium model with a nontraded sector where only child labour is used to render services to the richer segment of the society. The analysis shows how economic growth via inflows of foreign capital can increase the size of the services sector, even though it lowers the overall enormity of the child labour problem in the society and improves the welfare of the poor families that supply child labour. Finally, a composite policy has been recommended that can deal with all of the issues favourably.

Finally, Chapter 9 summarizes the findings of the previous chapters and discusses the policy implications of the results. As a final point, we identify issues relating to the problem of child labour that future research should address.

Notes

1 We find references of child labour in an ancient Indian text, *Arthashastra*, compiled by Kautilya probably about 150 C.E. References were made to bonded child labour, recruited both from Aryan and non-Aryan communities. Children were employed to collect and prepare the ingredients for the liquor industry. As attendants to the king and other nobles, they were primarily engaged in the works of shampooing, preparing the bath, making garlands and perfumery and carrying the regalia of office. (Translated by Rangarajan (1992), pp 69, 88).
2 Other industrializing countries like Belgium, the U.S. and Japan also experienced similar situations.
3 Generally, children used to work for 12 to 14 hours a day, although in some cases the working day was up to 19 hours.
4 According to the Census of England and Wales in 1861, 36.9 per cent of boys in the 10–14 age group were labourers, and the corresponding figure for girls was 20.5 per cent (figures cited in Basu 1999). These figures are clearly higher than the participation rate of children in the present world.
5 Grootaert and Kanbur (1995), Basu (1999), Grimsrud (2001) Cigno, Rosati and Tzannatos (2002) and others have discussed this issue in detail.

6 While under normal circumstances, 15 years is the minimum age, Convention 138 specifies some special cases. For example, Article 2 of the Convention points out that "a Member whose economy and educational facilities are insufficiently developed may, after consultation with the organizations of employers and workers concerned, where such exist, initially specify a minimum age of 14 years". Article 3 says, "The minimum age for admission to any type of employment or work which by its nature or the circumstances in which it is carried out is likely to jeopardize the health, safety or morals of young people shall not be less than 18 years". Again for 'light work', the minimum age for admission to employment was 13 years (12 years for countries with poor educational facilities). (See Article 7.)

7 While using the data on child labour, one must accept that the estimation heavily depends on the definition and survey methodology. A study by Jayaraj and Subramanian (1997) has shown how the estimated outcome can change considerably if we follow different definitions. Their calculation for the state of Tamil Nadu shows that for the 5–14 age group in 1983, if they use the restrictive definition of the kind that the ILO uses, 13 per cent of all children were labourers. Using the more liberal definition, the figure jumps to 33 per cent.

8 The figure is much higher at 168 million (11 per cent of the child population) if we consider children of the 5–17 age group. More than half of them, about 85 million children, were found to be engaged in hazardous activities. Some of them were caught in the worst forms of child labour, including slavery, trafficking, debt bondage and other forms of forced labour, forced recruitment for armed conflict, prostitution, pornography and other illicit activities.

9 Grootaert and Kanbur (1995) present an overview of early writings on child labour. Basu (1999) reviewed the literature on child labour with special emphasis on concepts, theory and policy debates. Cigno, Rosati and Tzannatos (2002) and Basu and Tzannatos (2003) revisited the existing theoretical literature on child labour. For an overview of empirical literature on child labour, one can go through Canagarajah and Nielsen (1999), Grootaert and Patrinos (1999), Andvig (2001), Dar et al. (2002) and Bhalotra and Tzannatos (2003). For a more recent review of the existing literature on child labour, see Fors (2012).

10 Basu (1999), Basu (2000) and Basu and Tzannatos (2003) have also considered parents as altruistic towards their children because they send their offspring to work only when they are compelled to do so due to utter poverty.

11 Rogers and Swinnerton (2000) extended the model further using a more general utility function. They find that a more equal distribution of income can reduce child labour in high-productivity countries; nevertheless, in low-productivity countries, such redistribution may be ineffective and can even exacerbate the child labour problem.

12 Grootaert and Kanbur (1995) noted, "General economic development the fruits of which are equally distributed among the population, is the best and most sustainable way of reducing child labour". Fallon and Tzannatos (1998) also recognize that distribution considerations are important.

13 A study of India by the PROBE team (1999) found that the state of basic education was appalling even though parents had valued education in its own right. They also believed that their offspring were unlikely to benefit from education in its current state. UNICEF (1997) cited the low quality of schooling as an important reason for high dropout rates among primary school students in developing countries. Based on these observations, Jafarey and Lahiri (2002) have shown that child labour can coexist with child schooling even if credit markets are perfect. However, Psacharopoulos (1994) reported that the returns to all levels of education (both private and social) are much higher than the returns to physical capital for all regions of the world.

14 For a comprehensive overview of the literature on family size and its effect on time allocation of children, see Grootaert and Kanbur (1995).

15 Less schooling, however, does not necessarily imply more child labour. Empirical findings in this area reveal that, in general, child work affects schooling adversely. However, in some cases there may be complementarity between them.
16 Estimates from Sri Lankan and Indonesian data by Deaton and Muellbauer (1986) suggest that children cost their parents about 30-40 per cent of what they spend on themselves.
17 For a survey on intrahousehold bargaining models, see Xu (2007).
18 Prevailing laws do not allow parents to undertake debts that can be passed on by them as the responsibility of their children in future.
19 There are, however, disagreements on this issue. Some studies have found that child labour does not have a significantly adverse effect on schooling. Patrinos and Psacharopoulos (1997) have shown that child labour is not detrimental to schooling (in Peru) and even that, in some cases, "working actually makes it possible for the children to go to school". Nonetheless, it is hard to believe that the human capital accumulation of a child is not impaired by having to work. Psacharopoulos (1997) shows that the educational attainment of children who work is significantly lower than that of nonworking children in Bolivia and Venezuela (see also evidence found in Canagarajah and Coulombe (1997), Jensen and Nielsen (1997) and Wahba (2000)).
20 See UNICEF (1997).
21 Under the threat of such a measure, employers in the booming garment industry of Bangladesh sacked about 50,000 child labourers (most of them girls). Subsequent studies found them working in more hazardous conditions, such as brick making, leatherwork and even prostitution (UNICEF 1997, p. 23).
22 Bhalotra and Tzannatos (2003) categorize the primary forces behind child labour in terms of *incentives, constraints* and *agency*. They argue that, if of these three the *incentive* factor (determined by the return to work relative to alternative uses of time such as schooling) dominates, the right policy should be making schools more attractive. If households are compelled by poverty and/or credit constraints, we need to focus on poverty alleviation and credit subsidy policies. In certain cases, where parental *agency* (parents are not altruistic towards their children) is behind the working of children, one should go for legislative interventions.
23 Using cross-country information, empirical investigation by Braun and Busse (2003), however, indicates that child labour, on the contrary, deters foreign direct investment.

References

Admassie, A. (2002): 'Explaining the high incidence of child labor in Sub-Saharan Africa', *African Development Review*, 14(2), 251–275.

Andvig, J.C. (2000): 'An essay on child labour in Sub-Saharan Africa – A bargaining approach', Norwegian Institute of International Affairs Working Paper No. 613.

Andvig, J.C. (2001): 'Family-controlled child labor in Sub-Saharan Africa – A survey of research', Social Protection Discussion Paper Series, No. 0122, Human Development Network, The World Bank.

Ashagrie, K. (1993): 'Statistics on child labor', Bulletin of Labor Statistics, Issue No. 3, International Labor Organization, Geneva.

Ashagrie, K. (1998): *Statistics on Working Children and Hazardous Child Labour in Brief*, International Labour Office, Geneva.

Baland, J. and Robinson, J.A. (2000): 'Is child labour inefficient?', *Journal of Political Economy*, 108(4), 663–679.

Barros, R., Mendonca, R. and Velazco, T. (1994): 'Is poverty the main cause of child work in urban Brazil?', Texto Para Discussao No. 351, Servico Editorial.

Basu, K. (1999): 'Child labour: Cause, consequence, and cure, with remarks on international labour standards', *Journal of Economic Literature*, 37(September), 1083–1119.

Basu, K. (2000): 'The intriguing relationship between adult minimum wage and child labour', *The Economic Journal*, 110(462), C50–C61.

Basu, K. (2005): 'Child labor and the law: Notes on possible pathologies', *Economics Letters*, 87(2), 169–174.

Basu, K. (2006): 'Gender and say: A model of household behaviour with endogenously determined balance of power', *Economic Journal*, 116(511), 558–580.

Basu, K., Das, S. and Dutta, B. (2010): 'Child labor and household wealth: Theory and empirical evidence of an inverted-U', *Journal of Development Economics*, 91, 8–14.

Basu, K. and Tzannatos, Z. (2003): 'The global child labour problem: What do we know and what can we do?', *The World Bank Economic Review*, 17(2), 147–173.

Basu, K. and Van, P.H. (1998): 'The economics of child labour', *American Economic Review*, 88(3), 412–427.

Becker, G.S. (1964): *Human Capital*, Columbia University Press, New York.

Becker, G.S. and Lewis, H.G. (1973): 'On the interaction between the quantity and quality of children', *The Journal of Political Economy*, 81(2) Part 2: New Economic Approaches to Fertility (March–April, 1973), S279–S288.

Bhagwati, J. (1995): 'Trade liberalization and "Fair Trade" demands: Addressing environmental and labour standard issues', *World Economy*, 18(6), 745–759.

Bhalotra, S. (2000): 'Is child work necessary?', Discussion Paper No. 26, STICERD, London School of Economics, August.

Bhalotra, S. (2004): 'Parent altruism, cash transfers and child poverty', Discussion Paper No. 04/562, University of Bristol.

Bhalotra, S. and Heady, C. (2003): 'Child farm labor: The wealth paradox', *World Bank Economic Review*, 17(2), 197–228.

Bhalotra, S. and Tzannatos, Z. (2003): 'Child labour: What have we learnt?', Social Protection Discussion Paper Series, No. 0317, Human Development Network, The World Bank.

Blunch, N.-H. and Verner, D. (2001): 'Revisiting the link between poverty and child labor: The Ghanaian experience', Working Paper 01–03, Centre for Labour Market and Social Research Department of Economics, The Aarhus School of Business.

Bonnet, M. (1993): 'Child labour in Africa', *International Labour Review*, 132(3), 371–389.

Braun, S. and Busse, M. (2003): 'Export structure, FDI and child labour', HWWA Discussion Paper No. 216.

Browning, M., Bourguignon, F., Chiappori, P.A. and Lechene, V. (1994): 'Income and outcomes: A structural model of intrahousehold allocation', *Journal of Political Economy*, 102(6), 1067–1096.

Burra, N. (1997): *Born to Work: Child Labour in India*, Oxford University Press, New Delhi.

Canagarajah, S. and Coulombe, H. (1997): 'Child labor and schooling in Ghana', Policy Research Working Paper No. 1844, World Bank, Washington, DC.

Canagarajah, S. and Nielsen, H.S. (1999): 'Child labor and schooling in Africa: A comparative study', Social Protection Discussion Paper Series, No. 9916, Human Development Network, The World Bank.

Cartwright, K. (1999): 'Child labor in Colombia', in: Christiaan Grootaert and Harry Anthony Patrinos (eds.), *The Policy Analysis of Child Labor, a Comparative Study*, World Bank, Washington, DC, 63–102.

Cartwright, K. and Patrions, A. (1999): 'Child labor in urban Bolivia', in: Christiaan Grootaert and Harry Anthony Patrinos (eds.), *The Policy Analysis of Child Labor, a Comparative Study*, World Bank, Washington, DC, 103–130.

Chaudhuri, S. and Dwibedi, J.K. (2007): 'Foreign capital inflow, fiscal policies and incidence of child labour in a developing economy', *The Manchester School*, 75(1), 17–46.

Chaudhuri, S. and Gupta, M.R. (2004): 'Child labour and trade liberalization in a developing economy', *Japanese Economic Review*, 55(2), 201–211.

Chernichovsky, D. (1985): 'Socioeconomic and demographic aspects of school enrollment and attendance in rural Botswana', *Economic Development and Cultural Change*, 33(2), 319–332.

Cigno, A., Rosati, F.C. and Guarcello, L. (2002): 'Does globalization increase child labor?', *World Development*, 30(9), 1579–1589.

Cigno, A., Rosati, F.C. and Tzannatos, Z. (2001): 'Child labor, nutrition and education in rural India: An economic analysis of parental choice and policy options', Social Protection Discussion Paper Series, No. 0131, Human Development Network, The World Bank.

Cigno, A., Rosati, F.C. and Tzannatos, Z. (2002): 'Child labour handbook', Social Protection Discussion Paper Series, No. 0206, Human Development Network, The World Bank.

Cunningham, H. and Viazzo, P.P. (eds.). (1996): *Child Labor in Historical Perspective, 1800–1985: Case Studies from Europe, Japan and Colombia*, UNICEF, Florence.

Dar, A., Blunch, N.-H., Kim, B. and Sasaki, M. (2002): 'Participation of children in schooling and labour activities: A review of empirical studies', Social Protection Discussion Paper Series, No. 0221, Human Development Network, The World Bank.

Dasgupta, P. (1995): 'The population problem: Theory and evidence', *Journal of Economic Literature*, 33, 1879–1902.

Deaton, A.S. and Muellbauer, J. (1986): 'On measuring child costs: With application to poor countries', *Journal of Political Economy*, 94(4), 720–744.

DeGraff, D.S., Bilsborrow, R.E. and Herrin, A.N. (1993): 'The implication of high fertility for children's time use in Philippines', in: C.B. Lloyd (ed.), *Fertility, Family Size and Structure- Consequences for Families and Children*, Proceedings of a Population Council Seminar, New York, 9–10 June 1992. New York, The Population Council.

Dehejia, R. and Gatti, R. (2002): 'Child labor: The role of income variability and access to credit across countries', Working Paper No. 9018, National Bureau of Economic Research, Cambridge, MA.

Dessy, S.E. (2000): 'A defense of compulsory measures against child labour', *Journal of Development Economics*, 62, 261–275.

Duryea, S. and Arends-Kuenning, M.P. (2003): 'School attendance, child labor, and local labor markets in urban Brazil', *World Development*, 31, 1165–1178.

Dwibedi, J.K. and Marjit, S. (2015): 'Relative affluence and child labor – Explaining a paradox', MPRA Working Paper No. 66379.

Edmonds, E.V. (2005): 'Does child labor decline with improving economic status?', *Journal of Human Resources*, 40(1), 77–99.

Edmonds, E.V. and Pavcnik, N. (2005): 'The effect of trade liberalization on child labour', *Journal of International Economics*, 65(2), 401–419.

Edmonds, E.V. and Pavcnik, N. (2006): 'International trade and child labor: Cross-country evidence', *Journal of International Economics*, 68(1), 115–140.

Edmonds, E.V. and Turk, C. (2002): 'Child labor in transition in Vietnam', World Bank Policy Research Paper No. 2774.

Emerson, P. and Souza, A. (2003): 'Is there a child labor trap? Intergenerational persistence of child labor in Brazil', *Economic Development and Cultural Change*, 51(2), 375–398.

Eswaran, M. (1996): 'Fertility, literacy, and the institution of child labour', CRESP Discussion Paper No. 36, The University of British Columbia.

Fallon, P. and Tzannatos, Z. (1998): *Child Labor: Issues and Directions for the World Bank*, The World Bank, Washington, DC.

Fors, H.C. (2012): 'Child labour: A review of recent theory and evidence with policy implications', *Journal of Economic Surveys*, 26(4), 570–593.

Galasso, E. (1999): 'Intra-household allocation and child labor in Indonesia', Mimeograph, Boston College.

Grimsrud, B. (1999): 'Child labor and development', Mimeograph, Oslo.

Grimsrud, B. (2001): 'Measuring and analyzing child labor: Methodological issues', Social Protection Discussion Paper Series, No. 0123, Human Development Network, The World Bank.

Grootaert, C. (1999): 'Child labour in Cote d'Ivoire: Incidence and determinants', in: C. Grootaert and H. Patrinos (eds.), *The Policy Analysis of Child Labour: A Comparative Study*, Manuscript, World Bank, Washington.

Grootaert, C. and Kanbur, R. (1995): 'Child labour: An economic perspective', *International Labour Review*, 134(2), 187–203.

Grootaert, C. and Patrinos, H. (eds.). (1999): *The Policy Analysis of Child Labor*, St. Martin's Press, New York.

Grootaert, C. and Patrinos, H. (2002): 'A four-country comparative study of child labor', Mimeograph, The World Bank.

Gupta, M.R. (2000): 'Wage determination of a child worker: A theoretical analysis', *Review of Development Economics*, 4(2), 219–228.

Gupta, M.R. (2002): 'Trade sanctions, adult unemployment and the supply of child labour: A theoretical analysis', *Development Policy Review*, 20(3), 317–332.

Ilahi, N. (2001): 'Children's work and schooling: Does gender matter? Evidence from the Peru LSMS', World Bank Policy Research Working Paper No. 2745, The World Bank.

ILO. (1996): *Economically Active Populations: Estimates and Projections, 1950–2010*, International Labour Office, Geneva.

ILO. (2002): *Every Child Counts: New Global Estimates on Child Labour*, International Labour Office, Geneva.

ILO. (2012): *Making Progress against Child Labour: Global Estimates and Trends 2000–2012*, International Labour Office, Geneva.

Jacoby, H.G. and Skoufias, E. (1997): 'Risk, financial markets, and human capital in a developing country', *The Review of Economic Studies*, 64(3), 311–335.

Jafarey, S. and Lahiri, S. (2002): 'Will trade sanctions reduce child labour? The role of credit markets', *Journal of Development Economics*, 68(1), 137–156.

Jafarey, S. and Lahiri, S. (2005): 'Food for education and funds for education quality: Policy options to reduce child labour', *Canadian Journal of Economics*, 38(2), 394–419.

Jayaraj, D. and Subramanian, S. (1997): 'Child labour in Tamil Nadu: A preliminary account of its nature, extent and distribution', Working Paper No. 151, Madras Institute of Development Studies, Chennai.

Jensen, E.R. (1990): 'An econometric analysis of the old-age security motive for childbearing', *International Economic Review*, 31, 953–968.

Jensen, P. and Nielsen, H.S. (1997): 'Child labour or school attendance? Evidence from Zambia', *Journal of Population Economics*, 10, 407–424.

Kambhampati, U.S. and Rajan, R. (2005): 'Does child work decrease with parental income? The luxury axiom revisited in India', *The European Journal of Development Research*, 17(4), 649–680.

Knodel, J., Havanon, N. and Sittitrai, W. (1990): 'Family size and education of children in the contest of rapid fertility decline', *Population and Development Review*, 16(1), 31–62.

Knodel, J. and Wongsith, M. (1991): 'Family size and children's education in Thailand: Evidence from a national sample', *Demography*, 28(1), 119–131.

Krueger, A. (1996): 'International labor standards and trade', in: Michael Bruno and Boris Pleskovic (eds.), *Annual World Bank Conference on Development Economics*, The World Bank, Washington, DC, 281–302.

Kruger, D.I. (2007): 'Coffee production effects on child labor and schooling in rural Brazil', *Journal of Development Economics*, 82, 448–463.

Lieten, G.K. (2003): 'Globalisation and child labour: Possible consequences', International conference on "Child labour within the context of globalisation: Problem outline and action points", Hattingen, Germany, 26–28 September 2003.

Lloyd, C.B. (1994): 'Investing in the next generation: The implication of high fertility at the level of the family', Research Division Working Paper No. 63, The Population Council, New York.

Loker, W. (1999): 'Grit in the prosperity machine: Globalization and the rural poor in Latin America', in: William Loker (ed.), *Globalization and the Rural Poor in Latin America*, Lynne Rienner, Boulder, CO, 9–40.

Lopez-Calva, L.F. (2002): 'A social stigma model of child labour', *Estudios Económicos*, 17(2), 193–217.

Moehling, C.M. (1998): 'State, child labour laws and the decline of child labour', Mimeograph, Ohio State University.

Moehling, C.M. (2005): '"She has suddenly become powerful": Youth employment and household decision-making in the early twentieth century', *The Journal of Economic History*, 65, 414–438.

Montegomery, M., Kouame, A. and Oliver, R. (1995): 'The tradeoff between number of children and child schooling: Evidence from Cote d'Ivoire and Ghana', Living Standards Measurement Study (LSMS) Working Paper No. 112, The World Bank, Washington, DC.

Nagaraj, K. (2002): 'Female and child workers in a household industry: A case study of beedi industry in Karnataka and Tamil Nadu', Mimeograph, Madras Institute of Development.

Nandi, T.K. (2015): 'The effect of employment guarantee scheme on school attendance in rural India', CTRPFP Working Paper No. 7, CSSS, Calcutta.

Nardinelli, C. (1990): *Child Labor and the Industrial Revolution*, Indiana University Press, Bloomington.

Neumayer, E. and Soysa, I. (2005): 'Trade openness, foreign direct investment and child labour', *World Development*, 33(1), 43–63.

Patrinos, H.A. and Psacharopoulos, G. (1995): 'Educational performance and child labor in Paraguay', *International Journal of Educational Development*, 15(1), 47–60.

Patrinos, H.A. and Psacharopoulos, G. (1997): 'Family size, schooling and child labor in Peru: An empirical analysis', *Journal of Population Economics*, 10, 387–405.

PROBE. (1999): *Public Report on Basic Education in India*, Oxford University Press, New Delhi.

Psacharopoulos, G. (1994): 'Returns to investment in education: A global update', *World Development*, 22, 1325–1343.

Psacharopoulos, G. (1997): 'Child labor versus educational attainment: Some evidence from Latin America', *Journal of Population Economics*, 10(4), 377–386.

Rangarajan, L.N. (1992): *Kautilya: The Arthashastra*, Penguin Books, New Delhi.

Ranjan, P. (1999): 'An economic analysis of child labour', *Economic Letters*, 64, 99–105.

Ranjan, P. (2001): 'Credit constraints and the phenomenon of child labour', *Journal of Development Economics*, 64, 81–102.

Ravallion, M. and Wodon, Q. (2000): 'Does cheaper schooling mean less child labour? Evidence from behavioural responses to an enrollment subsidy', *Economic Journal*, 110, C158–C175.

Ray, R. (2000a): 'Analysis of child labour in Peru and Pakistan: A comparative study', *Journal of Population Economics*, 13, 3–19.

Ray, R. (2000b): 'Child labour, child schooling and their interaction with adult labour: Empirical evidence from Peru and Pakistan', *The World Bank Economic Review*, 14(2), 347–367.

Rodgers, G. and Standing, G. (eds.). (1981): *Child Work, Poverty, and Underdevelopment*, International Labor Office, Geneva.

Rogers, C.A. and Swinnerton, K. (2000): 'Inequality, productivity, and child labor: Theory and evidence', Georgetown University Working Paper. Available at: http://ssrn.com/abstract=223795

Rosenzweig, M.R. and Everson, R. (1977): 'Fertility, schooling and the economic contribution of children in rural India: An econometric analysis', *Econometrica*, 45(5), 1065–1079.

Sasaki, M. and Temesgen, T. (1999): 'Children in different activities: Child labor and schooling in Peru', Draft, World Bank, Washington, DC.

Sharif, M. (1994): 'Child participation, nature of work and fertility demand: A theoretical analysis', *The Indian Economic Journal*, 40(4).

Skoufias, E. and Parker, S. (2001): 'Conditional cash transfers and their impact on child work and schooling', FCND Discussion Paper No. 123, International Food Policy Research Institute, Washington, DC.

Srinivasan, T.N. (1996): 'International trade and labour standards from an economic perspective', in: P. Van Dyck and G. Faber (eds.), *Challenges to the New World Trade Organization*, Kluwer Publishers, Amsterdam, 219–224.

Swaminathan, M. (1998): 'Economic growth and the persistence of child labor: Evidence from an Indian city', *World Development*, 26(8), 1513–1528.

Swinnerton, K.A. and Rogers, C.A. (1999): 'The economics of child labor: Comment', *American Economic Review*, 89(5), 1382–1385.

Thomas, D. (1990): 'Intra-household resource allocation: An inferential approach ', The Journal of Human Resources, 25(4), 635–664.

UNICEF. (1997): *The State of the World's Children, 1997*, Oxford University, Oxford.

Wahba, J. (2000): 'Do market wages influence child labor and child schooling?', Social Protection Discussion Paper Series, No. 0024, Human Development Network, The World Bank.

Weiner, M. (1991): *The Child and the State in India: Child Labor and Education Policy in Comparative Perspective*, Oxford University Press, New Delhi.

World Development Report. (1995): Published by Oxford University Press for The World Bank.

Xu, Z. (2007): 'A survey on intra-household models and evidence', MPRA Paper No. 3763. Available at: http:// mpra.ub.uni-muenchen.de/ 3763/

Zelizer, V.A. (1985): *Pricing the Priceless Child: The Changing Social Value of Children*, Basic Books, New York.

2 Derivation of supply functions of child labour from household behaviour

2.1 Introduction

In this chapter, we are going to derive the supply function of a working family from its optimizing behaviour. The key assumption behind our exercise is that children in the family have no bargaining power. Hence, they cannot decide on their own supply of labour. It is the guardian of the family who takes the decision on behalf of the family. In other words, we are not considering intrahousehold bargaining.[1]

A couple of certain other issues require clear explanations before we proceed. One such issue is the relationship between adult labour and child labour. Are these two complementary or substitutes? If they are substitutes, are they perfect substitutes?

The so-called *nimble fingers argument* claims that only children can do certain jobs or can do them better than adults. According to this line of thinking, child labour is essential in certain production activities like garments and carpet because their 'nimble fingers' are typically suited to perform activities like carpet weaving, stitching buttons, and the like. Hence, if this argument is valid, at least in some cases, two types of labour are complementary rather than substitutes.

The ILO (1996) had examined the validity of the nimble figures argument in the handwoven carpet, glass bracelet (bangles), diamond polishing, gem polishing, slate, and limestone and mosaic chip quarrying industries in India. These studies by the ILO (1996) undoubtedly refuted the nimble fingers argument that had claimed that only children could do certain jobs or could do them better than adults. "Very often," the studies found, "the jobs that only children perform consist of menial unskilled work that adults could do at least as quickly." "Some of the best carpets, those having the greatest density of small knots, are woven by adults," states the report. If child dexterity is not uniquely necessary to knot the finest carpets, it is difficult to imagine other trades for which the nimble fingers argument could be valid.

These arguments lead to the conclusion that child labour and adult labour are indeed substitutes but not complementary. This lends a helping hand to the substitution axiom of Basu and Van (1998). Then comes the question relating to the degree of substitutability between the two types of labour. First, let us consider the simple case (as in Basu (1999)) where these are perfect substitutes. If these are indeed perfect substitutes, we may assume that an adult's labour is equivalent to

μ units of a child's labour, where $0 < \mu > 1$. In other words, each adult, working all day, produces 1 unit of labour, whereas each child, working all day, produces $\left(\frac{1}{\mu}\right)$ units of labour. Thus, adult and child labour are perfect substitutes, subject to a child-equivalent scale correction of μ. If the adult wage is W, the child wage, denoted W_C would be equal to $\left(\frac{W}{\mu}\right)$.

However, the idea that child labour and adult labour are perfect substitutes is too simplistic. This is because there are quite a few numbers of intermediate stages of production even in agriculture adult labour that cannot be substituted by child labour although, as per ILO (2012), the concentration of child labour is the highest in the rural sector of a developing economy, and child labour is used intensively directly or indirectly in agriculture.[2] Farming in backward agriculture is mostly done by using bullocks and ploughs, and the cattle feeding is done entirely by child labour.[3] Besides, during peak season when there is a temporary scarcity of adult labour, demand for child labour remains high. Children are often used in the family farms for helping adult members of the family. However, in certain activities even in backward agriculture—digging wells, applying fertilizers and weedicides and thrashing crops—children are seldom used. Besides, in advanced agriculture, labour-saving technologies are used that rely heavily on modern machines. This reduces and eliminates use of child labour. Thus, if we consider agriculture as a vertically integrated sector comprised of both backward agriculture and advanced agriculture, it would be proper if adult labour and child labour are considered imperfect substitutes. Hence, the child wage, W_C, is not a fixed fraction of the adult wage, W.

On the other hand, the objective of the guardian may differ across families. First, some guardians might be altruistic, and the others are not. An altruistic guardian does care for his children and derives utility from the children's leisure. The luxury axiom of Basu and Van (1998) and Basu (1999) is applicable in such a case. The luxury axiom suggests that child labour is a luxury commodity to the poor household. If the income of the family from its nonchild sources (e.g. adult wage income) is below a certain critical level, it considers itself as poor and decides to send some of its children out to work in the job market to supplement low family income. This is the *poverty hypothesis* of Basu and Van (1998) and Basu (1999). Second, there could be families that do not care about the well-being of their children and maximize their own consumption. We rule out such a possibility on the basis of evidence provided in the literature review section of the previous chapter. We rather consider a static framework where a representative altruistic guardian decides on the supply of child labour from his family where there is no room for human capital formation.

Next, we consider a situation where the guardian is maximizing the intertemporal or lifetime income (welfare). In such a case, human capital formation through education plays a very crucial role. Children who go to schools in the current period become skilled workers in the future and earn skilled wages, which are greater than unskilled wages. On the contrary, children who go to the job market and work as child workers in the current period grow up as unskilled workers in future. The family maximizes its lifetime utility and decides on the supply of child labour in the current period. In this case, children's leisure does not come into consideration of the family.

Hence, we will be going to consider the following three cases: (1) the family is altruistic, but the two types of labour are not perfect substitutes; (2) the family is altruistic, and child labour and adult labour are perfect substitutes; (3) the family maximizes its intertemporal utility, and there is scope for human capital formation through education. However, in the first two cases, the question of human capital formation does not arise because the analysis is static in nature. Let us consider these three cases one by one and derive the supply function of child labour by each family.

2.2 Derivations of the supply function of child labour of a working family

Let us first consider a static framework with an altruistic family and discuss how its decision on the supply of child labour is taken.

2.2.1 Case I: a static framework and imperfect substitutability between child labour and adult labour

The supply function of child labour is derived from the utility maximizing behaviour of the representative altruistic household. We assume that all of the working families who supply child labour, although they do care about the well-being of their children, are identical in every respect and that each household consists of only one adult member and n number of children. There exists a critical adult wage income (income from nonchild sources), say $\bar{W}$, such that any family whose adult wage income is less than or just equal to $\bar{W}$ considers itself as poor and decides to send some of its children out to work in the child labour market at the competitive child wage, W_C. Adult workers whose adult incomes are greater than $\bar{W}$ do not send their children to the job market. In the absence of any scope skill formation through education in schools, these children are kept at homes that gives utility to these families.[4] We are here considering the case where adult labour and child labour are not perfect substitutes to each other. Although the adult wage, W, is greater than the child wage, W_C, there is no strict proportional relationship between the two wages. For the sake of simplicity, we assume that the owners of other factors of production like capital and land are separate classes and that they do not supply any child labour.[5]

The altruistic adult member of the family (guardian) decides on the number of children to be sent to the workplace (l_C). The rest, ($n - l_C$), are kept at home. Hence, ($n - l_C$) measures the aggregate amount of leisure of its children. Suppose that the family consumes three other commodities.[6] The utility function of the representative household is given by

$$U = U\left[C_1, C_2, C_3, (n - l_C)\right] \tag{2.1}$$

The household derives utility from the consumption of the three commodities, C_is for $i = 1, 2, 3$, and from the children's leisure. For the sake of analytical simplicity let us consider the following Cobb-Douglas type utility function for each household.

$$U = A(C_1)^{\alpha}(C_2)^{\beta}(C_3)^{\rho}(n - l_C)^{\gamma} \qquad (2.2)$$

with $A > 0$, $1 > \alpha$, β, ρ, $\gamma > 0$, and $(\alpha + \beta + \rho + \gamma) = 1$.

It satisfies all the standard properties, and it is homogeneous of degree 1. The parameter γ denotes the degree of altruism of the guardian towards the well-being of his children. The value of γ crucially depends on the social values and norms of the society towards child labour. In a relatively educationally advanced society, the value of γ is likely to be comparatively high.

Ruling out the possibility for any child worker attending school to undertake any part-time job, the budget constraint of the representative poor household is given by the following.

$$P_1C_1 + P_2C_2 + P_3C_3 = (W_C l_C + W) \qquad (2.3)$$

where W is the income of the adult worker, and $W_C l_C$ measures the income from child labour. P_i denotes the price of the ith commodity for $i = 1, 2, 3$. The household takes the commodity prices and the two wage rates as datum.

The household maximizes its utility subject to its budget constraint. This is a constrained optimization problem. The relevant Lagrange expression is given by the following.

$$\Omega = A(C_1)^{\alpha}(C_2)^{\beta}(C_3)^{\rho}(n - l_C)^{\gamma} + \eta[W_C l_C + W - P_1C_1 - P_2C_2 - P_3C_3] \qquad (2.4)$$

where η is the Lagrange multiplier and $\eta > 0$.

The problem of the household is to maximize this expression with respect to C_1, C_2, C_3, l_C, and η. The first-order conditions are as follows.

$$\left(\frac{\partial \Omega}{\partial C_1}\right) = \alpha A(C_1)^{\alpha-1}(C_2)^{\beta}(C_3)^{\rho}(n - l_C)^{\gamma} - \eta P_1 = 0 \qquad (2.5.1)$$

$$\left(\frac{\partial \Omega}{\partial C_2}\right) = \beta A(C_1)^{\alpha}(C_2)^{\beta-1}(C_3)^{\rho}(n - l_C)^{\gamma} - \eta P_2 = 0 \qquad (2.5.2)$$

$$\left(\frac{\partial \Omega}{\partial C_3}\right) = \rho A(C_1)^{\alpha}(C_2)^{\beta}(C_3)^{\rho-1}(n - l_C)^{\gamma} - \eta P_3 = 0 \qquad (2.5.3)$$

$$\left(\frac{\partial \Omega}{\partial l_C}\right) = -\gamma A(C_1)^{\alpha}(C_2)^{\beta}(C_3)^{\rho}(n - l_C)^{\gamma-1} + \eta W_C = 0 \qquad (2.5.4)$$

$$\left(\frac{\partial \Omega}{\partial \eta}\right) = [W_C l_C + W - P_1C_1 - P_2C_2 - P_3C_3] = 0 \qquad (2.5.5)$$

Using equations (2.2) and (2.5.1)–(2.5.4), eliminating η and simplifying the first-order conditions may be rewritten as follows.

$$((\alpha U) / P_1C_1) = ((\beta U) / (P_2C_2)) = ((\rho U) / (P_3C_3)) = ((\gamma U) / (n - l_C)W_C) \qquad (2.6)$$

From (2.6) we get the following expressions.

$$C_1 = \{\alpha(n - l_C)W_C / \gamma P_1\} \tag{2.7.1}$$

$$C_2 = \{\beta(n - l_C)W_C / (\gamma P_2)\} \tag{2.7.2}$$

$$C_3 = \{\rho(n - l_C)W_C / (\gamma P_3)\} \tag{2.7.3}$$

Substitution of the values of C_1, C_2 and C_3 in (2.5.5) and further simplifications give us the following child labour supply function of each poor working household.

$$l_C = \left\{(1 - \gamma)n - \gamma \frac{W}{W_C}\right\} \tag{2.8}$$

However, for l_C to be positive, we require that

$$(1 - \gamma)n > \left(\frac{\gamma W}{W_C}\right) \tag{2.9}$$

The condition as given by (2.9) puts some restrictions on the system parameters.

Using (2.8) from equation (2.7.2) we can derive the demand function for commodity of the family as follows.

$$C_2 = \beta \frac{(W + nW_C)}{P_2} \tag{2.8.1}$$

From equation (2.8), the consumption of children's leisure by the family may be obtained as follows.

$$(n - l_C) = \gamma \left(\frac{W + nW_C}{W_C}\right) \tag{2.8.2}$$

Let us now analyze the properties of the child labour supply function as given by equation (2.8). A rise in W produces a positive income effect so that the adult worker chooses more leisure for his children and therefore decides to send a fewer number of children to the place of work. An increase in W_C, on the other hand, implies increased opportunity cost of leisure and hence produces a negative price effect. This leads to a decrease in children's leisure and hence raises the supply of child labour by each family.[7]

If there are F number of homogeneous poor families that supply child labour and each of them sends l_C number of children to workplace, the aggregate supply function of child labour in the economy is given by

$$L_C = \left[(1 - \gamma)n - \gamma \frac{W}{W_C}\right]F \tag{2.10}$$

Case II: a static framework with perfect substitutability between adult labour and child labour

We now consider the case where adults can do whatever children do and vice versa. Hence, adult labour and child labour are perfect substitutes subject to a child-equivalent scale correction of μ where, $\mu > 1$. This implies that 1 unit of adult labour is equivalent to μ units of child labour. Hence, under competitive labour market conditions, the child wage rate, W_C, must be $\left(\frac{W}{\mu}\right)$ when the adult wage rate is W.

Substituting $W_C = \left(\frac{W}{\mu}\right)$ in equation (2.8), we find

$$l_C = \{(1-\gamma)n - \mu\gamma\} \tag{2.11}$$

l_C is thus constant. Hence, if child labour and adult labour are perfect substitutes and households are altruistic, the supply of child labour by each family does not depend on wages and is constant. This is because the income effect and the price effect are equally strong so that they cancel out each other's effects.

A special case

Let us now see whether this supply function undergoes any changes if there are public incentives in the form of scholarships, distribution of free school uniforms and books and midday meals designed to keep children in school even though the two types of labour are perfect substitutes.

We assume that only a public educational system is available to the children in the economy and that it is entirely financed by government subsidy on this account.[8,9] In a society with high fertility rate, the poor perception by the parents of the future benefits of children's education, the low quality of schooling and households' objectives to maximize present income, one of the main motives behind the decision of the poorer households in sending some of their offspring to public schools is to derive the immediate benefits of the free education policy.[10] In the public education system in the developing economies, there are provisions for the children from the poorer families to get stipends, free educational goods and free midday meals. It is sensible to assume that higher the subsidy on education, E, the higher would be the free educational facilities and the related benefits, B, associated with child schooling. On the other hand, the larger the number of children sent to schools, the higher would be the aggregate benefits accrued to the poor families. We make the simplifying assumption that the money value of such benefits is strictly proportional to the number of children sent to schools.

The household derives utility from the consumption of the final goods and from the children's leisure. However, children's leisure here does not imply that the children who are not sent out to work are kept at home. They are sent to schools.[11] The altruistic guardian of the family derives utility from this source because at least some of the children have been kept out of the work hazards. Besides, by sending some of the children to school, the family secures current income gain from access to the different incentives that the free education scheme provides.

We continue to assume the same family welfare (utility) function for the household as given by equation (2.2). Nonetheless, the family budget equation undergoes changes. This is now given by the following.

$$P_1 C_1 + P_2 C_2 + P_3 C_3 = (W_C l_C + W) + (n - l_C)B(E) \tag{2.12}$$

where $(n - l_C)B(E)$ is the money value of the benefits derived by the household from sending $(n - l_C)$ number of children to schools. Note that $B'(.)$ is positive. Here the effective child wage rate is $(W_C - B(E))$.[12]

We use the same Lagrange technique. Maximizing, eliminating the Lagrange multiplier and simplifying, we arrive at the following first-order conditions.

$$((\alpha U) / (P_1 C_1)) = ((\beta U) / (P_2 C_2)) = ((\rho U) / (P_3 C_3)) = ((\gamma U) / (n - l_C)(W_C - B(E))) \quad (2.13)$$

From (2.13) we get the following expressions.

$$C_1 = \{\alpha(n - l_C)(W_C - B(E)) / (\gamma P_1)\} \quad (2.14)$$

$$C_2 = \{\beta(n - l_C)(W_C - B(E)) / (\gamma P_2)\} \quad (2.15)$$

$$C_3 = \{\rho(n - l_C)(W_C - B(E)) / (\gamma P_3)\} \quad (2.16)$$

Substituting the values of C_1, C_2 and C_3 in the budget equation (equation 2.12) and simplifying, we finally arrive at the following family supply function of child labour.

$$l_C = \frac{\left[n\{(\alpha + \beta + \rho)W_C - B(E)\} - \gamma W\right]}{(W_C - B(E))} \quad (2.17)$$

We now analyze its properties. First, l_C varies negatively with the adult wage rate, W. A rise in W produces a positive income effect so that the adult worker sends a larger number of children to schools and therefore decides to send a lower number of children to the workplace. An increase in W_C (or an increase in $(W_C - B(E))$), on the other hand, produces a negative price effect, which increases the supply of child labour from the family.

Because adult labour and child labour are perfect substitutes in this model subject to a child-equivalent scale correction of μ, the child wage rate, W_C, must be (W/μ) when the adult wage rate is W. Substituting (W/μ) in place of W_C in (2.17), we get

$$l_C = \frac{\left[n\{(\alpha + \beta)(W / \mu) - B(E)\} - \gamma W\right]}{((W / \mu) - B(E))} \quad (2.18)$$

Differentiating (2.18) with respect to W, we get

$$(dl_C / dW) = \left[B(E)\gamma\left(1 + \frac{n}{\mu}\right)\left(\frac{1}{(W / \mu) - B(E)}\right)^2\right] > 0.$$ In this case, the nega-

tive price effect of an increase in the adult wage rate, W, taking place through an increase in the effective child wage rate, $((W/\mu) - B(E))$, outweighs the positive income effect so that the net effect would be an increase in the supply of child labour. Consequently, an increase in the adult wage, W, leads to an increase in the supply of child labour by each poor working family when the two types of labour are perfect substitutes and there are certain immediate monetary benefits from sending children to school.

2.2.2 *Intertemporal utility-maximizing household*

In this sub-section, let us consider a dynamic set-up where the family decides on the supply of child where its objective is to maximize the intertemporal utility of the family.

2.2.2.1 *Case III: child labour supply decision of an intertemporal utility-maximizing family*

We consider a dynamic partial equilibrium framework to analyze the behaviour of the representative household that maximizes its intertemporal utility and derive the supply function of child labour. Because this analysis is dynamic in nature, there is scope for human capital formation through education. If a child goes to school in the current period, in the next period he grows up and comes out as a skilled worker. On the contrary, if he works as child labour in the current period, he cannot acquire skills and grows up as an unskilled worker. Because the skilled wage in the current period, W_S, is greater than the unskilled wage, W, and the intertemporal utility depends positively on the income level in each period, the household finds it profitable to send some of its children to school so that they can earn a higher wage in future.

In this two-period optimizing problem, the representative working family consists of one adult member (the guardian) and a child. In the economy, there are L and S numbers of unskilled and skilled working families, respectively. Besides, the economy is endowed with a fixed amount of capital, K_D. We assume that workers are the owners of capital and the income from capital is equally distributed among the working families.[13] Each working family, irrespective of whether skilled or unskilled, receives an equal share, $\left(\frac{RK_D}{L+S}\right)$, of the capital income where R and K_D stand for return to capital and size of capital stock, respectively. The guardian of each working family in the first period works in the adult labour market and earns a wage W_0.[14] In this period, he takes decisions about his child's work effort and schooling. Total child time is 1, a part of which (l_C) is sent out to work at the wage rate W_C. Nonexistence of a market for loans against future earnings compels the parent to use income from child work to smooth out the family consumption.[15] Time not spent on working is spent in school.[16] Hence $(1 - l_C)$ is the child's schooling. Hence, the l_C part of the child labour time earns the child wage, (W_C), in the first period and the unskilled adult wage (W) in the second period while the $(1 - l_C)$ fraction earns nothing in the first period but the skilled wage (W_S) in the second period.[17] In the presence of positive return to education, W_S is greater than W. In the second period, the guardian earns nothing and lives on his family share of rental income and the income he receives from his child who has become an adult worker by this time.

We assume that the parent cares only about the lifetime family consumption. The utility is therefore a function of consumption levels in the two periods (1 and 2) and is represented as follows.

$$U = \frac{C_1^{-\rho}}{-\rho} + \beta\frac{C_2^{-\rho}}{-\rho}; -1 < \rho < \infty \qquad (2.19)$$

β is the time discount factor with $\beta < 1$, and $\left(\frac{1}{1+\rho}\right)$ is the constant intertemporal elasticity of substitution.

For algebraic simplicity, we consider the special case where $\rho = 0$, which implies a logarithmic utility function with unitary intertemporal elasticity of substitution.[18]

$$U = \log C_1 + \beta \log C_2 \quad \text{with } C_1, C_2 > 0 \tag{2.20}$$

The first period's consumption (C_1) consists of wage income of the guardian and child wage from the working time of the child and the rental income; that is

$$C_1 = (W_0 + l_C W_C) + \frac{RK_D}{(L+S)} \tag{2.21}$$

The second period's consumption (C_2) can be thought of as the sum of the skilled wage of the educated adult (schooled in the first period) labour and the unskilled wage of the uneducated adult labour (worked in the first period) and the household share of rental income.[19]

$$C_2 = (l_C W + (1 - l_C)W_S) + \frac{RK_D}{(L+S)} \tag{2.22}$$

We assume that the only cost of education is the opportunity cost in terms of the forgone earnings of children.[20]

The guardian maximizes the lifetime utility (equation (2.20)) with respect to l_C and subject to (2.21) and (2.22). Using (2.21) and (2.22), equation (2.20) may be rewritten as follows.

$$U = \log\left[(W_0 + l_C W_C) + \frac{RK_D}{(L+S)}\right] + \beta \log\left[(l_C W + (1 - l_C)W_S) + \frac{RK_D}{(L+S)}\right] \tag{2.20.1}$$

Thus, the maximization problem has been converted to an unconstrained one. Equation (2.20.1) is now maximized through a choice of l_C.

Maximization gives the following first-order condition.[21]

$$\left[\frac{l_C W + (1 - l_C)W_S + \frac{RK_D}{(L+S)}}{W_0 + l_C W_C + \frac{RK_D}{(L+S)}}\right] = \frac{\beta(W_S - W)}{W_C} \tag{2.23}$$

Solving equation (2.23), the following child labour function by each working family is obtained.

$$l_C = \left[\left\{\frac{W_S + R_H}{(1+\beta)(W_S - W)}\right\} - \beta\left\{\frac{W_0 + R_H}{(1+\beta)W_C}\right\}\right] \tag{2.24}$$

where

$$R_H = \frac{RK_D}{(L+S)} > 0$$

Because, there are two groups of workers, skilled and unskilled, the family supply curves of them are given as follows, respectively.

$$l_{CS} = \frac{W_S + R_H}{(1+\beta)(W_S - W)} - \frac{\beta\{W_S + R_H\}}{(1+\beta)W_C}$$

and

$$l_{CU} = \frac{W_S + R_H}{(1+\beta)(W_S - W)} - \frac{\beta\{W + R_H\}}{(1+\beta)W_C}$$

$$(2.25)$$

If both skilled and unskilled working families supply child labour, then from equation (2.25) it follows that[22]

$$l_{CS} > 0 \text{ if and only if } W_C > \beta(W_S - W) \text{ and}$$
$$l_{CU} > 0 \text{ if } W_C \geq \beta(W_S - W)$$

$$(2.26)$$

$W_C > \beta(W_S - W)$ implies that the child wage rate has to be greater than the discounted present value of the skill premium for both types of working families to supply child labour.

The properties of the child labour supply function, given by (2.24), are as follows. An increase in current income, W_0 (income from nonchild sources), raises C_1 directly and lowers l_C following a positive income effect so as to increase C_2. An increase in the child wage rate implies an increase in the opportunity cost of education and hence leads to more child labour supply (i.e. less schooling). Any changes in skilled and/or unskilled wage impinge on the return to education and therefore influence the guardian's decision regarding allocation of child time between education and work. For example, an increase in skilled wage (W_S) or a decrease in unskilled wage (W) will make education more attractive and raise the schooling time of the child, thereby lowering the supply of child labour by the household. An increase in rental income of the household, R_H, produces two opposite effects on l_C. On the one hand, it increases the current income, which raises C_1 directly and lowers l_C following a positive income effect, so as to increase C_2, and on the other, it increases the future income (and also C_2) and raises l_C so that C_1 can increase. The net effect on l_C depends on the relative strengths of the two opposite effects. It can be easily shown[23] that an increase in R_H raises l_C because we have assumed that $W_C > \beta(W_S - W)$.

An important matter to mention at this juncture is that in section 2.2.1 in one of the cases, we have derived the supply function of child labour by each family in the presence of education subsidy. We considered only the immediate monetary benefits arising out of the subsidy appropriated by the family through sending some of its children to school. Nonetheless, we could not consider the aspect of skill formation because the structure was static. We have already pointed out that the issue of skill formation is a dynamic one that should be addressed only by using a dynamic framework. Because the present analysis is dynamic in nature, it is the appropriate structure to analyze the consequence of different incentive schemes, such as midday meal programs and/or cash stipend schemes, on the supply of child labour by each family, where not only short-term gains but also long-term benefits accrue to the family through sending some of its children to school.

2.2.2.2   *Child labour supply decision in the presence of an incentive scheme*

Let us assume that there are provisions for midday meals and cash stipends for children attending school and that the immediate (i.e. in the current period) monetary value of that is b per unit of child time attending school. Hence, l_C fraction of child time earns the child wage (W_C) in the first period and the unskilled adult wage (W) in the second period while the remaining ($n - l_C$) units of child time earn b in the first period and the skilled wage (W_S) in the second period. We assume that $W_C > b$; otherwise no children will be sent out to work.

Equation (2.21) will now undergo some changes and is rewritten as follows.

$$C_1 = \left[\{W_0 + l_C W_C + b(1 - l_C)\} + \frac{RK_D}{(L + S)} \right] \tag{2.21.1}$$

The second period's consumption (C_2) given by equation (2.22), however, does not change.

The intertemporal utility of the household is now given by the following equation.

$$U = \log \left[\{W_0 + l_C W_C + b(1 - l_C)\} + \frac{RK_D}{(L + S)} \right] + \beta \log \left[(l_C W \right.$$

$$\left. + (1 - l_C)W_S) + \frac{RK_D}{(L + S)} \right] \tag{2.20.2}$$

The household now maximizes this utility function with respect to l_C.

From the first-order condition, l_C can be solved as follows.

$$l_C = \frac{W_S + R_H}{(1 + \beta)(W_S - W)} - \frac{\beta(W_0 + b) + R_H}{(1 + \beta)(W_C - b)} \tag{2.24.1}$$

From equation (2.24.1), it can be easily verified that an increase in the pecuniary benefits from the midday meal program, b, lowers the effective child wage rate, ($W_C - b$), thereby leading to less child labour supply, l_C, by the family.

Appendix 2.1

The supply functions of child labour by skilled and unskilled working families are given by the following two equations, respectively.

$$l_{CS} = \frac{W_S + R_H}{(1+\beta)(W_S - W)} - \frac{\beta\{W_S + R_H\}}{(1+\beta)W_C}$$

and

$$l_{CU} = \frac{W_S + R_H}{(1+\beta)(W_S - W)} - \frac{\beta\{W + R_H\}}{(1+\beta)W_C}$$

$$(2.A.1)$$

where

$$R_H = \frac{RK_D}{(L+S)} > 0$$

If we now assume that each skilled working family supplies child labour, it implies that $l_{CS} > 0$. From equation (2.25), it then follows that

$$\frac{W_S + R_H}{(1+\beta)(W_S - W)} > \frac{\beta.(W_0 + R_H)}{(1+\beta)W_C}$$

or

$$\frac{W_S + R_H}{(W_S + R_H)} > \frac{\beta.(W_S - W)}{W_C}$$

or

$$1 > \frac{\beta.(W_S - W)}{W_C}$$

that is

$$W_C > \beta(W_S - W)$$

Hence, a necessary and sufficient condition for $l_{CS} > 0$ is that

$$W_C > \beta(W_S - W)$$

$$(2.A.2)$$

On the other hand, $l_{CU} > 0$ if and only if

$$\frac{(W_S + R_H)}{(W + R_H)} > \frac{\beta.(W_S - W)}{W_C}$$

As $W_S > W$ from the preceding expression, it follows that $l_{CU} > 0$ under the sufficient condition that $W_C \geq \beta(W_S - W)$.

Notes

1 This may not always be the case. There are empirical evidences (see, for example, Andvig 2000; Yasuyuki et al. 2006) in support of the fact that teenage workers do have significant intrahousehold bargaining power in determining their labour supply and consumption decision. One has recourse to collective models like those of Bourguignon and Chiappori (1994) and Moehling (1995) for analyzing intrahousehold bargaining.

2 According to the ILO (2012), more than 59 per cent of economically active children in the developing countries are engaged in agriculture and allied sectors. In the case of India, this figure is as high as 68 per cent (National Sample Survey Organisation 2006).

3 See Gupta (2000) in this context.

4 Because skill formation takes place over time, it is a dynamic issue. Hence, it cannot be captured in a static framework like this. In a subsequent section, however, we use a dynamic set-up to address this aspect.

5 Alternatively, one can assume that rental incomes are equally divided among the L number of working families. Consequently, the share of rental incomes enters into the household maximization exercise.

6 Because this supply function of child labour would be used in different general equilibrium models in the subsequent chapters, the number of goods consumed by the family would differ from case to case.

7 It may be checked that the results of the models in the subsequent chapters where this function has been used hold for any utility function generating a supply function of child labour that satisfies these two important properties.

8 Governments all over the world devote substantial resources to their education sector. This is especially true in developing countries. In 1995, public spending on education accounted for 15.7 per cent of total government expenditure in developing countries (see Bedi and Garg (2000). Furthermore, the majority of students in developing countries are educated in publicly funded and publicly managed educational institutions. According to Jimenez and Lockheed (1995), almost 90 per cent of all primary and 70 per cent of all secondary enrollments in developing countries are in public schools.

9 The present analysis does not deal with an important aspect of child labour – its relation to education and human capital. However, Basu and Van (1998) also share the same limitation.

10 In this context, mention should be made of an empirical paper by Ravallion and Wodon (2000), who have found that the school enrollment subsidy substantially increased the number of schoolgoing children from the poorer segment of the households in Bangladesh. Nonetheless, the magnitude of decline in the incidence of child labour as a proportion of the total amount of enrollment subsidy was insignificant. This is because parents were clearly substituting other uses of their children's time, so as to secure the current income gain from access to the program with modest impact on earnings from their children's work.

11 This is a static framework. Hence, the aspects of education and human capital formation and their effect on the supply of child labour have not been dealt with in this section.

12 We assume that $W_C > B(E)$. Otherwise, no children are sent to the job market.

13 There is no harm if this assumption is dropped. This would be clear from the analyses of some of the subsequent chapters.

14 W_0 can take two values, W (unskilled wage) and W_S (skilled wage), depending on the type of the representative working household.

15 In the developing countries, informal credit markets serve as a substitute for missing formal credit market, but they mainly deal in short-term loans. Poor households need long-term credit to be able to substitute for the foregone earnings of their children, which is missing in the developing countries. The crucial role of credit constraint in explaining the inefficient child labour has been empirically verified by Beegle et al. (2003) and Dehejia and Gatti (2003) etc. This aspect has been theoretically dealt with in Ranjan (1999, 2001), Baland and Robinson (2000) and Jafarey and Lahiri (2002, 2005), among others.

16 This is a simplifying assumption that ignores the existence of nonlabour non-schoolgoers.

17 The introduction of uncertainty in securing a skilled job in the second period would be an interesting theoretical exercise. However, the results of the model still hold if the probability in finding a high-skill job is given exogenously.

18 See Ranjan (1999) for a similar treatment.

19 Because family composition and number of working families remain constant, each family's share of rental income in the second period also remains the same.

20 One can incorporate direct schooling costs without affecting the qualitative results of the model.

21 The second-order condition of maximization is satisfied because

$$\left(\frac{d^2U}{dl_c^2}\right) = -\left[\frac{(W_C)^2}{\{W_0 + l_C W_C + (RK_D / (L+S))\}^2}\right]$$
$$-\left[\frac{\beta(W_s - W)^2}{\{W_s - l_C(W_s - W) + (RK_D / (L+S))\}^2}\right] < 0$$

22 See appendix 2.1 in this connection.

23 From (2.24), it follows that $\left(\frac{\partial l_C}{\partial R_H}\right) = \left[\frac{\{W_C - \beta(W_s - W)\}}{(1+\beta)(W_s - W)W_C}\right] > 0$ iff $W_C > \beta(W_s - W)$.

References

Andvig, J.C. (2000): 'An essay on child labour in Sub-Saharan Africa – A bargaining approach', Norwegian Institute of International Affairs Working Paper No. 613.

Baland, J. and Robinson, J.A. (2000): 'Is child labour inefficient?', *Journal of Political Economy*, 108(4), 663–679.

Basu, K. (1999): 'Child labour: Cause, consequence, and cure, with remarks on international labour standards', *Journal of Economic Literature*, 37(September), 1083–1119.

Basu, K. and Van, P.H. (1998): 'The economics of child labour', *American Economic Review*, 88(3), 412–427.

Bedi, A.S. and Garg, A. (2000): 'The effectiveness of private versus public schools: The case of Indonesia', *Journal of Development Economics*, 61, 463–494.

Beegle, K., Dehejia, R.H. and Gatti, R. (2003): 'Child labour, crop shocks, and credit constraints', NBER Working Paper No. W10088.

Bourguignon, F. and Chiappori, P.A. (1994): 'The collective approach to household behaviour', in: R. Blundell, I. Preston and I. Walker (eds.), *The Measurement of Household Welfare*, Cambridge University Press, Cambridge, 70–85.

Dehejia, R.H. and Gatti, R. (2003): 'Child labour: The role of income variability and credit constraints across countries', NBER Working Paper No. 9018.

Gupta, M.R. (2000): 'Wage determination of a child worker: A theoretical analysis', *Review of Development Economics*, 4(2), 219–228.

ILO. (1996): 'Child labour: Refuting the "nimble fingers" argument', International Labour Office. Available at: http://www.citinv.it/associazioni/CNMS/archivio/paesi/clabour_today.html

ILO. (2012): *Making Progress against Child Labour: Global Estimates and Trends 2000–2012*, International Labour Office, Geneva.

Jafarey, S. and Lahiri, S. (2002): 'Will trade sanctions reduce child labour? The role of credit markets', *Journal of Development Economics*, 68(1), 137–156.

Jafarey, S. and Lahiri, S. (2005): 'Food for education versus school quality: A comparison of policy options to reduce child labour', *Canadian Journal of Economics*, 38(2), 394–419.

Jimenez, E. and Lockheed, M. (1995): 'Public and private secondary education in developing countries: A comparative study', World Bank Discussion Paper No. 309, The World Bank, Washington, DC.

Moehling, C.M. (1995): 'The intra-household allocation of resources and the participation of children in household decision-making: Evidence from early twentieth century America', Mimeograph, Northwestern University.

NSSO. (2006): 'Employment and unemployment situation in India 2004–05', Government of India, Ministry of Statistics and Programme Implementation.

Ranjan, P. (1999): 'An economic analysis of child labour', *Economic Letters*, 64, 99–105.

Ranjan, P. (2001): 'Credit constraints and the phenomenon of child labour', *Journal of Development Economics*, 64, 81–102.

Ravallion, M. and Wodon, Q. (2000): 'Does child labour displace schooling? Evidence on behavioural responses to an enrollment subsidy', *The Economic Journal*, 110(462), C158–C175.

Yasuyuki, S., Kensuke, K., Nobuhiko, F., Seiro, I. and Kurosaki, T. (2006): 'On the mother and the child labour nexus under credit constraints: Findings from rural', *Developing Economies*, 44(4), 465–499.

3 Trade sanction and child labour

3.1 Introduction

Child labour is considered a social evil. Statutory provisions and efforts have been concerted towards its eradication and prevention in different parts of the world. However, despite all efforts and statutory provisions, child labour continues to be a problem of enormous dimension, especially in the developing countries. According to ILO (2002), one in every six children between 5 and 17 years of age – or 246 million children – is involved in child labour. Out of the 246 million, about 170 million child workers were found in different hazardous and illegal activities. There is no gainsaying that the incidence of child labour worldwide has decreased over the last few years both in absolute and percentage terms. According to ILO (2013) estimates, 168 million children aged 5–17 were involved in child labour in 2012 (10.6 per cent) compared to 215 million in 2008 (13.6 per cent). However, the aggregate number of child labour is still quite high. Besides, if the invisible workers who perform unpaid and household jobs are included, the estimates are likely to shoot up significantly.

Poverty has been attributed as the single largest factor behind the incidence of child labour in a developing economy. It compels people to have large families and children to go out into the job market and earn their own means of livelihood. Apart from poverty, the supply of child labour has also been attributed to factors such as failure of the educational system, the objectives of households to maximize present income, a dualistic economy characteristic of developing countries with the coexistence of formal and informal sectors, and so on.

The *World Development Report (1995)*, recognizing poverty as the greatest single force behind the incidence of child labour, called for a multifaceted approach with programs that increase income security, reduce education costs and improve the quality of schooling. However, policy prescriptions directed towards poverty alleviation are difficult to implement properly due to various bottlenecks and vicious circles typical of developing economies; even if implemented, they take a long time to mitigate the problem, so that legal restrictions can be more instrumental in dealing with child labour. Legislative fiats to combat child labour range from an outright ban on child labour to social labeling of products. The imposition of trade sanctions on products, which are produced using child labour, is related to the agitation for minimal international labour standards. Use of child labour in production is one way of violating labour standards, and the imposition of sanctions on the import of commodities produced using child labour is one such social clause. The argument in favour of the clause is that the use of child labour gives the developing countries a trading advantage in labour-intensive goods, which is illegitimate because the use of child labour in production activities is socially unethical and unacceptable. Those who oppose the inclusion of the clause argue that trade sanctions will encourage protectionism and that it will hurt not only the workers in the developing countries but also the consumers in the developed countries. According to them, the international campaign against child labour, waged by bodies, is hardly guided by any ethical or humanitarian motive. On the contrary, their sole motive is to preserve the interests of the developed countries by depriving the labour-intensive export industries of the developing countries of cost advantages in the international market. Several economists, for example, Bhagwati (1995) and Srinivasan (1996), have argued that a social clause in the WTO is not the right response to child labour.[1] It is therefore important to have a close look at trade sanctions as a means of reducing child labour.

There are some theoretical papers that have studied the efficacy of trade sanctions as a policy of reducing the incidence of child labour. Jafarey and Lahiri (2002) have examined the interaction between credit markets, trade sanctions and the child labour incidence in a two-commodity, two-period model. However, they have laid special emphasis on the role of the credit market in financing the cost of children's education. Trade sanctions may have an adverse effect on the incidence of child labour, which however, diminishes as the accessibility of the poor households to the credit market increases. Gupta (2002), on the other hand, has considered a three-sector general equilibrium model where an incentive wage mechanism on the part of the firms to overcome the moral hazard problem leads to the existence of unemployment in the adult labour market. The supply of child labour varies negatively with the rate of unemployment in the adult labour market. The paper shows that trade sanctions may increase the incidence of child labour. Nevertheless, trade and fiscal policies, which impact the effective producers' price of the good produced by adult workers, may help in reducing the prevalence of the evil in the system. Davis (2005) has found that if firms producing commodities with or without child labour are engaged in Bertrand competition among themselves, social labeling is not likely to drive out products produced by child labour even if consumers prefer commodities that are free of child labour. Finally, Basu and Zarghamee (2009) have shown that consumer product boycotts can, in a wide class of situations, have an adverse reaction that causes child labour to rise rather than fall.

The issue of trade sanctions as an instrument in eliminating child labour has again come into the limelight after a social activist in India, a strong advocator of such a policy, was awarded the Nobel Peace Prize in 2014. Such an important event may be seen as giving a formal recognition to imposing social labeling on the products that have used child labour in any of their production processes, although Bhagwati warned about the possible disastrous consequences of the policy a long time ago.[2] In the circumstances, further research on the consequences of trade sanctions on the incidence of child labour and other related aspects like adult unemployment and the welfare of poor families supplying child labour has become a necessity. The theoretical exercise in this chapter aims at addressing these aspects in terms of two general equilibrium models with child labour that are reasonable for small open developing economies. In the first model, we have developed a three-sector, full-employment general equilibrium model with child labour and a nontraded final good. There are two agricultural sectors. One of them produces an export good while the other produces a nontraded final commodity that is consumed by the poorer segment of the working population. Both of these two sectors use adult labour, child labour and land-capital as inputs.[3] The remaining sector is the import-competing sector that produces a manufacturing commodity by means of adult labour and capital. Here trade sanction has been captured through a reduction in the price of the product produced by the exports sector. It is found that the policy accentuates the prevalence of child labour in the society and makes the poor families that supply child labour worse off under reasonable factor intensity conditions. Next, we have developed a two-period, three-commodity, specific-factor Harris-Todaro type of general equilibrium model with child labour and endogenous skill formation. The supply function of child labour of each working family is derived from its intertemporal utility-maximizing behaviour. Sector 1 in the general equilibrium model is the rural sector, where child labour is used along with adult unskilled labour and capital to produce an agricultural commodity. Sector 2 is an urban sector where a low-skill manufacturing good is produced by means of adult unskilled labour and capital. Finally, sector 3, another urban sector, employs skilled labour and capital to produce a high-skill commodity. There are imperfections in the market for unskilled labour in sector 2 where the unskilled workers receive a high unionized wage while their counterparts in the rural sector earn a competitive wage. There is unemployment of unskilled labour in the urban sector although there is perfect mobility of factor between the rural and urban sectors. Using such a set-up, we show that although trade sanction lowers the incidence of child labour, the policy affects the urban unemployment situation of unskilled labour and the welfare of the child labour supplying families adversely. We therefore conclude that a trade sanction is not the right approach to address the child labour problem because on the one hand, the policy is likely to make many unskilled workers jobless and the working families worse off and, on the other, may fail to mitigate even the incidence of child labour under some plausible situations.

3.2   A static model without skill formation

We consider a small open economy with three sectors: two agricultural and one manufacturing. Sector 1 produces an exportable agricultural commodity, X_1, by means of adult labour (L), child labour (L_C) and land-capital (N). Sector 2 is another agricultural sector that uses the same three inputs to produce a nontraded final commodity, X_2, which is consumed by the poorer segment of the working population. The input, land-capital, is broadly conceived to include land, material inputs like fertilizers, pesticides, weedicides and durable capital equipment, tractors and harvesters and the like (see Bardhan 1972; Chaudhuri 2007 in this context). The land-capital-output ratios in sector 1 and sector 2 (a_{N1} and a_{N2}) are assumed to be technologically given. This assumption not only simplifies the algebra but can be also justified as follows. In one hectare of land, the number of saplings that can be sown is given. There should be a minimum gap between two saplings and land cannot be substituted by other factors of production.

The formal sector (sector 3) is the import-competing sector of the economy producing a manufacturing commodity, X_3. It uses adult labour and capital in its production. Because it is the formal sector of the economy, the use of child labour in this sector is strictly prohibited by government laws. We assume that the *substitution axiom*[4] of Basu and Van (1998) holds so that, in the two agricultural sectors, adult labour and child labour are substitutes, although how intensively child labour is used in these two sectors with respect to other inputs differs. Owing to effective wage legislation and unionization of labour, the adult wage rate in the formal sector is fixed at W^*. This is greater than the competitive adult wage rate, W, prevailing in the two agricultural sectors of the economy. Capital is specific to sector 3 (manufacturing sector). Both adult labour and child labour are perfectly mobile between sector 1 and sector 2, while adult labour is imperfectly mobile between the agricultural and the manufacturing sectors of the economy.

Production functions satisfy constant returns to scale (CRS) with positive but diminishing returns to each factor.[5] Markets, except the formal sector (adult) labour market, are perfectly competitive. The adult labour allocation mechanism is of the following type. Adult workers first try to get employment in the formal manufacturing sector that offers an institutionally given high wage, W^*, and those who are unable to find employment in the said sector are automatically absorbed in the two agricultural sectors at the competitive wage, W with $W^* > W$, because there is complete wage flexibility in the latter sectors. Child labour and land-capital are perfectly mobile between sector 1 and sector 2. Owing to the small open economy assumption, the prices of the two traded commodities, P_1 and P_3, are internationally given. The price of the nontraded commodity 2, P_2, is domestically determined by the demand–supply forces.

The following three equations present the zero-profit conditions relating to the three sectors of the economy.

$$Wa_{L1} + W_C a_{C1} + Ra_{N1} = P_1 \tag{3.1}$$

$$Wa_{L2} + W_C a_{C2} + Ra_{N2} = P_2 \tag{3.2}$$

$$W^* a_{L3} + ra_{K3} = 1 \tag{3.3}$$

where R, r and W_C stand for return to land, return to capital and child wage rate, respectively. Besides, a_{ji}s are input–output ratios. The other symbols have already been defined.

Complete utilization of adult labour, land-capital, capital and child labour implies the following four equations, respectively.

$$a_{L1}X_1 + a_{L2}X_2 + a_{L3}X_3 = L \tag{3.4}$$

$$a_{N1}X_1 + a_{N2}X_2 = N \tag{3.5}$$

$$a_{K3}X_3 = K \tag{3.6}$$

$$a_{C1}X_1 + a_{C2}X_2 = L_C \tag{3.7}$$

The supply function of child labour by each poor working family is given by the following.[6]

$$l_C = \left[(1-\gamma) - \frac{\gamma W}{W_C}\right] \tag{3.8}$$

Because there are $(L - a_{L3}X3)$ number of poor working families, each of which supplying l_C amount of child labour, the aggregate supply function of child labour in the economy is given by the following.

$$L_C = \left[(1-\gamma) - \frac{\gamma W}{W_C}\right](L - a_{L3}X_3) \tag{3.8.1}$$

Using (3.8.1), equation (3.7) can be rewritten as follows.

$$a_{C1}X_1 + a_{C2}X_2 = \left[(1-\gamma) - \frac{\gamma W}{W_C}\right](L - a_{L3}X_3) \tag{3.7.1}$$

The aggregate demand for the nontraded final commodity (commodity 2), which is consumed by the poorer segment of the working population, is given as follows.[7]

$$X_2^D = \left[\frac{\alpha(W + W_C)}{P_2}\right](L - a_{L3}X_3) \tag{3.9}$$

The market for the nontraded good must clear domestically by demand–supply forces. Hence, in equilibrium we must have

$$X_2^D = X_2 \tag{3.10}$$

Using (3.9), equation (3.10) can be rewritten as follows.

$$\left[\frac{\alpha(W + W_C)}{P_2}\right](L - a_{L3}X_3) = X_2 \tag{3.10.1}$$

Using (3.6), equation (3.4) can be rewritten as follows.

$$a_{L1}X_1 + a_{L2}X_2 = \left[L - \frac{a_{L3}}{a_{K3}}K\right] \tag{3.4.1}$$

The general equilibrium system consists of ten equations, (3.1)–(3.10) with ten unknowns. The unknown variables are W, W_C, R, r, P_2, X_1, X_2, X_3, X_2^D and L_C. The price system consists of equations (3.1)–(3.3) with five unknowns, W, W_C, R, r and P_2. This is an indecomposable system. r is obtained from (3.3) because W^* is exogenously given. X_3 is then found from (3.6). The values of W, W_C, R, X_1 and X_2 are determined as functions of P_1 and P_2 solving equations (3.1), (3.2), (3.4.1), (3.5) and (3.7.1) simultaneously. The equilibrium value of the price of the nontraded final commodity, P_2, is then determined from equation (3.10.1).

Finally, X_2^D and L_C are found from equations (3.9) and (3.8.1), respectively. It is to be noted that all of the endogenous variables, except r and X_3, come out as functions of the parameter, P_1. Hence, the equilibrium values of these variables would change if P_1 changes.

Although sector 1 and sector 2 use the same three inputs – adult labour (L), child labour (C) and land-capital (N) – it is quite realistic to assume that the concentration of both types of labour are higher in the nontraded agriculture (sector 2) vis-à-vis the exportable agricultural sector. The non-traded sector produces a low-quality agricultural commodity for the poorer segment of the population. Therefore, it is expected to use more labour-intensive technology of production than sector 1. In other words, sector 2 is more intensive in the uses of both adult labour and child labour relative to sector 1 with respect to land-capital. Hence, we write

$$
\left.
\begin{aligned}
&\frac{a_{C2}}{a_{N2}} > \frac{a_{C1}}{a_{N1}}; and \; \frac{a_{L2}}{a_{N2}} > \frac{a_{L1}}{a_{N1}} \text{ which in turn implies} \\[2mm]
&\frac{\lambda_{C2}}{\lambda_{N2}} > \frac{\lambda_{C1}}{\lambda_{N1}}; \frac{\lambda_{L2}}{\lambda_{N2}} > \frac{\lambda_{L1}}{\lambda_{N1}} \\[2mm]
&\text{Because factor price are the same in} \quad \frac{\theta_{C2}}{\theta_{N2}} > \frac{\theta_{C1}}{\theta_{N1}}; \frac{\theta_{L2}}{\theta_{N2}} > \frac{\theta_{L1}}{\theta_{N1}} \\
&\text{these two sector we have}
\end{aligned}
\right\}
\quad (3.11)
$$

Here θ_{ji} and λ_{ji}, respectively, denote the distributive and allocative shares of the jth input in the ith sector for $j = L, L_C, N$ and $i = 1, 2, 3$. This means that sector 2 is more intensive in the uses of both types of labour with respect to the other input, land-capital vis-à-vis sector 1 in both the physical and the value senses.

3.2.1   Effects of trade sanction on factor prices and child labour

In this section of the chapter, we are interested in examining the consequences of the imposition of trade sanctions by large trading nations on the exports good of this small open economy. In this model, the country exports the output of sector 1 that uses a small amount of child labour in its production. If large trading giants decline to purchase this commodity on humanitarian or any other grounds, the demand for the product in the international would fall significantly, leading to a fall in the world price of commodity 1 (i.e. P_1). We would now like to see the outcomes of this price reduction on the different endogenous variables, including the aggregate supply of child labour in the economy.

Differentiating equations (3.1), (3.2), (3.4.1), (3.5), (3.7.1), (3.8.1), (3.9) and (3.10.1), using the stability condition in the market for commodity 2 and simplifying, the following two propositions can be proved.[8]

Proposition 3.1: In the stable equilibrium, trade sanctions on commodity 1 leads to (i) an increase in the price of the nontraded good, P_2; (ii) a decrease in the competitive adult wage, W; and (iii) an increase in the child wage rate, W_C. The levels of production of the different commodities, however, do not change.

Proposition 3.2: A trade sanction on commodity 1 unambiguously raises the incidence of child labour in the society. Besides, the policy makes the child labour–supplying families worse off.

We explain propositions 3.1 and 3.2 in the following fashion. A trade sanction in this model is captured through a decrease in the price of commodity 1, P_1. It cannot change the return to capital, r, because the unionized wage in sector 3, W^*, is exogenously given (see equation 3.3). This implies that the factor-coefficient in sector 3 (i.e. a_{13} and a_{K3}) do not change. Because capital is specific to sector 3, the level of production in sector 3, $X_3 \left(= \dfrac{K}{a_{K3}} \right)$, and the level of employment of adult labour, $a_{13}X_3$, cannot change. Hence, the number of poor child labour–supplying families employed in the two agricultural sectors, $(L - a_{13}X_3)$, remains unchanged. Hence, the effect of the policy on the aggregate supply of child labour depends solely on the change in the supply of child labour by each family, l_C.

Now from equations (3.1) and (3.2), it is clear that the policy affects the two wage rates both directly and indirectly (through a change in the price of the non-traded commodity, P_2). Because sector 1 uses child labour less intensively vis-à-vis sector 2 with respect to the other inputs, a decrease in P_1 lowers the adult wage, W, and raises that of child labour, W_C, given the return to land-capital, R.[9,10] The immediate (direct) effect would be a fall in aggregate maximum possible income of each poor family, $(Z = W + W_C)$.[11] Consequently, the demand for the nontraded final commodity 2, which is solely consumed by the poorer segment of the working population, falls while its supply remains unchanged. As a sequel, the price of the nontraded good, P_2, falls in the stable equilibrium.[12] A fall in P_2 this time lowers W_C and raises W via another *Stolper-Samuelson type effect*. These are the induced effects on the two wages that work through a change in P_2. However, our analysis shows that the direct effects dominate over the induced effects. Hence, the net effects would be a fall in the adult wage, W, and an increase in the child wage, W_C.[13] The aggregate income of each family also decreases, worsening their welfare because their consumption levels of all of the commodities, including children's leisure, fall.[14] For the reason that the children's leisure of the family falls, the supply of child labour by each family rises. Consequently, the aggregate supply of child labour also rises since the number of child labour–supplying families has not changed.[15,16]

3.3 A dynamic model with skill formation

Most of the existing theoretical works virtually have pointed out the potential counterproductiveness of trade sanctions as a policy in combating the child labour problem in the developing world. In other words, these works show that there might be several cases, where the policy, instead of curing the problem, may end up in accentuating it. The analysis of section 2 of this chapter also has demonstrated such a possibility by means of a static general equilibrium model with two agricultural sectors, one of which produces a nontraded final commodity. However, it is important to note that there might be reasons as to why this policy should not be undertaken even if it is effective in ameliorating the child labour incidence. The objective of the present section is to demonstrate such a possibility.

Because the analytical structure that we have followed in section 3.2 is static in nature, it cannot take into consideration the aspects like skill formation on the part of the children, unemployment problem of adult labour and the like. These issues are extremely important in the context of a developing economy because provision for skill formation has a direct beneficial impact on the magnitude of child labour. On the other hand, child labour is often held responsible for the existence of a high magnitude of adult unemployment in the developing nations because it acts a cheaper substitute to adult employment, accentuating the adult unemployment problem.

The objective of the analysis in this section is to show that a trade sanction that lowers the international price of an exportable commodity produced with the help of child labour should not be resorted to, even though it is effective in controlling the prevalence of the evil in the system. This is because of its potential harmful effects on the unemployment problem of adult labour and the welfare of the working class.

In this section, we have developed a two-period, three-commodity specific-factor Harris-Todaro type of general equilibrium model with child labour and endogenous skill formation. There are four factors of production: adult unskilled labour (L), child labour (C), skilled labour (S) and capital (K). All of the working households, irrespective of whether the guardian of the family is himself an unskilled worker or a skilled worker, are the potential suppliers of child labour. The supply function of child labour of each working family is derived from its intertemporal utility-maximizing behaviour.[17] Sector 1 in the general equilibrium model is the rural sector where child labour is used along with adult unskilled labour and capital to produce an agricultural commodity. Sector 2 is an urban sector where a low-skill manufacturing good is produced by means of adult unskilled labour and capital. Finally, sector 3, another urban sector, employs skilled labour and capital to produce a high-skill commodity. There is imperfec tion in the market for unskilled adult labour in sector 2 where the unskilled adult workers receive a high unionized wage, W^*, while their counterparts in the rural sector earn a competitive wage, W. There is unemployment of adult unskilled labour in the urban sector (L_U). Using such a set-up, we show that, although a trade sanction lowers the incidence of child labour, the policy adversely affects the unemployment situation of adult unskilled labour and the welfare of the child labour supplying families. The analysis of this section establishes that trade sanctions are not the right approach to mitigate the child labour problem because it may make not only many adult unskilled workers jobless but also the poor unskilled working families worse off.

3.3.1   *The general equilibrium model*

We consider a small open dual economy with two broad sectors: rural and urban. The urban sector is further subdivided into two subsectors so that in all we have three sectors. Sector 1 produces an agricultural commodity, X_1, using adult unskilled labour, child labour and capital. The capital-output ratio in sector 1, a_{K1}, is assumed to be technologically given.[18] Sector 2 is an urban sector that produces a low-skill manufacturing good, X_2, by means of capital and adult unskilled labour.[19] Finally, sector 3, another urban sector, uses capital and skilled labour (S) to produce a high-skill commodity, X_3. Skilled labour is a specific input in sector 3, while child labour is specific to sector 1. Adult unskilled labour is perfectly mobile between sector 1 and sector 2, while capital is completely mobile among all the three sectors of the economy. The possibility of the use of child labour in the two urban (formal) sectors is strictly prohibited by government laws.

Sector 2 faces a unionized adult unskilled labour market where workers receive a contractual wage, W^*, while the adult unskilled wage rate in the rural sector, W, is market determined with $W^* > W$.[20] The two wage rates are related by the Harris and Todaro (1970) condition of migration equilibrium where the expected urban wage equals the rural wage rate. Hence, there is urban unemployment of unskilled labour. Sector 2 uses capital more intensively with respect to adult unskilled labour vis-à-vis sector 1 in the value sense.[21] Production functions exhibit constant returns to scale with positive and diminishing marginal productivity to each factor.[22] Markets, except the urban adult unskilled labour market, are perfectly competitive. All of the three commodities are traded internationally. Hence their prices, P_i, are given internationally. Finally, commodity 3 is chosen as the numeraire so that $P_3 = 1$.

A general equilibrium of the system is represented by the following set of equations.

$$Wa_{L1} + W_C a_{C1} + Ra_{K1} = P_1 \tag{3.12}$$

$$W^* a_{L2} + Ra_{K2} = P_2 \tag{3.13}$$

$$W_S a_{S3} + Ra_{K3} = 1 \tag{3.14}$$

where a_{ji}s are input–output ratios. R is the return to capital, while W_C and W_S are the child wage and skilled wage, respectively.

$$a_{C1} X_1 = L_C \tag{3.15}$$

$$a_{K1} X_1 + a_{K2} X_2 + a_{K3} X_3 = K \tag{3.16}$$

$$a_{S3} X_3 = S \tag{3.17}$$

$$a_{L1} X_1 + a_{L2} X_2 + L_U = L \tag{3.18}$$

Equations (3.12)–(3.14) are the three competitive industry equilibrium conditions in the three sectors. On the other hand, equations (3.15)–(3.17) are the full-employment conditions for child labour, capital and skilled labour, respectively. The adult unskilled labour endowment is given by (3.18).

Since the probability of finding a job in the low-skill urban manufacturing sector is $a_{L2} X_2 / (a_{L2} X_2 + L_U)$, the expected adult unskilled wage in the urban area is $(W^* a_{L2} X_2) / (a_{L2} X_2 + L_U)$. Therefore, the rural–urban migration equilibrium condition of adult unskilled labour is given by

$$(W^* a_{L2} X_2) / (a_{L2} X_2 + L_U) = W$$

Using (3.18), this can be rewritten as follows.

$$(W^* / W) a_{L2} X_2 + a_{L1} X_1 = L \tag{3.19}$$

The firms in the low-skill urban sector have well organized trade unions. One of the most important roles of the labour unions is to bargain with their respective employers in respect to the betterment of the working conditions. Through offer of negotiation, threat of strike, actual strike and other tactics, trade unions exert pressure on the employers (firms) in order to secure higher wages, reduced hours of work, share in profits and other benefits. Organized workers in large firms leave no stones unturned to reap wages higher than their reservation wage (i.e. the rural sector unskilled wage).[23] The relationship for the unionized wage rate is specified as[24]

$$W^* = W^* (W, U) \tag{3.20}$$

This function satisfies the following properties.

$W^* = W$ for $U = 0$

$W^* > W$ for $U > 0$

and

$$(\partial W^* / \partial W), (\partial W^* / \partial U) > 0$$

Equation (3.20) states that, in the absence of any bargaining power of the trade unions (i.e. when $U = 0$), the rural and the urban adult unskilled wage rates are equal. However, the urban sector wage rate, W^*, exceeds the competitive rural sector wage rate, W, when the trade unions have at least some power. The unionized wage is scaled upward as the rural sector wage rate rises. Also with an increase in the bargaining power, the unions bargain for a higher wage.

Using (3.20), equations (3.13) and (3.19) can be rewritten as follows.

$$W^* (W, U) a_{L2} + R a_{K2} = 1 \tag{3.13.1}$$

$$(W^* (W, U) / W) a_{L2} X_2 + a_{L1} X_1 = L \tag{3.19.1}$$

Both unskilled and skilled working families are potential suppliers of child labour and their current wage incomes (W_0) are W and W_S, respectively.[25] Besides, there are L and S numbers of unskilled and skilled working families in the economy, respectively. Using equation (2.24) and assuming that workers are not the owners of capital, the aggregate child labour supply in the economy is obtained as follows.

$$L_C = \left(\frac{1}{1+\beta}\right)\left[L\left\{\frac{nW_S}{(W_S - W)} - \frac{\beta W}{W_C}\right\} + S\left\{\frac{nW_S}{(W_S - W)} - \frac{\beta W_S}{W_C}\right\}\right] \quad (3.21)$$

Using (3.21), equation (3.15) can be rewritten as follows.

$$a_{C1}X_1 = \left(\frac{1}{1+\beta}\right)\left[L\left\{\frac{nW_S}{(W_S - W)} - \frac{\beta W}{W_C}\right\} + S\left\{\frac{nW_S}{(W_S - W)} - \frac{\beta W_S}{W_C}\right\}\right] \quad (3.15.1)$$

3.3.2 Comparative statics

The general equilibrium structure consists of nine equations, (3.12), (3.13.1), (3.14), (3.15.1), (3.16)–(3.18), (3.19.1) and (3.21), and exactly the same number of variables namely: W, W_C, W_S, R, X_1, X_2, X_3, L_C and L_U. This is an indecomposable system. Hence, factor prices depend on both commodity prices and factor endowments. Given the child wage rate, sector 1 and sector 2 together effectively form a miniature Heckscher-Ohlin system because they use both adult unskilled labour and capital. It is sensible to assume that sector 1 is more adult labour–intensive vis-à-vis sector 2 with respect to capital in the value sense.

In this section of the chapter, we will study the efficacy of trade sanctions on the supply of child labour in the economy. We also intend to examine the consequences of the policy on the urban unemployment of unskilled labour and the welfare of the child labour–supplying families. Because child labour is used to produce the exportable agricultural commodity (commodity 1), a worldwide trade sanction is captured through a reduction in the price of commodity 1.

3.3.2.1 Trade sanctions, factor prices and output composition

Totally differentiating equations (3.12), (3.13.1), (3.14), (3.15.1), (3.16), (3.17) and (3.19.1) and solving the following proposition can be established.[26]

Proposition 3.3: A worldwide trade sanction against the commodity produced by using child labour leads to (i) an increase in the return to capital; (ii) decreases in both adult unskilled wage and adult skilled wage rates; (iii) a deterioration in the skilled–unskilled wage inequality provided the low-skill sector is capital-intensive in the Jones and Neary (1984) sense.[27,28] The policy is also likely to lower the child wage rate. Furthermore, the rural sector unambiguously contracts while the low-skill urban sector expands due to this policy.

Proposition 1 can be intuitively explained in the following fashion. A policy of trade sanction lowers the price of the agricultural commodity, P_1. This produces a *Stolper-Samuelson effect* in the *Heckscher-Ohlin subsystem (HOSS)* and lowers the adult unskilled wage in the rural sector, W, and an increase in the return to capital, R, as the rural sector (sector 1) is more intensive in the use of adult unskilled labour with respect to capital relative to the low-skill urban sector (sector 2) in the value sense. This produces a *Rybczynski type effect* in the HOSS and causes sector 1 to contract and sector 2 to expand.[29] As the cost of capital rises the skilled wage, W_S falls to satisfy the zero-profit condition in sector 3 (see equation (3.14)). This causes the producers in sector 3 to substitute capital by skilled labour that lowers the capital-output ratio, a_{K3}, and raises the skilled labour-output ratio, a_{S3}. Because the supply of skilled labour is given, sector 3 contracts and releases capital to the expanding sector 2. As both W and W_s fall, what happens to the relative wage inequality must depend upon the rates of fall in the two wages. Our analysis shows that the wage inequality worsens and the return to education, $\left(\dfrac{(W_S - W)}{W_S} \right)$, increases if the low-skill urban sector is capital-intensive in the Jones and Neary (1984) sense. This should also be clear if one looks at the price system of the production structure given by equations (3.12), (3.13.1) and (3.14). On the other hand, there would be two opposite effects on the child wage rate, W_C. As sector 1 has contracted, the demand for the sector-specific input, child labour, falls. This exerts a downward pressure on W_C. On the contrary, as the two wages have gone down and the return to education has increased, the supply of child labour by the working families declines, exerting an upward pressure on W_C. It can be easily seen that the demand side effect dominates over the supply side effect under the sufficient condition: $(E + S_{CL}^1) \geq 0$. However, there can be some other sufficient conditions under which the child wage rate drops.

3.3.2.2   Trade sanctions and incidence of child labour

For examining the consequence of trade sanctions on the supply of child labour in the economy after totally differentiating equation (3.21), we can establish the following proposition.[30]

Proposition 3.4: An imposition of trade sanctions on the commodity that uses child labour lowers the incidence of child labour in the economy if the low-skill sector is capital-intensive relative to the high-skill sector.

We intuitively explain proposition 3.4 as follows. In proposition 3.3 we stated how different factor prices and the relative wage inequality (return to education) respond to trade sanctions on commodity 1. We find that changes in different wages produce two opposite effects on the problem of child labour. First, the initial incomes from nonchild sources of both the unskilled and skilled working families have decreased, increasing the supply of child labour by each family via the negative income effect. Second, a fall in the child wage rate, W_C, means a decrease in the opportunity cost of education. This lowers the supply of child labour and raises the number schoolgoing children. Finally, the return to education rises as the wage inequality rises, which also causes child labour to decline. The favourable effects of a fall in the child wage and an increase in the skill-premium dominate over the unfavourable effect of decreases in the skilled and unskilled wages on the problem of child labour under the sufficient condition that the low-skill sector is capital-intensive relative to the high-skill sector. Hence, trade sanctions on the commodity that uses child labour can effectively improve the child labour situation in the society.

3.3.2.3   Trade sanctions and unemployment of adult unskilled labour

We are now going to examine the result of trade sanctions on the unemployment of unskilled labour in the urban sector. Subtraction of (3.19.1) from (3.18) yields

$$L_U = a_{L2}X_2\left(\frac{W^*}{W} - 1\right) \qquad (3.22)$$

Differentiating (3.22), the following proposition can be established.[31]

Proposition 3.5: A trade sanction on commodity 1 unambiguously worsens the urban unemployment problem of unskilled labour.

We explain proposition 3.5 as follows. In the migration equilibrium, the expected urban wage for a prospective unskilled rural migrant equals the actual unskilled rural wage. From proposition 1, we find that a trade sanction on commodity 1 lowers the rural adult unskilled wage and expands the low-skill urban sector. Thus, the policy influences the migration equilibrium in two ways. First, as the low-skill urban manufacturing sector expands, the number of unskilled jobs available in this sector shoots up. The expected urban wage for a prospective rural migrant, $[W^*/\{1+(L_U/a_{12}X_2)\}]$, increases as the probability of getting a job in this sector rises for every unskilled worker. This is the *centrifugal force*, which paves the way for fresh migration from the rural to the urban sector. On the other hand, because the rural adult unskilled wage has declined the *negative centripetal force* also lowers the incentive for the unskilled workers to remain in the rural sector, which in turn encourages migration to the urban sector. Hence, both the centrifugal and centripetal forces work in the same direction and cause more migration to the urban sector. The number of new jobs created in sector 2 falls short of the number of new migrants into the urban sector. Consequently, the urban unemployment problem unambiguously worsens.

3.3.2.4   *Trade sanctions and the welfare of working families*

How do trade sanctions affect the welfare of the families that supply child labour? We would like to address this question in this section. Differentiating equations (2.20)–(2.22) and using (2.24), the final proposition of the model can be established as follows.[32]

Proposition 3.6: Trade sanctions on the exportable commodity affects the welfare of the child labour supplying families adversely if

(i) $E \geq 0$ or $(S_{CL}^1 + E) \geq 0$

and

(ii) $\left[nW_C\dfrac{W_S}{W}(W_S - W)\right] \geq \beta \geq nW_C(W_S - W)$

From proposition 3.3, we find that following trade sanctions, the skilled and unskilled wages unequivocally decline. The child wage rate also falls if $E \geq 0$ or $(S_{CL}^1 + E) \geq 0$. Both the aggregate (L_C) and the family supply of child labour (l_c) drop if $(\theta_{K3}E_W\theta_{12} \leq \theta_{S3}\theta_{K2})$ (proposition 3.4). From equation (2.21), it then follows that the consumption level of each working family in period 1, C_1, declines if (i) $E \geq 0$ or $(S_{CL}^1 + E) \geq 0$ and (ii) $(\theta_{K3}E_W\theta_{12} \leq \theta_{S3}\theta_{K2})$. However, the effect on the consumption level in period 2, C_2, is not so obvious. This is because C_2 falls as the income from unskilled family members, Wl_c (who worked as child labour in period 1), falls (see equation (2.22)). But the effect on the income from skilled family members, $(n - lc)W_S$ (who went to school in period 1), is ambiguous. However, the negative effects on the welfare of the family dominate over the positive effect (if any) under the sufficient conditions as stated in the proposition. Consequently, the welfare of the child labour supplying families worsens owing to trade sanctions.[33]

3.4 Concluding remarks

Child labour is a slur on the fair face of the globalized world. Different policies are advocated in reducing the prevalence of the evil in the system. The imposition of trade sanctions on the exportable commodities of the developing countries that are produced using child labour is the most controversial and hotly debated policy suggested by representatives of the developed countries in this context at the WTO meeting. It is argued that the use of child labour gives the developing countries a trading advantage in labour-intensive goods, which is illegitimate because the use of child labour in production activities is socially unethical and unacceptable. On the other hand, many of the economists are of the opinion that the international campaign against child labour is not guided by any ethical or humanitarian motive. The sole motive of the advocators of the policy is to help the developed nations in preserving their interests by depriving the labour-intensive export industries of the developing countries of cost advantages in the international market. Some theoretical works have shown how trade sanctions on the commodities that have directly or indirectly used child labour in their production might be counterproductive and accentuate not only the gravity of the problem but also compel them to shift to more hazardous and exploitative activities. Very recently, the issue again came into the limelight when the Nobel Peace prize 2014 was awarded to a social activist in India who consistently has advocated in favour of impositing trade sanctions to eliminate child labour from society.

It is now more or less accepted among economists that child labour in general is not bad given the widespread poverty, massive adult unemployment and very low return to education in the developing nations. However, one should be concerned about the use of child labour in hazardous and exploitative activities. Besides, in the developing countries, child labour should be viewed along with the associated problems like adult unemployment and the welfare of the poorer segment of the working population. It is not desirable to eradicate child labour at the cost of accentuating its associated tribulations. Because the existing literature has not adequately addressed the related issues, we have felt the necessity to reevaluate the trade sanction as an instrument to deal with child labour in view of the related problems.

We have carried out the theoretical exercise using two general equilibrium models with child labour. The first one is a three-sector, full-employment model with two agricultural sectors, one traded and the other nontraded. There is a manufacturing sector in the scene as well that happens to be the import-competing sector of the economy. Although the two agricultural sectors use the same three inputs, adult labour, child labour, and land-capital, the nontraded agricultural sector (sector 2) uses child labour far more extensively relative to the traded sector (sector 1) with respect to other inputs. The nontraded sector produces a final agricultural commodity for the poorer segment of the working population. We have captured trade sanctions in terms of a reduction in the international price of the exports good, produced by sector 1. Our analysis has found that a trade sanction not only accentuates the incidence of child labour but also makes the poor families worse off. Then, using a two-period, three-commodity, specific-factor Harris-Todaro type of general equilibrium model with endogenous skill formation, we have shown that although trade sanction lowers the incidence of child labour, the policy adversely affects both the unemployment situation of unskilled adult labour and the welfare of the child labour–supplying families. All of these findings have led us to conclude that trade sanction is not the right approach to eradicate child labour because the policy might not only sometimes be counter-productive but also might make many unskilled adult workers jobless and the poor families worse off.

Appendices
The static model without skill formation

Appendix 3.1 Direct effects of a fall in P_1 and a change in P_2 on factor prices and output composition

Differentiating equations (3.1), (3.2), (3.4.1), (3.5) and (3.7.1), simplifying and arranging in a matrix notation, we get the following.

$$
\begin{bmatrix}
\theta_{L1} & \theta_{C1} & \theta_{N1} & 0 & 0 \\
\theta_{L2} & \theta_{C2} & \theta_{N2} & 0 & 0 \\
-A & A & 0 & \lambda_{L1} & \lambda_{L2} \\
0 & 0 & 0 & \lambda_{N1} & \lambda_{N2} \\
B & -B & 0 & \lambda_{C1} & \lambda_{C2}
\end{bmatrix}
\begin{bmatrix}
\hat{W} \\
\hat{W}_C \\
\hat{R} \\
\hat{X}_1 \\
\hat{X}_2
\end{bmatrix}
=
\begin{bmatrix}
\hat{P}_1 \\
\hat{P}_2 \\
0 \\
0 \\
0
\end{bmatrix}
\tag{3.A.1}
$$

where

$$
\left.
\begin{aligned}
A &= [\lambda_{L1}S_{LC}^1 + \lambda_{L2}S_{LC}^2] > 0 \\
B &= \left[\lambda_{C1}S_{CL}^1 + \lambda_{C2}S_{CL}^2 + \frac{\gamma W}{W_C l_C}\right] > 0
\end{aligned}
\right\}
\tag{3.A.2}
$$

Here θ_{ji} and λ_{ji}, respectively, denote the distributive and allocative share of the jth input in the ith sector for $j = L, L_C, N, K$ and $i = 1, 2, 3$. S_{ji}^k = the degree of substitution between factors j and i in the kth sector, $j,i = L,L_C$, and $k = 1, 2 = 1,2,3$. For example, $S_{LC}^1 \equiv (W_C / a_{L1})(\partial a_{L1} / \partial W_C)$, $S_{LL}^1 \equiv (W / a_{L1})(\partial a_{L1} / \partial W)$ and so on. $S_{ji}^k > 0$ for $j \neq i$, and $S_{jj}^k < 0$. '^' denotes proportional change, for example,

$$\hat{X} \equiv \frac{dX}{X}.$$

From (3.A.1), it can be easily seen that the determinant to the coefficient-matrix, denoted Δ, is given by the following.

$$
\Delta = (|\theta|_{LN} + |\theta|_{CN})(A|\lambda|_{CN} + B|\lambda|_{LN}) > 0
\tag{3.A.3}
$$
$$
\quad\ (-) \qquad\ (-) \qquad\ (-) \qquad\quad (-)
$$

where

$$|\theta|_{LN} = (\theta_{L1}\theta_{N2} - \theta_{L2}\theta_{N1}) < 0; |\theta|_{CN} = (\theta_{C1}\theta_{N2} - \theta_{C2}\theta_{N1}) < 0$$
$$|\lambda|_{LN} = (\lambda_{L1}\lambda_{N2} - \lambda_{L2}\lambda_{N1}) < 0; |\lambda|_{CN} = (\lambda_{C1}\lambda_{N2} - \lambda_{C2}\lambda_{N1}) < 0$$

$$(3.A.4)$$

Solving (3.A.1) and simplifying, the following expressions can be obtained.

$$\left(\frac{\hat{W}}{\hat{P}_1}\right) = -\left(\frac{\theta_{N2}}{\Delta}\right)\left[A|\lambda|_{CN} + B|\lambda|_{LN}\right] > 0$$
$$(+) \quad (+)(-) \quad (+)(-);$$

$$\left(\frac{\hat{W}}{\hat{P}_2}\right) = \left(\frac{\theta_{N1}}{\Delta}\right)\left[A|\lambda|_{CN} + B|\lambda|_{LN}\right] < 0$$
$$(+) \quad (+)(-) \quad (+)(-)$$

$$\left(\frac{\hat{W}_C}{\hat{P}_1}\right) = \left(\frac{\theta_{N2}}{\Delta}\right)\left[A|\lambda|_{CN} + B|\lambda|_{LN}\right] < 0$$
$$(+) \quad (+)(-) \quad (+)(-)$$

$$(3.A.5)$$

$$\left(\frac{\hat{W}_C}{\hat{P}_2}\right) = -\left(\frac{\theta_{N1}}{\Delta}\right)\left[A|\lambda|_{CN} + B|\lambda|_{LN}\right] > 0$$
$$(+) \quad (+)(-) \quad (+)(-)$$

$$\left(\frac{\hat{X}_1}{\hat{P}_1}\right); \left(\frac{\hat{X}_1}{\hat{P}_2}\right); \left(\frac{\hat{X}_2}{\hat{P}_1}\right); \left(\frac{\hat{X}_2}{\hat{P}_2}\right) = 0$$

From (3.A.5) we find that a reduction in P_1 directly lowers the adult wage, W, and raises the child wage rate, W_C, although it keeps the two output levels, X_1 and X_2, unchanged. On the contrary, a fall in P_2 raises the adult wage, lowers the child wage directly but cannot change the production levels of the two commodities.

The aggregate income (adult income plus maximum possible child income) of each poor child labour–supplying family, denoted Z, is given by the following.

$$Z = (W + W_C) \tag{3.A.6}$$

Differentiating (3.A.6), using (3.A.5) and simplifying, we find the following.

$$\left(\frac{\partial Z}{\partial P_1}\right) = \left(\frac{\partial W}{\partial P_1}\right) + \left(\frac{\partial W_C}{\partial P_1}\right) = -\left[\left(A|\lambda|_{CN} + B|\lambda|_{LN}\right)\left(\frac{\theta_{N2}}{P_1\Delta}\right)(W - W_C)\right] > 0$$
$$(+)(-) \quad (+)(-) \quad (+) \quad (+)$$

$$\left(\frac{\partial Z}{\partial P_2}\right) = \left(\frac{\partial W}{\partial P_2}\right) + \left(\frac{\partial W_C}{\partial P_2}\right) = \left[\left(A|\lambda|_{CN} + B|\lambda|_{LN}\right)\left(\frac{\theta_{N1}}{P_2\Delta}\right)(W - W_C)\right] < 0$$
$$(+)(-) \quad (+)(-) \quad (+) \quad (+)$$

$$(3.A.7)$$

Hence, the direct effect of a reduction in P_1 would be a decline in Z while a fall in P_2 raises Z directly.

Appendix 3.2   The stability condition in the market for commodity 2 and the effect of a trade sanction on P_2

Totally differentiating equation (3.9), one finds the following.

$$dX_2^D = \left[\frac{\alpha(L - a_{L3}X_3)}{(P_2)^2} \right] \left[P_2 \left(\frac{\partial W}{\partial P_1} + \frac{\partial W_C}{\partial P_1} \right) dP_1 + \left\{ P_2 \left(\frac{\partial W}{\partial P_2} + \frac{\partial W_C}{\partial P_2} \right) \right. \right.$$

$$\left. \left. - (W + W_C) \right\} dP_2 \right]$$ (3.A.8)

Now, using (3.A.5) and simplifying, it is easily seen that

$$\left(\frac{\partial W}{\partial P_1} + \frac{\partial W_C}{\partial P_1} \right) = \left[\left\{ \frac{\overset{(+)(-)}{\theta_{N2}}(A|\lambda|_{CN} + B|\lambda|_{LN})}{P_1\Delta} \right\} \overset{(+)(-)}{(W_C - W)} \right] > 0$$
$$\qquad\qquad\qquad\qquad (+) \qquad\qquad\quad (-)$$

$$\left(\frac{\partial W}{\partial P_2} + \frac{\partial W_C}{\partial P_2} \right) = \left[\left\{ \frac{\overset{(+)(-)}{\theta_{N1}}(A|\lambda|_{CN} + B|\lambda|_{LN})}{P_2\Delta} \right\} \overset{(+)(-)}{(W - W_C)} \right] < 0 \qquad (3.A.9)$$
$$\qquad\qquad\qquad\qquad (+) \qquad\qquad\quad (+)$$

$$\left[P_2 \left(\frac{\partial W}{\partial P_2} + \frac{\partial W_C}{\partial P_2} \right) - (W + W_C) \right] = \frac{\left(\overset{(+)(-)}{(A|\lambda|_{CN}} + \overset{(+)(-)}{B|\lambda|_{LN}}) \right)}{\Delta}$$
$$[2W\theta_{N1} - \theta_{N2}(W + W_C)]$$
$$(+)$$

Using (3.A.9) from (3.A.8), we can write

$$dX_2^D = \left[\frac{\alpha(L - a_{L3}X_3)}{(P_2)^2} \right] \left[\left\{ \left(\frac{P_2\theta_{N2} \left(A|\lambda|_{CN} + B|\lambda|_{LN} \right)}{P_1\Delta} \right) (W_C - W) \right\} dP_1 \right.$$

$$\left. + \left\{ \left(\frac{\left(A|\lambda|_{CN} + B|\lambda|_{LN} \right)}{\Delta} \right) [2W\theta_{N1} - \theta_{N2}(W + W_C)] \right\} dP_2 \right] \qquad (3.A.10)$$

The Walrasian stability condition in the market for commodity 2 requires the following.

$$\left[\left(\frac{\partial X_2^D}{\partial P_2} \right) - \left(\frac{\partial X_2}{\partial P_2} \right) \right] < 0 \qquad (3.A.11)$$

Because $\left(\frac{\partial X_2}{\partial P_2} \right) = 0$ (see equation (3.A.5)), the stability condition boils down to

$$\left(\frac{\partial X_2^D}{\partial P_2}\right) < 0 \tag{3.A.11.1}$$

From (3.A.10), we get

$$\left(\frac{\partial X_2^D}{\partial P_2}\right) = \left[\frac{\overset{(+)}{\alpha(L - a_{L3}X_3)}}{(P_2)^2}\right]\left[\left(\frac{\overset{(+)(-)}{A|\lambda|_{CN}} + \overset{(+)(-)}{B|\lambda|_{LN}}}{\Delta}\right)\right.$$

$$\left.\underset{(+)}{\{2W\theta_{N1} - \theta_{N2}(W + W_C)\}}\right] \tag{3.A.12}$$

Hence, from (3.A.11.1) and (3.A.12) it follows that the stability condition in the market for commodity 2 ultimately requires the following.

$$2W\theta_{N1} > \theta_{N2}(W + W_C) \tag{3.A.13}$$

Now differentiating (10.1), using (3.A.13), and simplifying, we get the following result.

$$\left(\frac{\hat{P}_2}{\hat{P}_1}\right) = -\left[\frac{\overset{(-)}{\theta_{N2}(W_C - W)}}{\underset{(+)}{2W\theta_{N1} - \theta_{N2}(W + W_C)}}\right] > 0 \tag{3.A.14}$$

Hence, a reduction in P_1 lowers the price of the nontraded good, P_2.

Appendix 3.3   Aggregate (direct plus induced) effect of a reduction in P_1 on the two wages

Solving (3.A.1), we find

$$\hat{W} = \left[A|\lambda|_{CN} + B|\lambda|_{LN}\right]\left[\frac{\theta_{N1}\hat{P}_2 - \theta_{N2}\hat{P}_1}{\Delta}\right]; \text{ and}$$

$$\hat{W}_C = \left[A|\lambda|_{CN} + B|\lambda|_{LN}\right]\left[\frac{\theta_{N2}\hat{P}_1 - \theta_{N1}\hat{P}_2}{\Delta}\right] \tag{3.A.15}$$

Dividing both sides of each of the two expressions by $\hat{P}_1$, we get

$$\left(\frac{\hat{W}}{\hat{P}_1}\right) = \left(\frac{A|\lambda|_{CN} + B|\lambda|_{LN}}{\Delta}\right)\left[\theta_{N1}\left(\frac{\hat{P}_2}{\hat{P}_1}\right) - \theta_{N2}\right]$$

$$\left(\frac{\hat{W}_C}{\hat{P}_1}\right) = \left[\frac{A|\lambda|_{CN} + B|\lambda|_{LN}}{\Delta}\right]\left[\theta_{N2} - \theta_{N1}\left(\frac{\hat{P}_2}{\hat{P}_1}\right)\right] \tag{3.A.15.1}$$

Now from (3.A.14), we can write

$$\left[\left(\frac{\hat{P}_2}{\hat{P}_1}\right)\theta_{N1} - \theta_{N2}\right] = \left[\frac{\theta_{N2}\theta_{N1}(W - W_C)}{2W\theta_{N1} - \theta_{N2}(W + W_C)}\right] - \theta_{N2}$$

Simplifying and using (3.A.13) from these expression we get

$$\left[\left(\frac{\hat{P}_2}{\hat{P}_1}\right)\theta_{N1} - \theta_{N2}\right] = \left[\frac{\overset{(-)}{\theta_{N2}(W + W_C)(\theta_{N2} - \theta_{N1})}}{2W\theta_{N1} - \theta_{N2}(W + W_C)}\right] < 0 \qquad (3.A.16)$$
$$\underset{(+)}{}$$

With the help of (3.A.16), the expressions presented in (3.A.15.2) can finally be rewritten as follows.

$$\left.\begin{array}{l}
\left(\dfrac{\hat{W}}{\hat{P}_1}\right) = \left[\dfrac{\overset{(+)(-)}{A|\lambda|_{CN}} + \overset{(+)(-)}{B|\lambda|_{LN}}}{\Delta}\right]\left[\dfrac{\overset{(-)}{\theta_{N2}(W + W_C)(\theta_{N2} - \theta_{N1})}}{2W\theta_{N1} - \theta_{N2}(W + W_C)}\right] > 0 \\[6pt]
\qquad\qquad\quad \underset{(+)}{} \qquad\qquad\qquad\quad \underset{(+)}{} \\[10pt]
\left(\dfrac{\hat{W}_C}{\hat{P}_1}\right) = -\left[\dfrac{\overset{(+)(-)}{A|\lambda|_{CN}} + \overset{(+)(-)}{B|\lambda|_{LN}}}{\Delta}\right]\left[\dfrac{\overset{(-)}{\theta_{N2}(W + W_C)(\theta_{N2} - \theta_{N1})}}{2W\theta_{N1} - \theta_{N2}(W + W_C)}\right] < 0 \\[6pt]
\qquad\qquad\quad \underset{(+)}{} \qquad\qquad\qquad\quad \underset{(+)}{}
\end{array}\right\} \qquad (3.A.15.2)$$

Hence, the aggregate effect of a reduction in P_1 would be a fall in W and a rise in W_C.

Appendix 3.4   Effect of a trade sanction on the relative wage, $\dfrac{W}{W_C}$

Let the relative wage be denoted by M where

$$M = \frac{W}{W_C} \qquad (3.A.17)$$

Differentiating (3.A.17), we get

$$\hat{M} = (\hat{W} - \hat{W}_C)$$

Now, $\left(\dfrac{\hat{M}}{\hat{P}_1}\right) = \left(\dfrac{\hat{W}}{\hat{P}_1} - \dfrac{\hat{W}_C}{\hat{P}_1}\right) \qquad (3.A.18)$

Using (3.A.15.2) and simplifying from (3.A.18), we find the following expression.

$$
\left(\frac{\hat{M}}{\hat{P_1}}\right) = \left(\frac{\hat{W}}{\hat{P_1}} - \frac{\hat{W_C}}{\hat{P_1}}\right) = 2 \overset{(-)}{\left[\frac{\theta_{N2}(W + W_C)(\theta_{N2} - \theta_{N1})}{2W\theta_{N1} - \theta_{N2}(W + W_C)}\right]}
$$
$$
(+)
$$

$$
\overset{(+)(-)\quad(+)(-)}{\left(\frac{A|\lambda|_{CN} + B|\lambda|_{LN}}{\Delta}\right)} > 0
$$
$$
(+)
$$

(3.A.18.1)

Thus, a reduction in P_1 lowers $\dfrac{W}{W_C}$.

Appendix 3.5 Effect of a trade sanction on the aggregate supply of child labour, L_C

Differentiating equation (3.8.1), we get

$$
\hat{L}_C = -\left[\left(\frac{\gamma W}{l_C W_C}\right)(\hat{W} - \hat{W_C})\right]
$$

Hence,

$$
\left(\frac{\hat{L}_C}{\hat{P_1}}\right) = -\left[\left(\frac{\gamma W}{l_C W_C}\right)\left(\frac{\hat{W}}{\hat{P_1}} - \frac{\hat{W_C}}{\hat{P_1}}\right)\right]
$$

(3.A.19)

Using equation (3.A.18.1) from (3.A.19), we obtain the following expression.

$$
\left(\frac{\hat{L}_C}{\hat{P_1}}\right) = -\left[\left(\frac{2\gamma W}{l_C W_C}\right)\overset{(-)}{\left[\frac{\theta_{N2}(W + W_C)(\theta_{N2} - \theta_{N1})}{2W\theta_{N1} - \theta_{N2}(W + W_C)}\right]}\overset{(+)(-)\quad(+)(-)}{\left(\frac{A|\lambda|_{CN} + B|\lambda|_{LN}}{\Delta}\right)}\right] < 0
$$
$$
(+)\qquad\qquad\qquad\qquad(+)
$$

(3.A.19.1)

Appendix 3.6 Direct and total (direct plus induced) effects of trade sanction on aggregate income of each child labour–supplying family

The aggregate income (adult income plus maximum possible child income), denoted Z, is given by

$$
Z = W + W_C
$$

(3.A.20)

For getting only the direct effect of a reduction in P_1 on Z partially differentiating equation with respect to Z, we find the following.

$$\left(\frac{\partial Z}{\partial P_1}\right) = \left(\frac{\partial W}{\partial P_1}\right) + \left(\frac{\partial W_C}{\partial P_1}\right)$$

Using (3.A.5) from this equation and simplifying, we obtain

$$\left(\frac{\partial Z}{\partial P_1}\right) = -\left[\left(A|\lambda|_{CN} + B|\lambda|_{LN}\right)\left(\frac{\theta_{N2}}{P_1\Delta}\right)(W - W_C)\right] > 0 \tag{3.A.21}$$
$$(+)(-)(+)(-)(+)(+)$$

Hence, the direct effect of a reduction in P_1 would be a fall in Z.

Now, for getting the total (direct plus induced) effect of a fall in P_1 on Z after totally differentiating equation (3.A.20), we get

$$\left(\frac{dZ}{dP_1}\right) = \left(\frac{\partial W}{\partial P_1}\right) + \left(\frac{\partial W_C}{\partial P_1}\right) + \left[\left(\frac{\partial W}{\partial P_2}\right) + \left(\frac{\partial W_C}{\partial P_2}\right)\right]\left(\frac{\partial P_2}{\partial P_1}\right) \tag{3.A.22}$$

Using (3.A.15.2) from (3.A.22) and simplifying, we obtain the following expression.

$$(+)(-)(+)(-)(-)$$
$$\left(\frac{dZ}{dP_1}\right) = \left[\frac{A|\lambda|_{CN} + B|\lambda|_{LN}}{P_1\Delta}\right]\left[\frac{\theta_{N2}(W + W_C)(\theta_{N2} - \theta_{N1})}{2W\theta_{N1} - \theta_{N2}(W + W_C)}\right] > 0 \tag{3.A.22.1}$$
$$(+)(+)$$

Hence, trade sanction lowers the aggregate maximum possible income of each family. Because each commodity in the consumption basket is normal, the consumption levels of all commodities, including children's leisure, decrease, thereby lowering the optimum welfare of each family.

The dynamic model with skill formation

Appendix 3.7 Determination of the unionized wage in the urban low-skill sector

We consider a competitive formal sector industry (sector 2). Each homogeneous firm in the industry has a separate trade union, and the unionized wage is determined through collective bargaining. Labour and capital are the two factors of production. The capital market facing each firm is perfect. Capital is perfectly mobile between the two sectors, and its economy-wide return is r. Although capital is another input of production in the process of determining the unionized wage, labour is considered the only variable input of production.[34] Here, the unionized wage is determined as a solution to the Nash bargaining game between the representative firm and the representative labour union, which would be the same across firms in this sector. Let us denote it by W^*. After dropping capital, the production function of the kth firm in sector 2 is written as $Q = Q(L_{2k})$, $Q'(.) > 0$; $Q''(.) < 0$ where L_{2k} is the number of workers employed by the kth firm.

The representative firm's profit function is given by routine

$$\Pi_{2k} = P_2 Q(L_{2k}) - W * L_{2k} \tag{3.A.23}$$

where P_2 is the exogenously given price of the product of the firm.

The representative labour union maximizes the aggregate wage income of its members net of their opportunity wage income; that is

$$\Omega_k = (W * -W)L_{2k} \tag{3.A.24}$$

where the rural sector wage, W, is the reservation wage or the opportunity wage income of each of the workers in sector 2.[35]

We consider a cooperative game between the representative firm and the representative labour union that leads to the simultaneous determination of the unionized wage, $W*$, and the level of employment, L_{2k}, by the firm. If the two parties fail to reach an agreement, no production will take place, and the workers shall have to be satisfied with their reservation wage. Hence, given the objective functions of the two parties represented by equations (3.A.23) and (3.A.24), the disagreement pay-off vector is $[0, 0]$.

The Nash bargaining solution is obtained from the following optimization exercise.

$$\text{Max } J_k = [P_2 Q(L_{2k}) - W * L_{2k}]^{(1-U)} \times [(W * - W)L_{2k}]^{U} \tag{3.A.25}$$

$$W*, L_{2k}$$

where U is the bargaining strength of the labour union.[36] It may be noted that if the urban formal sector labour market were perfect, there would have been no trade unionism. In that case, we would have $U = 0$.

The first-order conditions for maximization are the following.

$$(1-U)[(W * -W)L_{2k}] = U[P_2 Q(.) - W * L_{2k}] \tag{3.A.26}$$

and

$$(1-U)(P_2 Q'(.) - W*)L_{2k} = -U[P_2 Q(.) - W * L_{2k}] \tag{3.A.27}$$

Using (3.A.26) and (3.A.27), we obtain

$$P_2 Q'(.) = W \tag{3.A.28}$$

From equation (3.A.28), the equilibrium employment in the kth firm is determined as follows.[37]

$$L_{2k} = L_{2k}(W, P_2) \tag{3.A.28.1}$$

Simplification from (3.A.27) and (3.A.28) yields

$$W^* = U\frac{P_2 Q(L_{2k})}{L_{2k}} + (1-U)W \tag{3.A.29}$$

With identical firms using equation (3.A.29) and dropping the k, equation (7), after generalizing, is rewritten as follows.

$$W^* = W^*(P_2, W, U) \tag{3.A.30}$$

Differentiating (3.A.28) and (3.A.29) and simplifying, we can easily show that

$$E_W = \left(\frac{\partial W^*}{\partial W}\frac{W}{W^*}\right) > 0$$

$$E_{P2} = \left(\frac{\partial W^*}{\partial P_2}\frac{P_2}{W^*}\right) > 0$$

and

$$E_U = \left(\frac{\partial W^*}{\partial U}\frac{U}{W^*}\right) > 0$$

where E_W, E_{P2} and E_U denote the elasticities of $W^*(.)$ with respect to W, P_2 and U, respectively, and $(E_W + E_{P2}) = 1$.

Differentiating equations (3.A.28) and (3.A.29), it is not difficult to verify that

$$\left(\frac{\partial W^*}{\partial P_2}\right) > 0 \text{ if } (Q'' L + Q') \leq 0 \text{ i.e. } \xi_L \geq 1$$

where $\xi_L = -\left(\frac{LQ_{LL}}{Q_L}\right)$ is the elasticity of the marginal product curve of labour. Quite naturally, $E_{P2} > 0$ if $\xi_L \geq 1$. For example, for the production function, $Q = \log L$; $L > 0$, $(Q' + LQ'' L) = 0$ and hence $E_{P2} > 0$.

Let us now consider a Cobb-Douglas production function for sector 2. From equations (3.A.28) and (3.A.29), we find that the unionized wage function becomes the following.

$$W^* = W\left[1 + \frac{U(1-\alpha)}{\alpha}\right] \tag{3.A.31}$$

where α is the output elasticity of labour.

From (3.A.31), it readily follows that $E_{P2} = 0$ and $E_W = 1$. But $W^* > W$ as long as $U > 0$.

Appendix 3.8   Effects of a trade sanction on factor prices and output composition

Totally differentiating equations (3.12), (3.13.1) and (3.14) and using envelope conditions, the following expressions are obtained.

$$\theta_{L1}\hat{W} + \theta_{C1}\hat{W}_C + \theta_{K1}\hat{R} = \hat{P}_1 \tag{3.A.32}$$

$$\theta_{L2}E_W\hat{W} + \theta_{K2}\hat{R} = 0 \tag{3.A.33}$$

$$\theta_{S3}\hat{W}_S + \theta_{K3}\hat{R} = 0 \tag{3.A.34}$$

Next, totally differentiating equations (3.15.1), (3.16), (3.17) and (3.19.1), collecting terms and simplifying, we get the following expressions.

$$\bar{S}_{LL}\hat{W} + \lambda_{L1}S_{LC}^1\hat{W}_C + \bar{S}_{LK}\hat{R} + \lambda_{L1}\hat{X}_1 + \lambda_{L2}\hat{X}_2 = 0 \tag{3.A.35}$$

$$\bar{S}_{KL}\hat{W} + A_2\hat{R} + A_1\hat{W}_S + \lambda_{K1}\hat{X}_1 + \lambda_{K2}\hat{X}_2 = \hat{K} \tag{3.A.36}$$

$$(S_{CL}^1 + E)W + (S_{CC}^1 - F)W_C + GW_S + X_1 = 0 \tag{3.A.37}$$

(Note that we have used $\hat{X}_3 = -S_{SS}^3\hat{W}_S - S_{SR}^3\hat{R}$ from (3.17).) where

$$\left.\begin{aligned}
&\bar{S}_{LL} = \left[\lambda_{L2}^*\{(E_W - 1) + S_{LL}^2\} + \lambda_{L1}S_{LL}^1)\right] < 0; \ \bar{S}_{LK} = \lambda_{L2}^*S_{LK}^2 > 0; \\
&\bar{S}_{KK} = (\lambda_{K2}S_{KK}^2 + \lambda_{K3}S_{KK}^3) < 0; \ \bar{S}_{KL} = \lambda_{K2}S_{KL}^2 > 0; \\
&A_1 = \lambda_{K3}(S_{SK}^3 + S_{KS}^3) > 0; \\
&A_2 = (\bar{S}_{KK} - \lambda_{K3}S_{SK}^3) < 0; \ \lambda_{L2}^* = \frac{W^*}{W}\lambda_{L2} > 0; \\
&A = \frac{W_S.W}{(1 + \beta)L_C(W_S - W)^2} > 0; \\
&B = \frac{\beta}{(1 + \beta)L_CW_C} > 0; \ E = (-nA(L + S) + BLW); \\
&F = B(LW + SW_S) > 0; \ G = [nA(L + S) + BSW_S] > 0.
\end{aligned}\right\} \tag{3.A.38}$$

Arranging (3.A.32)–(3.A.37) in matrix notation, we get the following.

$$\begin{bmatrix} \theta_{L1} & \theta_{C1} & \theta_{K1} & 0 & 0 & 0 \\ \theta_{L2}E_W & 0 & \theta_{K2} & 0 & 0 & 0 \\ 0 & 0 & \theta_{K3} & \theta_{S3} & 0 & 0 \\ \bar{S}_{LL} & \lambda_{L1}S_{LC}^1 & \bar{S}_{LK} & 0 & \lambda_{L1} & \lambda_{L2}^* \\ \bar{S}_{KL} & 0 & A_2 & A_1 & \lambda_{K1} & \lambda_{K2} \\ (S_{CL}^1 + E) & (S_{CC}^1 - F) & 0 & G & 1 & 0 \end{bmatrix} \begin{bmatrix} \hat{W} \\ \hat{W}_C \\ \hat{R} \\ \hat{W}_S \\ \hat{X}_1 \\ \hat{X}_2 \end{bmatrix} = \begin{bmatrix} \hat{P}_1 \\ 0 \\ 0 \\ 0 \\ 0 \\ 0 \end{bmatrix} \tag{3.A.39}$$

Solving (3.A.39), using (3.A.38) and simplifying, the following expressions are obtained.

$$\hat{W} = \left(\frac{\theta_{S3}\theta_{K2}\hat{P}_1}{\Delta}\right)\left[|\lambda|(S_{CC}^1 - F) - \lambda_{L1}\lambda_{K2}S_{LC}^1\right] \tag{3.A.40}$$

$$\hat{W}_C = -\left(\frac{\hat{P}_1}{\Delta}\right)\left[|\lambda|\theta_{K3}\theta_{L2}E_W G + \theta_{L2}E_W\lambda_{L2}^*(\theta_{K3}A_1 - \theta_{S3}A_2)\right.$$
$$+ \theta_{S3}\lambda_{K2}(\theta_{L2}E_W\bar{S}_{LK} - \theta_{K2}\bar{S}_{LL}) + \theta_{S3}\theta_{K2}$$
$$\left.\left\{\lambda_{L2}^*\bar{S}_{KL} + |\lambda|(E + S_{CL}^1)\right\}\right] \tag{3.A.41}$$

$$\hat{R} = -\left(\frac{\theta_{L2}E_W\theta_{S3}\hat{P}_1}{\Delta}\right)\left[|\lambda|(S_{CC}^1 - F) - \lambda_{L1}\lambda_{K2}S_{LC}^1\right] \tag{3.A.42}$$

$$\hat{W}_S = \left(\frac{\theta_{L2}E_W\theta_{K3}\hat{P}_1}{\Delta}\right)\left[|\lambda|(S_{CC}^1 - F) - \lambda_{L1}\lambda_{K2}S_{LC}^1\right]^\wedge \tag{3.A.43}$$

$$(\hat{W}_S - \hat{W}) = \left[\frac{(\theta_{L2}E_W\theta_{K3} - \theta_{S3}\theta_{K2})P_1}{\Delta}\right]\left[|\lambda|(S_{CC}^1 - F) - \lambda_{L1}\lambda_{K2}S_{LC}^1\right] \tag{3.A.44}$$

$$\left(\frac{\hat{X}_1}{\hat{P}_1}\right) = \left(\frac{S_{CC}^1 - F}{\Delta}\right)[\theta_{L2}E_W\{\theta_{K3}\lambda_{L2}^*A_1 + \theta_{S3}(\bar{S}_{LK}\lambda_{K2} - \lambda_{L2}^*A_2)$$
$$+ \theta_{K2}\theta_{S3}\lambda_{L2}^*\bar{S}_{KL}\}]$$
$$+ \left(\frac{S_{CL}^1 + F}{\Delta}\right)(\theta_{K2}\theta_{S3}\lambda_{K2}\lambda_{L2}^*)\{(E_W - 1) + S_{LL}^2\}$$
$$- \left(\frac{\lambda_{L1}\lambda_{K2}S_{LC}^1 G}{\Delta}\right)(\theta_{K2}\theta_{S3} - \theta_{L2}\theta_{K3}E_W) \tag{3.A.45}$$

$$\left(\frac{\hat{X}_2}{\hat{P}_1}\right) = \left(\frac{S_{LC}^1\lambda_{L1}}{\Delta}\right)[\theta_{L2}\theta_{K3}A_1 - \theta_{L2}\theta_{S3}E_W A_2 + \theta_{K2}\theta_{S3}\bar{S}_{KL}]$$
$$- \left(\frac{S_{CC}^1 - F}{\Delta}\right)[\theta_{L2}\theta_{K3}E_W\lambda_{L1}A_1 + \theta_{L2}\theta_{S3}E_W(\bar{S}_{LK}\lambda_{K1}$$
$$- \lambda_{L1}A_2) + \theta_{K2}\theta_{S3}\{\lambda_{L1}\bar{S}_{KL} - \lambda_{K1}\lambda_{L2}^*((E_W - 1) + S_{LL}^2)\}]$$
$$+ \left(\frac{\lambda_{L1}\lambda_{K1}S_{LC}^1 G}{\Delta}\right)(\theta_{K2}\theta_{S3} - \theta_{L2}\theta_{K3}E_W) \tag{3.A.46}$$

where

$$\Delta = |\theta|\theta_{S3}[|\lambda|(S_{CC}^1 - F) - \lambda_{L1}\lambda_{K2}S_{LC}^1] - \theta_{C1}\theta_{L2}E_W\theta_{K3}[\lambda_{L2}^*A_1 + G|\lambda|]$$
$$+ \theta_{C1}\theta_{L2}E_W\theta_{S3}(\lambda_{L2}^*A_2 - \lambda_{K2}\bar{S}_{LK}) - \theta_{C1}\theta_{K2}\theta_{S3}[(\lambda_{L2}^*\bar{S}_{KL} - \lambda_{K2}\bar{S}_{LL}) \tag{3.A.47}$$
$$+ |\lambda|(S_{CL}^1 + E)]$$

$$\left.\begin{aligned}|\lambda| &= (\lambda_{L1}\lambda_{K2} - \lambda_{K1}\lambda_{L2}^*) > 0 \text{ and}\\ |\theta| &= (\theta_{L1}\theta_{K2} - \theta_{K1}E_W\theta_{L2}) > 0\end{aligned}\right\} \tag{3.A.48}$$

(Note that $|\lambda|, |\theta| > 0$ because sector 2 is more capital-intensive than sector 1 with respect to adult unskilled labour in value sense.)

Using (3.A.38) and (3.A.48), from (3.A.47) it follows that

$$\Delta < 0 \text{ if } E \geq 0; \quad \text{or if, } (S^1_{CL} + E) \geq 0; \quad \text{or if, } [\lambda^*_{L2}\bar{S}_{KL} + |\lambda|$$
$$(S^1_{CL} + E)] \geq 0 \tag{3.A.49}$$

However, a few other sufficient conditions can be derived for Δ to be negative.

Using (3.A.38), (3.A.47) and (3.A.48), from (3.A.40)–(3.A.46) we can obtain the following results.

$$\left.\begin{array}{l}
\text{(i) } \hat{W} < 0 \text{ when } \hat{P}_1 < 0 \\[4pt]
\text{(ii) } \hat{W}_C < 0 \text{ when } \hat{P}_1 < 0 \text{ if } E \geq 0; \text{ or if, } (S^1_{CL} + E) \geq 0 \\[2pt]
\text{or if, } [\lambda^*_{L2}\bar{S}_{KL} + |\lambda|(S^1_{CL} + E)] \geq 0 \\[4pt]
\text{(iii) } \hat{R} > 0 \text{ when } \hat{P}_1 < 0 \\[4pt]
\text{(iv) } \hat{W}_S < 0 \text{ when } \hat{P}_1 < 0 \\[4pt]
\text{(v) } (\hat{W}_S - \hat{W}) > 0 \text{ when } \hat{P}_1 < 0 \text{ iff } \theta_{K3}E_W\theta_{L2} < \theta_{K2}\theta_{S3} \\[4pt]
\text{(vi) } \hat{X}_1 < 0 \text{ when } \hat{P}_1 < 0 \text{ if } \theta_{K3}E_W\theta_{L2} < \theta_{K2}\theta_{S3} \\[4pt]
\text{(vi) } \hat{X}_2 > 0 \text{ when } \hat{P}_1 < 0 \text{ if } \theta_{K3}E_W\theta_{L2} < \theta_{K2}\theta_{S3}
\end{array}\right\} \tag{3.A.50}$$

Appendix 3.9   Consequence on the incidence of child labour

We use equation (3.21) to examine the impact of foreign capital inflows on the incidence of child labour in the economy. Totally differentiating equation (3.21), we get

$$\hat{L}_C = -nA(L+S)(\hat{W}_S - \hat{W}) - LBW\hat{W} - SBW_S\hat{W}_S$$
$$+ B\hat{W}_C(W_S S + LW) \tag{3.A.51}$$

Using (3.A.40)–(3.A.44) and simplifying, the expression (3.A.51) may be rewritten as follows.

$$\left(\frac{\hat{L}_C}{\hat{P}_1}\right) = \left(\frac{1}{\Delta}\right)[(|\lambda| S^1_{CL} - \lambda_{L1}\lambda_{K2}S^1_{LL})G(\theta_{L2}E_W\theta_{K3} - \theta_{S3}\theta_{K2})$$
$$\quad\ (-)\quad\ (+)\qquad\qquad (-)\ (+)$$
$$- B(WL + W_S S)[\theta_{L2}E_W\lambda^*_{L2}(\theta_{K3}A_1 - \theta_{S3}A_2)]$$
$$\qquad\qquad (+)\qquad\qquad\quad (+)\quad (-)$$
$$+ \theta_{S3}(\lambda_{K2}\theta_{L2}E_W\bar{S}_{LK} + \theta_{K2}\lambda^*_{L2}\bar{S}_{KL})$$
$$- \theta_{S3}\theta_{K2}\lambda_{K2}\lambda^*_{L2}\{(E_W - 1) + S^2_{LL}\}]] \tag{3.A.52}$$
$$\quad (+)\qquad\qquad (\leq 0)\qquad (-)$$

From (3.A.52), we find that

$$\hat{L}_C < 0 \text{ when } \hat{P}_1 < 0 \text{ if } (\theta_{K3}E_W\theta_{L2} \leq \theta_{S3}\theta_{K2}) \qquad (3.A.52.1)$$

So the incidence of child labour decreases following trade sanctions under the sufficient condition $(\theta_{K2}\theta_{S3} \geq \theta_{K3}E_W\theta_{L2})$. This implies that sector 2 is not less capital-intensive relative to sector 2. However, this result may hold under other sufficient conditions as well.

Appendix 3.10   Effect on adult unskilled unemployment in the urban sector

Differentiating (3.18) one gets

$$\left(\frac{\hat{L}_U}{\hat{P}_1}\right) = \left(\frac{\hat{X}_2}{\hat{P}_1}\right) - \left[S_{LK}^2 E_W + \left(\frac{\lambda_{L2} + \lambda_{LU}}{\lambda_{LU}}\right)(1 - E_W)\right]\left(\frac{\hat{W}}{\hat{P}_1}\right) + S_{LK}^2 \left(\frac{\hat{R}}{\hat{P}_1}\right) \qquad (3.A.53)$$
$$(-) \qquad\qquad\qquad\qquad\qquad (\geq 0) \qquad (+) \qquad (-)$$

Using equations (3.A.40), (3.A.42), (3.A.46) and (3.A.49) and simplifying, from (3.A.53) we obtain

$$\left(\frac{\hat{L}_U}{\hat{P}_1}\right) < 0 \text{ if } (\theta_{K2}\theta_{S3} \geq \theta_{K3}E_W\theta_{L2}) \qquad (3.A.54)$$

Appendix 3.11   Outcome on the welfare of child labour–supplying families

Differentiation of equation (2.20) yields

$$dV = \hat{C}_1 + \beta\hat{C}_2 \qquad (3.A.55)$$

Substituting the expression for l_c from (2.24) in (2.21) and (2.22) and simplifying, we get

$$C_1 = \left[\frac{W(W_S - W) + nW_C W_S}{(1 + \beta)(W_S - W)}\right] \qquad (3.A.56)$$

and

$$C_2 = \beta\left[\frac{W(W_S - W) + nW_C W_S}{(1 + \beta)W_C}\right] \qquad (3.A.57)$$

Differentiating (3.A.56) and (3.A.57), we find

$$\hat{C}_1 = \left[\frac{(W_S - W)[W(W_S - W)^2\hat{W} + nW_C W_S\{(W_S - W)\hat{W}_C - W(\hat{W}_S - \hat{W})\}]}{[W(W_S - W) + nW_C W_S]}\right] \qquad (3.A.58)$$

and

$$\hat{C}_2 = \left| \frac{W_C\left[nW_S\hat{W}_S + \left(\dfrac{W}{W_C}\right)\{W_S\hat{W}_S + \hat{W}(W_S - 2W) - (W_S - W)\hat{W}_C\}\right]}{[W(W_S - W) + nW_CW_S]} \right. \quad (3.A.59)$$

Substitution of the expressions for $\hat{C}_1$ and $\hat{C}_2$ in (3.A.55) and simplification produce

$$dV = \left[\frac{1}{[W(W_S - W) + nW_CW_S]}\right][W(W_S - W)W\{(W_S - W)^2 + nW_CW_S + \beta\}$$

$$+ \beta W(W_S\hat{W}_S - W\hat{W}) + (W_S - W)\hat{W}_C\{nW_CW_S(W_S - W) - \beta W\}$$

$$+ nW_CW_S\hat{W}_S\{\beta - W(W_S - W)\}]$$

or

$$\left(\frac{dV}{dP_1}\right)[W(W_S - W) + nW_CW_S] = [(W_S - W)^3\left(\frac{dW}{dP_1}\right)$$

$$(+)$$

$$+ \left(\frac{W_S - W}{W_C}\right)\left(\frac{dW_C}{dP_1}\right)[nW_CW_S(W_S - W) - \beta W]$$

$$+ \left(\frac{dW}{dP_1}\right)[\beta(W_S - W) + \{nW_CW_S(W_S - W) - \beta W\}] \quad (3.A.60)$$

$$(+)$$

$$+ \left(\frac{dW_S}{dP_1}\right)[\beta nW_C + \{\beta W - nW_CW(W_S - W)\}]$$

$$(+)$$

From (3.A.60), it follows that

$$\left(\frac{dV}{dP_1}\right) > 0 \text{ if}$$

(i) if $E \geq 0$, or $(S_{CL}^1 + E) \geq 0$

and

(ii) $nW_C\dfrac{W_S}{W}(W_S - W) \geq \beta \geq nW_C(W_S - W)$ $\qquad$ (3.A.61)

(Note that $W_S > W$.)

However, from (3.A.60) it is easily seen that conditions (i) and (ii) are sufficient only for $\left(\dfrac{dV}{dP_1}\right) > 0$. One can find out several other sufficient conditions under which $\left(\dfrac{dV}{dP_1}\right) > 0$.

Notes

1 Social labeling might produce disastrous consequences on the developing economies, as the Bangladeshi experience has shown. Owing to the possible enactment of the U.S. Harkins Bill in 1994, which called for a complete ban on imports of any goods that were manufactured wholly or partly by child workers, the employers in the booming garments industry in Bangladesh that had employed a large number of child labourers began drastically removing the child workers. The consequence was a chaotic process that left many children worse off than they were before. See UNICEF (1997).

2 In an interview with the *Times of India* in 2001, the economist Jagdish Bhagwati grumbled: "Kailash Satyavarthi says that Biharis sell their children as bonded labour to work in Hoshiarpur in carpets. He wants foreign sanctions. If carpets are stopped, what will the Bihari parents do? They will send their children to some other conduit elsewhere. In Bangladesh, children were withdrawn from textiles. Many girls took to prostitution." Bhagwati said the solution was to have NGOs work at ground level and to fund families to send their children to school. (see V. Doctor (2014)). Also see http://articles.economictimes.indiatimes.com/2014-10-11/news/54899784_1_child-labour-child-labour-free-child-rights).

3 The input, land-capital, has been defined in section 3.2.

4 The substitution axiom emphasizes that adult and child labor are substitutes. In other words, it means that adults can do what children do. Some studies presume that certain tasks are specific to children. Expressions like 'nimble fingers' to describe child labour tended to perpetuate this belief. The substitution axiom expresses a completely opposite view on this. The nimble fingers argument, which once has been put forward, especially to carpet weaving, is an excuse given by employers and fails to convince researchers (see Burra (1997) and Weiner (1991)). A careful study of the technology of production involving children by Levison et al. (1998) lends strong support to the substitution axiom. They show that adults in India are as good, if not better, in producing hand-knotted carpets as children. Hence, even from a purely technical point of view, it is possible to replace child labour with adult labour. Nonetheless, because adults cost more, firms may be reluctant to make the transition to adults-only labor. This argument is also applicable to girl child labour helping household chore where, from a purely technical point of view, adult female labour can do what girls do.

5 The land/capital/output ratios in the two agricultural sectors (a_{N1} and a_{N2}) have been assumed to be technologically given. However, the other inputs exhibit CRS between themselves in these two sectors.

6 This supply function has been derived from the welfare-maximizing behaviour of each representative poor working household that supplies child labour (see equation 2.8 in chapter 2). The family consists of one adult member (the guardian) and a child. Total child time is 1, a part of which (l_C) is sent out to work at the wage rate, W_C. However, the family utility function has been slightly modified because in this model the family consumes only two commodities, X_2 and X_3.

7 This function has also been derived from the maximization exercise of the poor family. See equation (2.8.1) in chapter 2.

8 These propositions have been proved in appendices 3.1 and 3.2.

9 See appendix 3.1

10 This may be called a *Stolper-Samuelson type effect*. It may be noted that if we overlook the input, land-capital, sector 1 and sector 2 together would look like a *Heckscher-Ohlin Sub-System (HOSS)* using two common inputs, adult labour and child labour. This effect is different from the standard *Stolper-Samuelson effect*, which takes place only where two sectors use two common inputs, not a third one, like land-capital in the present case.

11 This has been proved in appendix 3.1.

12 This has been shown in appendix 3.2.

13 See appendix 3.3.

14 It has been proved in appendix 3.6.

15 That the output composition does not change and the number of child labour–supplying families remains the same has been shown in appendix 3.1.

16 See appendices 3.4 and 3.5 for the mathematical proof of this result.

17 See section 2.2.2.

18 Although this is a simplifying assumption, it is not completely without basis. Agriculture requires inputs like fertilizers, pesticides, weedicides and the like, which are to be used in recommended doses. Now if capital is used to purchase those inputs, the capital-output ratio becomes constant technologically. However, even if the capital-output ratio is not given technologically, the results of the model still hold under an additional sufficient condition relating to partial elasticities of substitution between capital and other inputs in sector 1.

19 Even if sector 2 is allowed to use child labour, the results of the model hold under different sufficient conditions.

20 How this contractual wage is endogenously determined will be explained subsequently.

21 This automatically implies that sector 2 is capital-intensive relative to sector 1 with respect to adult unskilled labour in the physical sense as well.

22 Even though the capital-output ratio in sector 1 is technologically given, adult labour and child labour are substitutes, and the production function displays the constant returns to scale property in these two inputs.

23 See Bhalotra (2002) in this context. Also, it is well known that in a Harris-Todaro type of economy, the rural sector (unskilled) wage is the average wage of all of the (unskilled) workers in the economy. This is known as the 'envelope property' of the Harris-Todaro model. See Chaudhuri and Mukhopadyay (2009) in this context.

24 The unionized wage function has been derived in appendix 3.7.

25 We assume that the representative working family has one adult member (the guardian) and n number of children with $n \geq 1$; l_C number of children are sent out to work at the wage rate, W_C. The remaining children who are not sent out to work are sent to school.

26 These results have been proved in appendix 3.8.

27 Three groups of unskilled workers in this system are earning different wages. Unskilled workers employed in the rural and the low-skill urban sectors receive a competitive wage, W, and the unionized wage, W^*, respectively, while the unemployed urban workers earn nothing. The average wage for unskilled labour is given by $W_A \equiv (W\lambda_{L1} + W^*\lambda_{L2})$, where λ_{L1} and λ_{L2} denote the proportion of unskilled labour employed in sectors 1 and 2, respectively. Using (13), we can write $W_A = W$. It may be mentioned that the average wage of the workers (unskilled workers in this case) in a Harris-Todaro economy is equal to the rural sector wage. This is known as the 'envelope property'. Hence, the change in relative skilled–unskilled wage inequality in this model is expressed as $(\hat{W}_S - \hat{W})$.

28 Here, sectors 2 and 3 use two different types of labour. However, there is one intersectorally mobile input, that is capital. So these two industries cannot be classified in terms of factor intensities that are usually used in the Hechscher-Ohlin-Samuelson model. Despite this, a special type of factor intensity classification in terms of the relative distributive shares of the mobile factor (i.e. capital) may be used for analytical purposes. The industry in which this share is higher relative to the other may be considered as capital-intensive in a special sense. See Jones and Neary (1984) for details.

29 A *Stolper-Samuelson effect* contains an element of *Rybczynski effect* if the production technologies are of the variable-coefficient type. This is a well-known theoretical result in the literature on international trade.

30 Derivations are available in appendix 3.9.

31 See appendix 3.10 for detailed derivations.

32 This result has been proved in appendix 3.11. Note that we have here denoted the intertemporal family utility by V instead of U and that workers are not the owners of capital.

33 Note that in the present case, both unskilled and skilled working families, each consisting of n number of children, supply child labour and that these families are not the owners of capital.

34 This is in line with Agell and Lundborg (1992, 1995) where while determining the 'fair wage' of the workers, w, the other variable input, Q (say, capital) , has been left aside on the plea that its rate of return, q, is the same in both the sectors of the economy. Chaudhuri (2003, 2016) and Chaudhuri and Ghosh Dastidar (2014) also have ignored capital in the process of determining the unionized wage on the same ground. In all these works, the determined unionized wage function has subsequently been fitted into the general equilibrium part of their models where all endogenous variables, including the unionized wage, are determined as functions of system parameters.

35 This is in line with Calvo (1978).

36 However, U is amenable to policy measures. If the government undertakes different labour market regulatory measures (e.g. partial or complete ban on resorting to strikes by the trade unions, reformation of employment security laws to curb union power), U takes on a lower value.

37 Each firm in industry 2 employs labour up to the point where the $VMPL$ is exactly equal to the reservation wage of the workers, W.

References

Agell, J. and Lundborg, P. (1992): 'Fair wages, involuntary unemployment and tax policy in the simple general equilibrium model', *Journal of Public Economics*, 47, 299–320.

Agell, J. and Lundborg, P. (1995): 'Fair wages in the open economy', *Economica*, 62, 325–351.

Bardhan, P.K. (1972): 'A model of growth of capitalism in a dual agrarian economy', in: J.M. Bhagwati and R.S. Eckaus (eds.), *Development and Planning: Essays in Honour of Paul Rosenstein-Rodan*, MIT Press, Cambridge, MA, 109–117.

Basu, K. and Van, P.H. (1998): 'The economics of child labour', *American Economic Review*, 88(3), 412–427.

Basu, K. and Zarghamee, H. (2009): 'Is product boycott a good idea for controlling child labor? A theoretical investigation', *Journal of Development Economics*, 88(2), 217–220.

Bhagwati, J. (1995): 'Trade liberalization and "Fair trade" demands: Addressing environmental and labour standard issues', *World Economy*, 18(6), 745–759.

Bhalotra, S. (2003): 'The impact of economic liberalization on employment and wages in India', ILO, Geneva.

Burra, N. (1997): *Born to Work: Child Labour in India*, Oxford University Press, Delhi.

Calvo, G. (1978): 'Urban unemployment and wage determination in LDCs: Trade unions in the Harris-Todaro model', *International Economic Review*, 19(1), 65–81.

Chaudhuri, S. (2003): 'How and how far to liberalize a developing country with informal sector and factor market distortions', *Journal of International Trade and Economic Development*, 12(4), 403–428.

Chaudhuri, S. (2007): 'Foreign capital, welfare and unemployment in the presence of agricultural dualism', *Japan and the World Economy*, 19(2), 149–165.

Chaudhuri, S. (2016): 'Trade unionism and welfare consequences of trade and investment reforms in a developing economy', *Metroeconomica*, 67(1), 152–171.

Chaudhuri, S. and Ghosh Dastidar, K. (2014): 'Corruption, efficiency wage and union leadership', *Pacific Economic Review*, 19(5), 559–576.

Chaudhuri, S. and Mukhopadhyay, U. (2009): *Revisiting the Informal Sector: A General Equilibrium Approach*, Springer, New York.

Davis, R.B. (2005): 'Abstinence from child labour and profit seeking', *Journal of Development Economics*, 76, 251–263.

Doctor, V. (2014): 'Nobel Prize 2014: Awarding Kailash Satyarthi & Malala Yousafzai is recognition for all social activists', *The Economics Times*, October 11, 2014. Available at: http://articles.economictimes.indiatimes.com/2014-10-11/news/54899784_1_child-labour-child-labour-free-child-rights

Gupta, M.R. (2002): 'Trade sanctions, adult unemployment and the supply of child labour: A theoretical analysis', *Development Policy Review*, 20(3), 317–332.

Harris, J.R. and Todaro, M.P. (1970): 'Migration, unemployment and development: A two-sector analysis', *American Economic Review*, 60, 126–142.

ILO. (2002): 'A future without child labour?', International Labour Conference, 90th Session June 2002, International Labour Office, Geneva.

ILO. (2012): 'Making progress against child labour: Global estimates and trends 2000–2012', International Labour Office, Geneva.

ILO. (2013): 'Global child labour trends 2008 to 2012', International Labour Office, International Programme on the Elimination of Child Labour (IPEC), Geneva.

Jafarey, S. and Lahiri, S. (2002): 'Will trade sanctions reduce child labour? The role of credit markets', *Journal of Development Economics*, 68(1), 137–156.

Jones, R.W. and Neary, P. (1984): 'Positive theory of international trade', in: R.W. Jones and P.B. Kenen (eds.), *Handbook of Development Economics*, Vol. 1, North-Holland, Amsterdam, 1–62.

Levison, D., Anker, R., Ashraf, S. and Barge, S. (1998): 'Is child labor really necessary in India's carpet industry?', in: R. Anker, S. Barge, S. Rajagopal and M.P. Joseph (eds.), *Economics of Child Labor in Hazardous Industries of India*, Hindustan Publishers, New Delhi, 95–133.

Srinivasan, T.N. (1996): 'International trade and labour standards from an economic perspective', in: P. Van Dyck and G. Faber (eds.), *Challenges to the New World Trade Organization*, Kluwer Publishers, Amsterdam, 219–224.

UNICEF. (1997): *The State of the World's Children*, Oxford University Press, Oxford.

Weiner, M. (1991): *The Child and the State in India: Child Labor and Education Policy in Comparative Perspective*, Oxford University Press, New Delhi.

World Development Report. (1995): Published by Oxford University Press for The World Bank.

4 Why do composite policies sometimes fail?

4.1 Introduction

The developing countries are plagued with a range of economic problems. Some of them are low economic growth, abject poverty, unemployment, moderate to severe inequality in income and wealth, incidence of child labour, inflation, corruption and so on. The governments in these countries undertake a wide set of policies to address the problems. Some of the policies are problem-specific in that they are designed to mitigate the problems directly, whereas others work on them indirectly. However, because different sectors of an economy are interlinked with one another, direct and indirect policies might work on a problem in the opposite directions, thereby leading to mild to moderate effects on the problem.

'Abject poverty' is thought to be the single largest factor behind the problem of child labour. Because the income from nonchild sources of a poor family is very low, the guardian of the family may decide to send some of its children to work instead of to school in order to supplement low family income. Free primary education policy with provisions for cash stipends and midday meals are the direct measures to keep children in school and restrain their parents from sending their children to the job market. However, given the abysmal condition of primary education system and very low return to education, the policy does not provide much incentive to the poor parents to send many of their children to school.[1] In many cases, they rather prefer to send their children to certain jobs that lead to some kind of on-the-job training, thereby increasing the possibility of earning more in future. On the other hand, the central authority in a developing country like India often resorts to agricultural subsidy policy as an instrument to fight against poverty because most of the poor people directly or indirectly rely on agriculture to earn their livelihoods. Nonetheless, it is also important to note that the concentration of child labour is the highest in agriculture. Hence, the possibility of the agricultural subsidy policy backfiring is always in the cards. Besides, because the developing countries have chosen free trade as their development strategy, as per their commitment to the IMF and the World Bank, they have been implementing liberalized trade and investment policies during the last three decades or so. The liberalized economic policies are believed to take the developing countries into higher growth orbits, the benefits of which are expected to percolate down to the poor people, thereby leading to lower poverty and hence less poverty-induced child labour incidence.

In the circumstances, a pertinent theoretical question is what could be the possible net effect of all of these diverse policies on the incidence of child labour. If we look at the reality, the ILO (2013) estimates that up to 2008, the rate of reduction in the worldwide incidence of child labour was not that as satisfactory as one would expect if all of the preceding policies had indeed been working in the same direction to curb the prevalence of the evil in the system. In this chapter, we intend to look at the issue in terms of a simple three-sector, full-employment general equilibrium model where child labour and adult labour are perfect substitutes.[2] There are two informal sectors and one formal sector. The formal sector faces a unionized labour market and cannot use child labour. The adult workers who are employed in the two informal sectors of the economy earn a low competitive wage and send many of their children to the job market instead of to school in order to supplement low income from nonchild sources. Because ours is a static model, we do not consider the aspect of skill formation on the part of the schoolgoing children, although there are some immediate monetary benefits for the school-attending children because of the provisions for receiving cash stipends, free educational and other goods and midday meals.[3] A price subsidy policy to agriculture is also present in the scene. Besides, the government also adopts liberalized trade and investment policies that take the forms of tariff reform and foreign direct investment (FDI). In this backdrop, we examine the effect of each of these four policies on the aggregate supply of child labour in the society. We find that while some of these policies produce favourable effects on child labour, the others always produce negative impact. Hence, when all of these policies are simultaneously adopted, the net outcome on the child labour could go either way.

4.2 The model

We consider a small open developing economy, which is divided into two informal sectors and one formal sector. One of the two informal sectors produces an agricultural product, X_1, with the help of labour and capital. The informal manufacturing sector (sector 2) uses labour and capital to produce an internationally nontraded input, X_2, for the formal manufacturing sector (sector 3).[4] In the two informal sectors, both adult labour and child labour are used, and these are assumed to be perfect substitutes for each other.[5] The formal sector (sector 3) produces a manufacturing commodity by means of adult labour, capital and the nontraded input produced by sector 2. Each adult worker in sector 3 receives a high (say, unionized) wage, W^*, while their compatriots in the two informal sectors receive a low competitive wage, W with $W^* > W$. The use of child labour in the formal sector is ruled out by virtue of government legislation. The economy is endowed with given endowments of labour (L) and domestic capital (K_D). The aggregate capital endowment of economy consists of both domestic capital, K_D and foreign capital, K_F, which are perfect substitutes.[6] There is perfect mobility of capital across sectors so that the return to capital, R, is the same in all of the three sectors. The endowment of child labour, is, however, endogenously determined. Following Basu and Van (1998), we make the assumption of 'substitution' in the informal sectors, which suggests that adult labour is a substitute for child labour or, more generally, that adults can do what children do. We go beyond this and assume that these two types of labour are perfect substitutes subject to a child-equivalent scale correction of μ. In other words, an adult worker is equivalent to μ numbers of child labourers where $\mu > 1$. Hence, under competitive conditions when the adult wage rate is W, the child wage rate, W_C, must be (W/μ). Complete mobility of both types of labour between these two sectors ensures that the wage rates must be the same across the two informal sectors.

Because the two types of labour are perfect substitutes, the economy's aggregate effective endowment of adult labour is $\left(L + \dfrac{L_C}{\mu}\right)$, where L_C is the aggregate supply of child labour. It is assumed that the number of adult workers employed in the formal sector (sector 3), $a_{L3}X_3$ is strictly less than the number of adult workers available in the economy, L. Let a_{ji} denote the amount of the jth input required to produce 1 unit of output of the ith commodity for $j = L, K$ and $i = 1, 2, 3$. Hence, a_{L3} denotes that labour-output ratio in sector 3. Besides, X_3 is the level of production in sector 3. Let R denote the return to capital. The prices of the two traded commodities are given by the small open economy assumption, while the price of the nontraded input produced by sector 2, P_2, is domestically determined. Sector 1 is the exports sector, and sector 3 is the import-competing sector. Sector 3 is protected by an import tariff at the ad valorem rate, t, so that the domestic (i.e. tariff-inclusive) price of the commodity is $(1 + t)P_3$.

On the other hand, agriculture in many countries is supported by government subsidies in the form of price support, export subsidy, credit support, energy support etc.[7] We here consider the case of a price subsidy policy to agriculture, which in this model is captured through a change in the producer price of the agricultural product, P_1. Therefore, P_1 is interpreted as the world price of commodity 1 plus the price subsidy.

Production functions in sector 1 and sector 2 satisfy constant returns to scale with positive but diminishing returns to each factor. On the contrary, fixed-coefficient technology is assumed for sector 3.[8] Except the formal sector labour market, the markets are perfectly competitive, and all inputs are fully employed. Finally, we assume that sector 2 and sector 3, as a whole, are more capital-intensive than sector 1.[9]

4.2.1   *The supply function of child labour*

We assume that the luxury axiom of Basu and Van (1998) holds. There are L numbers of altruistic working families in the economy, which are classified into two groups with respect to the earnings of their adult members. Each of the families consists of one adult member and n number of children. The adult workers who work in the higher-paid formal manufacturing sector comprise the richer segment of the working population, and they do not supply any child labour. On the contrary, workers who are engaged in the two informal sectors constitute the poorer segment. Adult workers belonging to this segment consider themselves as poor because of their low incomes from nonchild sources (competitive adult wage) and decide to send many of their children to the job market to supplement low family income (luxury axiom of Basu and Van 1998).

The supply function of child labour by each poor working family is derived from the utility-maximizing behaviour of the representative altruistic household. Because ours is a static model, we do not take into account the issue of human capital formation.[10] There is a free public education system in the economy where children from the poorer families get stipends, free educational goods and free midday meals. It is sensible to assume that higher the subsidy on education, E, the higher would be the free educational facilities and the related benefits, B, associated with child schooling. On the other hand, the larger the number of children sent to schools, the higher would be the aggregate benefits accrued to the poor families. We make the simplifying assumption that the money value of such benefits is strictly proportional to the number of children sent to schools. These suggest that $B(E)$ is given for any given value of E. Nonetheless, $B(E)$ increases with an increase in E, that is $B'(E) > 0$. The adult member maximizes the family welfare and decides on the number of children to be sent out to the job market. l_C. The remaining children, $(n - l_C)$, are sent to school. The detailed derivation of the supply function by the representative family has already been presented in chapter 2. The only difference is that instead of three material goods, the household in the present case consumes only two commodities 1 and 2. The supply function of child labour as derived in chapter 2 (equation 2.18), after appropriate modifications, is presented as follows.

$$l_C = \frac{[n\{(\alpha + \beta)W_C - B(E)\} - \gamma W]}{(W_C - B(E))} \tag{4.1}$$

The properties of this function have already been discussed in chapter 2.

There are $L_I (= L - a_{L3}X_3)$ number of adult workers engaged in the two informal sectors, and each of them sends l_C number of children to the workplace. Thus, the aggregate supply function of child labour in the economy is given by

$$L_C = \left[\frac{[n\{(\alpha + \beta)(W / \mu) - B(E)\} - \gamma W]}{((W / \mu) - B(E))}\right](L - a_{L3}X_3) \tag{4.2}$$

4.2.2 The general equilibrium analysis

Given the assumption of perfectly competitive markets, the usual price-unit cost equality conditions relating to the three sectors of the economy are given by the following three equations.

$$a_{L1}W + a_{K1}R = P_1 \tag{4.3}$$

$$a_{L2}W + a_{K2}R = P_2 \tag{4.4}$$

$$a_{L3}W^* + a_{K3}R + a_{23}P_2 = P_3(1 + t) \tag{4.5}$$

The formal sector faces a unionized labour market. The relationship for the unionized wage rate is specified as[11]

$$W^* = f(W, U) \tag{4.6}$$

$f(.)$ satisfies the following properties.

$$W^* = W \text{ for } U = 0, \ W^* > W \text{ for } U > 0: f_1, f_2 > 0.$$

Equation (4.6) states that in the absence of any bargaining power of the trade unions (i.e. when $U = 0$), the formal and informal sector wage rates are equal. However, the formal sector wage rate, W^*, exceeds the competitive informal sector wage rate, W, when there is at least some power to the trade unions. The unionized wage is scaled upward as the informal wage rate rises. Also with an increase in the bargaining power, the unions bargain for a higher wage.

Using (4.6), equation (4.5) may be rewritten as

$$a_{L3}f(W,U) + a_{23}P_2 + a_{K3}R = P_3(1+t) \tag{4.5.1}$$

Since the intermediate input, X_2, is used only in the production of X_3 its full-employment condition is as follows.

$$a_{23}X_3 = X_2 \tag{4.7}$$

The capital endowment equation is given by

$$a_{K1}X_1 + a_{K2}X_2 + a_{K3}X_3 = K$$

Using (4.7), this may be rewritten as follows.

$$a_{K1}X_1 + (a_{K2}a_{23} + a_{K3})X_3 = K \tag{4.8}$$

Because in the two informal sectors, child labour and adult labour are perfect substitutes, no separate market for child labour exists. The effective adult labour endowment of the economy is $(L + L_C/\mu)$ because 1 physical unit of adult labour is equivalent to μ physical units of child labour with $\mu > 1$. The full-employment condition in the adult labour market is given by the following.

$$a_{L1}X_1 + a_{L2}X_2 + a_{L3}X_3 = (L + L_C/\mu) = L^*$$

Using (4.7) and (4.3) and after simplification, this equation may be rewritten as follows.

$$a_{L1}X_1 + \left[a_{L2}a_{23} + a_{L3} \left\{ 1 + \frac{(n(\alpha + \beta)W - n\mu B(E) - \mu\gamma W)}{(W - \mu B(E))} \right\} \right] X_3$$
$$= L \left[1 + \frac{(n(\alpha + \beta)W - n\mu B(E) - \mu\gamma W)}{(W - \mu B(E))} \right] \tag{4.9}$$

In this model, there are eight endogenous variables (namely, W, W^*, R, P_2, X_1, X_2, X_3 and L_C) and eight independent equations (namely, equations (4.2) – (4.4), (4.5.1) and (4.6) – (4.9)). The parameters of the system are P_1, P_3, K, L, E, t, U, α, β, γ, μ and n. Equations (4.3), (4.4) and (4.5.1) constitute the price system.

Equation (4.6) describes the relationship between the adult informal and formal wages. The rest of the equations form the output system. We should note that the system possesses the decomposition property because the three unknown input prices, W, R and P_2, can be determined from the price system alone, independent of the output system. Once the factor prices are known, the factor-coefficients, a_{ji}s, are also known. Because W is already known, W^* is obtained from equation (4.6). X_1 and X_3 are simultaneously solved from equations (4.8) and (4.9). Given X_3, the equilibrium value of X_2 is found from (4.7). Finally, L_C is obtained from equation (4.2).

4.3 Comparative statics

The conventional wisdom suggests that an improvement in the educational facilities would bring about a significant reduction in the incidence of child labour. Besides, it is believed that liberalized trade and investment policies would take the developing countries into higher growth orbits, the benefits of which would percolate down to the poor people, thereby lowering the extent of poverty. Thus, these policies were expected to exert downward pressures on the incidence of poverty-induced child labour. In this section of the chapter, we will examine the effectiveness of these policies to mitigate the child labour problem. Although different liberalized trade and investment policies and the free primary education policy are undertaken simultaneously in a developing economy, to fix our ideas, we consider their effects one by one.

Totally differentiating equations (4.3), (4.4) and (4.5.1) and solving, the following expressions can be obtained.[12]

$$\hat{W} = \left(1 / |\theta|\right)\left[\hat{P_1}(\theta_{K2}\theta_{23} + \theta_{K3}) - \theta_{K1}T\hat{t}\right] \tag{4.10}$$

and

$$\hat{R} = \left(1 / |\theta|\right)\left[\theta_{L1}T\hat{t} - \hat{P_1}(\theta_{L2}\theta_{23} + \theta_{L3}E_W)\right] \tag{4.11}$$

where $|\theta| = \left[\theta_{L1}(\theta_{K2}\theta_{23} + \theta_{K3}) - \theta_{K1}(\theta_{L2}\theta_{23} + \theta_{L3}E_W)\right] > 0$ as the industrial sector as a whole (sector 2 and sector 3 taken together) is more capital-intensive than the agricultural sector (sector 1), $T = (t / (1 + t)) > 0$, $E_W = ((\partial W^* / \partial W)(W / W^*)) > 0$. E_W is the elasticity of the unionized wage rate, W^*, with respect to the informal sector wage rate, W.

Hence, a policy of trade liberalization in agriculture or a reduction in import tariff unequivocally raises the informal sector wage rate, W.

Now totally differentiating equations (4.9) and (4.8), one can derive the following expressions, respectively.[13]

$$\lambda_{L1}\hat{X_1} + \left\{\lambda_{L2} + \lambda_{L3}(1 + l_C / \mu)\right\}\hat{X_3} = A_1\hat{P_1} - A_2\hat{t} - A_3\hat{E} \tag{4.12}$$

and

$$\lambda_{K1}\hat{X_1} + (\lambda_{K2} + \lambda_{K3})\hat{X_3} = \hat{K} - A_4\hat{P_1} + A_5\hat{t} \tag{4.13}$$

where

$$A_1 = (1/|\theta|) \left[\begin{array}{l} (\lambda_{L1}\theta_{K1}\sigma_1 + \lambda_{L2}\theta_{K2}\sigma_2)(1 - \theta_{L3}(1 - E_W)) \\ + \dfrac{(L - a_{L3}X_3)W}{L*(W - \mu B)}\{n(\alpha + \beta) - \mu\gamma - l_C\}(\theta_{K2}\theta_{23} + \theta_{K3}) \end{array} \right] > 0;$$

$$A_2 = \left(\dfrac{T}{|\theta|}\right) \left[\begin{array}{l} (\lambda_{L1}\theta_{K1}\sigma_1 + \lambda_{L2}\theta_{K2}\sigma_2) \\ + \dfrac{\theta_{K1}(L - a_{L3}X_3)W\{n(\alpha + \beta) - \mu\gamma - l_C\}(\theta_{K2}\theta_{23} + \theta_{K3})\}}{L*(W - \mu B)} \end{array} \right] > 0;$$

$$A_3 = \left[\dfrac{\mu B' E(1 + n)(L - a_{LZ}X_3)}{L*(W - \mu B)} \right] > 0;$$

$$A_4 = \left[\{(\lambda_{K1}\theta_{L1}\sigma_1 + \lambda_{K2}\theta_{L2}\sigma_2)/|\theta|\}\{(1 - \theta_{L3}(1 - E_W))\} \right] > 0;$$

and

$$A_5 = \left[\{(\lambda_{K1}\theta_{L1}\sigma_1 + \lambda_{K2}\theta_{L2}\sigma_2)/|\theta|\}T \right] > 0 \qquad (4.14)$$

Solving (4.12) and (4.13), we get the following expression.

$$\hat{X}_3 = (1/|\lambda|) \left[\lambda_{K1}\hat{K} - (\lambda_{L1}A_4 + \lambda_{K1}A_1)\hat{P}_1 + (\lambda_{L1}A_5 + \lambda_{K1}A_2)\hat{t} + \lambda_{K1}A_3\hat{E} \right] \quad (4.15)$$

where $|\lambda| = \left[\lambda_{L1}(\lambda_{K2} + \lambda_{K3}) - \lambda_{K1}(\lambda_{L2} + \lambda_{L3}(1 + l_C/\mu)) \right]$ (4.16)

Hence, $|\lambda| > (<) 0$ iff $\{\lambda_{L1}(\lambda_{K2} + \lambda_{K3}) - \lambda_{K1}(\lambda_{L2} + \lambda_{L3})\} > (<)(\lambda_{K1}\lambda_{L3}l_C/\mu)$. Alternatively, $|\lambda| > (<) 0$ under the following necessary and sufficient condition.

$$\left[\dfrac{a_{L1}}{a_{K1}} - \dfrac{(a_{L2}X_2 + a_{L3}X_3)}{(a_{K2}X_2 + a_{K3}X_3)} \right] > (<) \left[\dfrac{(a_{L3}l_C/\mu)}{(a_{K2}X_2 + a_{K3}X_3)} \right] \qquad (4.17)$$

From equation (4.15), one can now establish the following proposition.[14]

Proposition 4.1: FDI or a hike in subsidy on education leads to a contraction (an expansion) of the formal sector (sector 3), in terms of both employment and output, if and only if $|\lambda| < (>) 0$. On the other hand, sector 3 contracts (expands) owing to an increase in the price subsidy to the agricultural sector or a reduction in the import tariff iff $|\lambda| > (<) 0$.

Let us now try to interpret the necessary and sufficient condition (given by (4.17)) for $|\lambda|$ to be negative (positive). We remember that each adult worker employed in the two informal sectors sends l_C number of his children to the job market, and the rest are sent to school. On the other hand, labourers engaged in the formal sector of the economy constitute the richer segment of the working class and do not send their children to the job market. In the two informal sectors, adult labour and child labour are perfect substitutes. Hence, the effective adult labour endowment of the economy, including child labour, is given by $L*(= L + L_C/\mu)$. The labour-capital ratio in sector 1 is given by (a_{L1}/a_{K1}). Sector 3 uses capital directly as well as indirectly through use of X_2 because production of one unit of X_3 requires a_{23} units of X_2 and sector X_2 also requires capital in its production. Thus, $(a_{K2}X_2 + a_{K3}X_3)$ gives the direct plus indirect requirement of capital in the production of X_3. Sector X_2 requires labour in its production. So this should be included in the calculation of labour requirement for sector X_3. The effective labour-capital ratio for sector X_3 is given by $\{(a_{L2}X_2 + a_{L3}X_3)/$

$(a_{K2}X_2 + a_{K3}X_3)\}$. The left-hand side of (4.17) gives the difference between the actual labour-capital ratio of sector 1 and the effective labour-capital ratio of sector 3. This difference is positive because it is sensible to assume that the agricultural sector (sector 1) is more labour-intensive vis-à-vis the aggregate industrial sector (i.e. sector 3 and sector 2 taken together). Now turning back to interpreting the right-hand side of (4.17), we note that $a_{L3}X_3$ number of workers who are engaged in sector 3 do not send their offspring to the job market. However, if they were employed in either of the two informal sectors, each of them would have sent l_C number of children to work. Because these $a_{L3}X_3$ numbers of workers are used in sector X_3, the economy is deprived of having $a_{L3}X_3l_C$ number of potential child workers, which is equivalent to $(a_{L3}X_3l_C/\mu)$ units of adult labour. Thus, the right-hand side of (4.17) gives the ratio between the forgone effective adult labour endowment and the aggregate amount of capital used in the industrial sectors. Thus, $|\lambda|$ is negative (positive) under the necessary and sufficient condition that the latter ratio must be greater (less) than the difference between the labour-capital ratios of the agricultural and the industrial sectors. We should note that a_{ji}s depends on the unknown factor prices, which in turn depend only on the parameters in the price system, like P_1, P_3, t and U. The value of l_C, on the other hand, depends on the values of μ, α, β, γ, P_1, P_3, t and U. Therefore, whether $|\lambda|$ would be negative or zero or positive would crucially hinge on the values of different parameters of the system.

Finally, totally differentiating equation (4.2) using (4.10), (4.15) and (4.16) and simplifying, we can derive the following expression.[15],[16]

$$\hat{L}_C = -\left(\frac{l_C a_{L3}X_3\lambda_{K1}}{L_C|\lambda|}\right)\hat{K}$$

$$+ \hat{P}_1\left(\frac{1}{L_C|\lambda||\theta|}\right)\left[\begin{array}{c}\dfrac{(L-a_{L3}X_3)W(\theta_{K2}\theta_{23}+\theta_{K3})(n(\alpha+\beta)-\mu\gamma-l_C)}{(W-\mu B)}\{\lambda_{L1}(\lambda_{K2}+\lambda_{K3})\\ -\{\lambda_{K1}(\lambda_{L2}+\lambda_{L3})\}+l_C a_{L3}X_3(1-\theta_{L3}(1-E_W))\\ \left[\lambda_{L1}(\lambda_{K1}\theta_{L1}\sigma_1+\lambda_{K2}\theta_{L2}\sigma_2)\\ \quad +\lambda_{K1}(\lambda_{L1}\theta_{K1}\sigma_1+\lambda_{L2}\theta_{K2}\sigma_2)\right]\end{array}\right]$$

$$-\hat{t}\left(\frac{T}{|\lambda||\theta|L_C}\right)\left[\begin{array}{c}\left\{\dfrac{\theta_{K1}W(L-a_{L3}X_3)(n(\alpha+\beta)-\mu\gamma-l_C)}{(W-\mu B)}\right\}\\ \{\lambda_{L1}(\lambda_{K2}+\lambda_{K3})-\lambda_{K1}(\lambda_{L2}+\lambda_{L3})\}+l_C a_{L3}X_3\\ \{\lambda_{L1}(\lambda_{K1}\theta_{L1}\sigma_1+\lambda_{K2}\theta_{L2}\sigma_2)+\lambda_{K1}(\lambda_{L1}\theta_{K1}\sigma_1+\lambda_{L2}\theta_{K2}\sigma_2)\}\end{array}\right]$$

$$-\hat{E}\left[\frac{\mu B'E(L-a_{L3}X_3)}{L_C|\lambda|(W-\mu B)}\right]\left[\begin{array}{c}(n-l_C)\{\lambda_{L1}(\lambda_{K2}+\lambda_{K3})-\lambda_{K1}(\lambda_{L2}+\lambda_{L3})\}\\ +l_C\lambda_{L3}\lambda_{K1}(1+l_C)\end{array}\right] \quad (4.18)$$

From (4.18) we find that

(i) $\hat{L}_C > (<)0$ when $\hat{K} > 0$ iff $|\lambda| < (>)0$

(ii) $\hat{L}_C > (<)0$ when $\hat{E} > 0$ iff $|\lambda| < (>)0$

Let us now explain these results intuitively. We note that any policy change affects the supply of child labour in two ways: (i) through a change in the size of the informal sector labour force, $(L_I = (L - a_{L3}X_3))$, because these families are the suppliers of child labour (we call this the *adult labour reallocation effect*), and (ii) through a change in l_C (the number of child workers supplied by each poor family), which results either from a change in the adult wage rate, W, or from a change in the benefit derived from sending children to schools, $B(E)$ (this may be termed the *direct effect*).

Foreign direct investment (FDI) cannot change the factor prices including the informal sector adult wage rate, W, because the production system possesses the decomposition property. Hence, the supply of child labour from each poor working family, l_C, does not change. However, it produces a *Rybczynski effect* leading to a contraction (expansion) of sector 3 and an expansion (contraction) of sector 1 if and only if $|\lambda| < (>)0$. Since sector 3 contracts (expands), more (less) adult workers would now be employed in the two informal sectors than previously. Consequently, the number of poor families, from which the supply of child labour comes, increases (decreases). This is the *adult labour reallocation effect*. Thus, the supply of child labour in the economy increases (decreases) following FDI if and only if $|\lambda| < (>)0$.

On the other hand, an increase in the subsidy on education affects the incidence of child labour in two ways. First, it lowers the effective price of child labour, $((W/\mu) - B(E))$. This lowers the supply of child labour from each family, l_C. This is the *direct effect* of the policy, which exerts a downward pressure on the incidence of child labour. Second, an induced effect is generated as the *direct effect* lowers the number of available child labour and hence the effective adult labour endowment of the economy.[17] This causes sector 3 to shrink (grow) and sector 1 to expand (contract) owing to *Rybczynski effect* if and only if $|\lambda| < (>)0$.[18] If the formal sector contracts, the number of child labour–supplying families employed in the two informal sectors increases. This is the *labour reallocation effect*, which tends to push up the number of child labourers in the society. The incidence of child labour gets a boost when the *adult labour reallocation effect* outweighs the contractionary *direct effect*. This happens under the necessary and sufficient condition that $|\lambda| < 0$. On the contrary, when $|\lambda| > 0$, a larger number of working families would now be engaged in the formal sector (sector 3), resulting in a decrease in the number of families supplying child labour. Hence, both the direct and induced effects of an education subsidy policy work together to lower the incidence of child labour in the society when $|\lambda| > 0$.

Hence, the following proposition can now be established.

Proposition 4.2: An increase in the subsidy on education and /or FDI will raise (lower) the supply of child labour iff $|\lambda| < (>)0$.

We are now interested in studying the consequences of tariff reform (trade liberalization) and the price subsidy policy to agriculture. If the price subsidy to agriculture rises, the effective producer price of the agricultural commodity P_1, takes on a higher value. On the contrary, tariff reform in the case of manufacturing product means a reduction in the import tariff, t, on commodity 3.

From (4.18). it is easy to check that

(iii) $\hat{L}_C > (<)0$ when $\hat{t} < 0$ iff $|\lambda| > (<)0$

and

(iv) $\hat{L}_C > (<)0$ when $\hat{P}_1 > 0$ iff $|\lambda| > (<)0$

If the effective producer price of the agricultural commodity, P_1, rises or the import tariff on sector 3 falls, the informal sector adult wage rate, W, rises, following a *Stolper-Samuelson effect* since sector 1 is more intensive in the use of labour vis-à-vis the formal sector with respect to capital. The child wage rate, W/μ, also rises as a consequence. The supply of child labour from each poor family, l_C, increases (see equation (4.1)). Consequently, the incidence of child labour rises. This is the *direct effect* of the agricultural price subsidy and/or trade liberalization policies, which exerts an upward pressure on the incidence of child labour. However, because the *direct effect* raises the number of available child labour and hence the effective adult labour endowment of the economy, sector 3 expands (contracts) if and only if $|\lambda| < (>)0$. If the formal sector expands, some workers move out of the two informal sectors to join the formal sector. Hence, the number of families supplying child labour decreases. This is the *adult labour reallocation effect*, which produces a favourable effect on the incidence of child labour. Our analysis finds that the net result would be a decrease in the aggregate supply of child labour because the *adult labour reallocation effect* outweighs the *direct effect*.[19] On the contrary, when $|\lambda| > 0$ sector 3 contracts. More adult workers are now employed in the two informal sectors, thereby raising the total number of families supplying child labour. Thus, in this case both the *direct effect* and the *adult labour reallocation effect* work in the same direction and accentuate the incidence of child labour in the society. This leads to the following proposition.

Proposition 4.3: Tariff reform in manufacturing import and/or a price subsidy policy to agriculture lowers (raises) the incidence of child labour in the society if and only if $|\lambda| < (>)0$.

A close look at propositions 4.2 and 4.3 reveals that when $|\lambda| > 0$, FDI and/or a hike in education subsidy lowers the incidence of child labour while a policy of tariff reform and/or a price subsidy to agriculture accentuates the problem. On the contrary, the former policies raise the incidence of child labour while the latter produce the opposite effect when $|\lambda| < 0$. In a developing economy, subsidy policies on education and agriculture and trade and investment liberalization policies are undertaken concurrently. In the given set-up, we find that if these policies are undertaken concurrently, some of these will work to reduce the incidence of child labour while the others will accentuate the problem, thereby counterbalancing each other's effects, partially if not fully. Thus, the net effect might sometimes be ambiguous irrespective of the sign of $|\lambda|$. This establishes the final proposition of the model.

Proposition 4.4: If an education subsidy policy and/or a price subsidy policy to agriculture and different trade and investment liberalization policies are concomitantly adopted in a developing economy, the net impact on the incidence of child labour could be uncertain.

4.4   Concluding remarks

Poverty and the lack of educational facilities are often cited in the literature as the primary factors responsible for the problem of child labour in the developing economies. Liberalized trade and investment policies and the provision of better and free education were often recommended as remedial measures. Trade and investment liberalization programs are supposed to reduce poverty by raising the growth rates of these economies, thereby putting a brake on the incidence of poverty-induced child labour. On the other hand, betterment of educational facilities, coupled with allied incentive schemes, would also be able to deliver the goods by keeping the children from poor families in school and restraining them from entering the job market. Over the last two decades and a half, the developing economies have gone in for economic liberalization in a big way. Several drastic measures have been implemented to ensure a freer international trade. Besides, provisions have been made for ensuring free and better educational opportunities. However, empirical evidence from several countries in transition reveal that in the first two decades after the initiation of economic reforms, the rate of decline in the number of working children was far from being satisfactory, both in absolute and percentage terms. Why globalization, poverty reduction programs through agricultural subsidy and the betterment of educational opportunities could not yield the desired results despite so many policies being in operation is puzzling. This chapter has provided a theoretical answer to this question in terms of a three-sector general equilibrium model with informal sector and child labour.

The analysis has shown that if different trade and investment liberalization programs, agricultural subsidies and free education policies are undertaken simultaneously in a transition economy, their overall effect on the supply of child labour may not be as satisfactory as expected because different policies produce mutually opposite effects on the incidence of child labour, thereby nullifying each other's effects, at least partially. For example, we have seen when $\lambda > 0$, FDI and/or an increase in education subsidy exerts a downward pressure on the incidence of child labour while a policy of tariff reform and/or a price subsidy policy to agriculture accentuates the problem. On the contrary, the first two policies raise the aggregate supply of child labour while the latter policies produce the opposite effect when $|\lambda| < 0$. The actual sign of $|\lambda|$ depends on the values of different parameters of the system. Hence, taking into account values of all of the system parameters, the policy makers of the country in question should decide which policies ought to be given priority and carried out in order to mitigate the incidence of poverty-induced child labour in the system.

Appendices

Appendix 4.1 Policy effects on factor prices

Totally differentiating equations (4.3), (4.4) and (4.5.1), we get the following expressions.

$$\theta_{L1}\hat{W} + \theta_{K1}\hat{R} = \hat{P}_1 \tag{4.A.1}$$

$$\theta_{L2}\hat{W} + \theta_{K2}\hat{R} - \hat{P}_2 = 0 \tag{4.A.2}$$

$$\theta_{L3}E_W\hat{W} + \theta_{K3}\hat{R} + \theta_{23}\hat{P}_2 = T\hat{t} \tag{4.A.3}$$

where $T = (t/(1 + t)) > 0$ and $E_W = ((\partial W^*/\partial W)(W/W^*))$. E_W is the elasticity of the unionized wage rate, W^*, with respect to the informal wage rate, W.

Solving equations (4.A.1)–(4.A.3), one gets expressions (4.10) and (4.11) as presented in the text.

Appendix 4.2 Consequences of different policies on output composition

Totally differentiating equation (4.9), one gets the following.

$$\lambda_{L1}\hat{X}_1 + \{\lambda_{L2} + \lambda_{L3}(1 + l_C / \mu)\}\hat{X}_3 = \lambda_{L1}\theta_{K1}\sigma_1(\hat{W} - \hat{R}) + \lambda_{L2}\theta_{K2}\sigma_2(\hat{W} - \hat{R})$$

$$+ \frac{(L - a_{L3}X_3)}{L*(W - \mu B)^2}\Big[(W - \mu B)\{n(\alpha + \beta)W\hat{W} - \mu\gamma W W\hat{W} - n\mu B'E\hat{E}\}$$

$$- \{n(\alpha + \beta)W - n\mu B - \mu\gamma W\}(W\hat{W} - \mu B'E\hat{E})\Big]$$

where $L*(= L + L_C/\mu)$ is the effective adult labour endowment of the economy. Thus, $\lambda_{Li} = (a_{Li}X_i/L*)$ for $i = 1, 2, 3$. Note that $\hat{a}_{Li} = -\theta_{Ki}\sigma_i(\hat{W} - \hat{R})$ where σ_i is the elasticity of substitution between the two factors in the ith sector for $i = 1, 2$. But $\sigma_3 = 0$ because we have assumed fixed-coefficient technology for sector 3.

Simplification gives

$$\lambda_{L1}\hat{X}_1 + \{\lambda_{L2} + \lambda_{L3}(1 + l_C / \mu)\}\hat{X}_3$$

$$= (\lambda_{L1}\theta_{K1}\sigma_1 + \lambda_{L2}\theta_{K2}\sigma_2)(\hat{W} - \hat{R})$$

$$+\frac{(L-a_{L3}X_3)}{L^*(W-\mu B)}\Big[W\hat{W}\{n(\alpha+\beta)-\mu\gamma\}-n\mu B'E\hat{E}-l_C(W\hat{W}-\mu B'E\hat{E})\Big]$$

Using (4.10) and (4.11) from the preceding expression, we write

$$\lambda_{L1}\hat{X}_1+\{\lambda_{L2}+\lambda_{L3}(1+l_C/\mu)\}\hat{X}_3=\frac{(\lambda_{L1}\theta_{K1}\sigma_1+\lambda_{L2}\theta_{K2}\sigma_2)}{|\theta|}\begin{bmatrix}\{1-\theta_{L3}(1-E_W)\}\\ \hat{P}_1-T\hat{t}\end{bmatrix}$$

$$+\frac{(L-a_{L3}X_3)W}{L^*(W-\mu B)|\theta|}\{n(\alpha+\beta)-\mu\gamma-l_C\}\Big[(\theta_{K2}\theta_{23}+\theta_{K3})\hat{P}_1-\theta_{K1}T\hat{t}\Big]$$

$$-\left[\frac{\mu B'E(1+n)(L-a_{L3}X_3)}{L^*(W-\mu B)}\right]\hat{E}$$

(4.A.4)

or

$$\lambda_{L1}\hat{X}_1+\{\lambda_{L2}+\lambda_{L3}(1+l_C/\mu)\}\hat{X}_3=A_1\hat{P}_1-A_2\hat{t}-A_3\hat{E}$$

where

$$A_1=(1/|\theta|)\Big[(\lambda_{L1}\theta_{K1}\sigma_1+\lambda_{L2}\theta_{K2}\sigma_2)(1-\theta_{L3}(1-E_W))$$

$$+\frac{(L-a_{L3}X_3)W}{L^*(W-\mu B)}\{n(\alpha+\beta)-\mu\gamma-l_C\}(\theta_{K2}\theta_{23}+\theta_{K3})\Big]>0$$

$$A_2=\left(\frac{T}{|\theta|}\right)\Big[(\lambda_{L1}\theta_{K1}\sigma_1+\lambda_{L2}\theta_{K2}\sigma_2)$$

$$+\frac{\theta_{K1}(L-a_{L3}X_3)W\{n(\alpha+\beta)-\mu\gamma-l_C\}(\theta_{K2}\theta_{23}+\theta_{K3})}{L^*(W-\mu B)}\Big]>0$$

and

$$A_3=\left[\frac{\mu B'E(1+n)(L-a_{L3}X_3)}{L^*(W-\mu B)}\right]>0$$

Similarly, totally differentiating equation (4.8), we obtain

$$\lambda_{K1}\hat{X}_1+(\lambda_{K2}+\lambda_{K3})\hat{X}_3=\hat{K}+\left[\frac{(\lambda_{K1}\theta_{L1}\sigma_1+\lambda_{K2}\theta_{L2}\sigma_2)\{T\hat{t}-\hat{P}_1(1-\theta_{L3}(1-E_W))\}}{|\theta|}\right]$$

(4.A.5)

$$=\hat{K}-A_4\hat{P}_1+A_5\hat{t}$$

where

$$A_4=\Big[\{(\lambda_{K1}\theta_{L1}\sigma_1+\lambda_{K2}\theta_{L2}\sigma_2)/|\theta|\}\{(1-\theta_{L3}(1-E_W))\}\Big]>0$$

and

$$A_5=\Big[\{(\lambda_{K1}\theta_{L1}\sigma_1+\lambda_{K1}\theta_{L2}\sigma_2)/|\theta|\}T\Big]>0$$

Solving (4.A.4) and (4.A.5), we get the following expression.

$$\hat{X}_3=(1/|\lambda|)\Big[\lambda_{K1}\hat{K}-(\lambda_{L1}A_4+\lambda_{K1}A_1)\hat{P}_1+(\lambda_{L1}A_5+\lambda_{K1}A_2)\hat{t}+\lambda_{K1}A_3\hat{E}\Big]\quad(4.15)$$

Appendix 4.3 Effects on child labour incidence

Totally differentiating equation (4.2), we write

$$L_C\hat{L}_C = \frac{(L - a_{L3}X_3)}{(W - \mu B)}\Big[nW(\alpha + \beta)\hat{W} - n\mu B'E\hat{E} - \mu\gamma W\hat{W} - l_C(W\hat{W} - \mu B'E\hat{E})\Big] - l_C a_{L3}X_3\hat{X}_3$$

or

$$\hat{L}_C = \frac{(L - a_{L3}X_3)}{L_C(W - \mu B)}\{n(\alpha + \beta) - \mu\gamma - l_C)\}W\hat{W} - \mu B'E(n - l_C)\frac{(L - a_{L3}X_3)}{L_C(W - \mu B)}\hat{E}$$
$$- (l_C a_{L3}X_3 / L_C)\hat{X}_3$$

Using (4.10) and (4.15), this expression can be rewritten as follows.

$$\hat{L}_C = \left[\frac{(L - a_{L3}X_3)W}{L_C(W - \mu B)|\theta|}\{n(\alpha + \beta) - \mu\gamma - l_C)\}\right]\Big[(\theta_{K2}\theta_{23} + \theta_{K3})\hat{P}_1 - \theta_{K1}T\hat{t}\Big]$$

$$- \frac{\mu B'E(n - l_C)(L - a_{L3}X_3)}{L_C(W - \mu B)}\hat{E}$$

$$- \left(\frac{l_C a_{L3}X_3}{L_C|\lambda|}\right)\Big[\lambda_{K1}\hat{K} - (\lambda_{L1}A_4 + \lambda_{K1}A_1)\hat{P}_1 + (\lambda_{L1}A_5 + \lambda_{K1}A_2)\hat{t} + \lambda_{K1}A_3\hat{E}\Big]$$

Rearranging terms, one finds

$$\hat{L}_C = -\left(\frac{l_C a_{L3}X_3\lambda_{K1}}{L_C|\lambda|}\right)\hat{K}$$

$$+ \hat{P}_1 \left[\begin{array}{c} \dfrac{(L - a_{L3}X_3)W\{n(\alpha + \beta) - \mu\gamma - l_C\}(\theta_{K2}\theta_{23} + \theta_{K3})}{L_C(W - \mu B)|\theta|} \\[2mm] + \dfrac{l_C a_{L3}X_3(\lambda_{L1}A_4 + \lambda_{K1}A_1)}{L_C|\lambda|} \end{array}\right]$$

$$- \hat{t} \left[\begin{array}{c} \dfrac{T\theta_{K1}W(L - a_{L3}X_3)\{n(\alpha + \beta) - \mu\gamma - l_C\}}{L_C(W - \mu B)|\theta|} \\[2mm] + \dfrac{l_C a_{L3}X_3(\lambda_{L1}A_5 + \lambda_{K1}A_2)}{L_C|\theta|} \end{array}\right]$$

$$\quad (4.A.6)$$

$$- \hat{E}\left[\frac{\mu B'E(n - l_C)(L - a_{L3}X_3)}{L_C(W - \mu B)} + \frac{l_C a_{L3}X_3\lambda_{K1}A_3}{L_C|\lambda|}\right]$$

Now let us simplify the different components of the right-hand side of (4.A.6) as follows. Consider the term

$$\left[\frac{\mu B'E(n - l_C)(L - a_{L3}X_3)}{L_C(W - \mu B)} + \frac{l_C a_{L3}X_3\lambda_{K1}A_3}{L_C|\lambda|}\right]$$

After substituting for A_3 from (4.14) in the preceding expression, we get

$$\left[\frac{\mu B'E(n-l_C)(L-a_{L3}X_3)}{L_C(W-\mu B)}+\frac{l_C a_{L3}X_3\lambda_{K1}A_3}{L_C|\lambda|}\right]$$

$$=\left[\frac{\mu B'E(n-l_C)(L-a_{L3}X_3)}{L_C(W-\mu B)}+\frac{l_C a_{L3}X_3\lambda_{K1}\mu B'(1+n)(L-a_{L3}X_3)}{L_C|\lambda|L*(W-\mu B)}\right]$$

$$=\left[\frac{\mu B'E(L-a_{L3}X_3)}{L_C|\lambda|(W-\mu B)}\right]\left[(n-l_C)|\lambda|+\lambda_{L3}l_C\lambda_{K1}(1+n)\right]$$

Inserting the value of $|\lambda|$ and after simplification, this expression becomes

$$\left[\frac{\mu B'E(n-l_C)(L-a_{L3}X_3)}{L_C(W-\mu B)}+\frac{l_C a_{L3}X_3\lambda_{K1}A_3}{L_C|\lambda|}\right]$$

$$=\left[\frac{\mu B'E(L-a_{L3}X_3)}{L_C|\lambda|(W-\mu B)}\right]\left[\begin{matrix}(n-l_C)\{\lambda_{L1}(\lambda_{K2}+\lambda_{K3})-\lambda_{K1}(\lambda_{L2}+\lambda_{L3})\}\\+l_C\lambda_{L3}\lambda_{K1}\{(1+n)-(n-l_C)/\mu\}\end{matrix}\right]$$ (4.A.7)

Again

$$\left[\frac{T\theta_{K1}W(L-a_{L3}X_3)\{n(\alpha+\beta)-\mu\gamma-l_C\}}{L_C(W-\mu B)|\theta|}+\frac{l_C a_{L3}X_3(\lambda_{L1}A_5+\lambda_{K1}A_2)}{L_C|\theta|}\right]$$

$$=\left[\frac{T\theta_{K1}W(L-a_{L3}X_3)\{n(\alpha+\beta)-\mu\gamma-l_C\}}{L_C(W-\mu B)|\theta|}+\left(\frac{l_C a_{L3}X_3T}{|\lambda|L_C|\theta|}\right)\{\lambda_{L1}(\lambda_{K1}\theta_{L1}\sigma_1+\lambda_{K2}\theta_{L2}\sigma_2)\right.$$

$$\left.+\lambda_{K1}(\lambda_{L1}\theta_{K1}\sigma_1+\lambda_{L2}\theta_{K2}\sigma_2)+\frac{\lambda_{K1}\theta_{K1}(L-a_{L3}X_3)W(n(\alpha+\beta)-\mu\gamma-l_C)}{L*(W-\mu B)}\}\right]$$

Inserting the value of $|\lambda|$ and after simplification, the preceding expression becomes

$$\left[\frac{T\theta_{K1}W(L-a_{L3}X_3)\{n(\alpha+\beta)-\mu\gamma-l_C\}}{L_C(W-\mu B)|\theta|}+\frac{l_C a_{L3}X_3(\lambda_{L1}A_5+\lambda_{K1}A_2)}{L_C|\theta|}\right]$$

$$=\left(\frac{T}{|\lambda||\theta|L_C}\right)\left[\left\{\frac{\theta_{K1}W(L-a_{L3}X_3)(n(\alpha+\beta)-\mu\gamma-l_C)}{(W-\mu B)}\right\}\{\lambda_{L1}(\lambda_{K2}+\lambda_{K3})-\lambda_{K1}(\lambda_{L2}+\lambda_{L3})\right.$$ (4.A.8)

$$+\lambda_{K1}\lambda_{L3}l_C(1-1/\mu)\}$$

$$\left.+l_C a_{L3}X_3\{\lambda_{L1}(\lambda_{K1}\theta_{L1}\sigma_1+\lambda_{K2}\theta_{L2}\sigma_2)+\lambda_{K1}(\lambda_{L1}\theta_{K1}\sigma_1+\lambda_{L2}\theta_{K2}\sigma_2)\}\right]$$

Finally.

$$\left[\frac{(L-a_{L3}X_3)W\{n(\alpha+\beta)-\mu\gamma-l_C\}(\theta_{K2}\theta_{23}+\theta_{K3})}{L_C(W-\mu B)|\theta|}+\frac{l_C a_{L3}X_3(\lambda_{L1}A_4+\lambda_{K1}A_1)}{L_C|\lambda|}\right]$$

$$=\left[\frac{(L-a_{L3}X_3)W\{n(\alpha+\beta)-\mu\gamma-l_C\}(\theta_{K2}\theta_{23}+\theta_{K3})}{L_C(W-\mu B)|\theta|}\right]$$

$$+\frac{l_C a_{L3} X_3}{|\theta| L_C |\lambda|}\{\lambda_{L1}(1-\theta_{L3}(1-E_W))(\lambda_{K1}\theta_{L1}\sigma_1+\lambda_{K2}\theta_{L2}\sigma_2)$$

$$+\lambda_{K1}(\lambda_{L1}\theta_{K1}\sigma_1+\lambda_{L2}\theta_{K2}\sigma_2)(1-\theta_{L3}(1-E_W))$$

$$+\lambda_{K1}\frac{(L-a_{L3}X_3)W(n(\alpha+\beta)-\mu\gamma-l_C)(\theta_{K2}\theta_{23}+\theta_{K3})}{L*(W-\mu B)}\Big\}\Big]$$

Inserting the value of $|\lambda|$ and after simplification, the expression becomes

$$\left[\frac{(L-a_{L3}X_3)W\{n(\alpha+\beta)-\mu\gamma-l_C\}(\theta_{K2}\theta_{23}+\theta_{K3})}{L_C(W-\mu B)|\theta|}+\frac{l_C a_{L3}X_3(\lambda_{L1}A_4+\lambda_{K1}A_1)}{L_C|\lambda|}\right]$$

$$=\left(\frac{1}{L_C|\lambda||\theta|}\right)\left[\frac{(L-a_{L3}X_3)W(\theta_{K2}\theta_{23}+\theta_{K3})(n(\alpha+\beta)-\mu\gamma-l_C)}{(W-\mu B)}\{\lambda_{L1}(\lambda_{K2}+\lambda_{K3})\right.$$

$$-\{\lambda_{K1}(\lambda_{L2}+\lambda_{L3})+\lambda_{K1}\lambda_{L3}l_C(1-1/\mu)\}$$

$$+l_C a_{L3}X_3(1-\theta_{L3}(1-E_W))\{\lambda_{L1}(\lambda_{K1}\theta_{L1}\sigma_1+\lambda_{K2}\theta_{L2}\sigma_2)$$

$$\left.+\lambda_{K1}(\lambda_{L1}\theta_{K1}\sigma_1+\lambda_{L2}\theta_{K2}\sigma_2)\}\right] \qquad (4.A.9)$$

Using (4.A.7), (4.A.8) and (4.A.9) from (4.A.6), we finally get

$$\hat{L}_C=-\left(\frac{l_C a_{L3}X_3\lambda_{K1}}{L_C|\lambda|}\right)\hat{K}$$

$$+\hat{P}_1\left(\frac{1}{L_C|\lambda||\theta|}\right)\left[\frac{(L-a_{L3}X_3)W(\theta_{K2}\theta_{23}+\theta_{K3})(n(\alpha+\beta)-\mu\gamma-l_C)}{(W-\mu B)}\{\lambda_{L1}(\lambda_{K2}+\lambda_{K3})\right.$$

$$-\{\lambda_{K1}(\lambda_{L2}+\lambda_{L3})\}+l_C a_{L3}X_3(1-\theta_{L3}(1-E_W))\{\lambda_{L1}(\lambda_{K1}\theta_{L1}\sigma_1+\lambda_{K2}\theta_{L2}\sigma_2)$$

$$\left.+\lambda_{K1}(\lambda_{L1}\theta_{K1}\sigma_1+\lambda_{L2}\theta_{K2}\sigma_2)\}]\right]$$

$$-\hat{t}\left(\frac{T}{|\lambda||\theta|L_C}\right)\left[\left\{\frac{\theta_{K1}W(L-a_{L3}X_3)(n(\alpha+\beta)-\mu\gamma-l_C)}{(W-\mu B)}\right\}\{\lambda_{L1}(\lambda_{K2}+\lambda_{K3})-\lambda_{K1}(\lambda_{L2}+\lambda_{L3})\}\right. \qquad (4.18)$$

$$\left.+l_C a_{L3}X_3\{\lambda_{L1}(\lambda_{K1}\theta_{L1}\sigma_1+\lambda_{K2}\theta_{L2}\sigma_2)+\lambda_{K1}(\lambda_{L1}\theta_{K1}\sigma_1+\lambda_{L2}\theta_{K2}\sigma_2)\}\right]$$

$$-\hat{E}\left[\frac{\mu B'E(L-a_{L3}X_3)}{L_C|\lambda|(W-\mu B)}\right][(n-l_C)\{\lambda_{L1}(\lambda_{K2}+\lambda_{K3})-\lambda_{K1}(\lambda_{L2}+\lambda_{L3})\}+l_C\lambda_{L3}\lambda_{K1}(1+l_C)]$$

Notes

1 A study of India by the PROBE team (1999) found that the state of basic education was appalling and that, even though parents valued education in its own right, they believed that their offspring were unlikely to benefit from education in its current state. UNICEF (1997) cited low quality of schooling as an important reason for high dropout rates among primary school students in the developing countries.

2 See note 5 in this context.

3 Some of these goods could be bicycles and/or shoes. It may be noted that the Government of West Bengal, India has very recently made provisions for distributing these items to schoolgoers to keep them in school and to lower the school dropout rate.

4 Empirical evidence suggests that the informal sector units produce mostly intermediate inputs for the formal sector. See for example, Joshi and Joshi (1976), Bose (1978), Papola (1981) and Romatet (1983). However, a few theoretical papers

like Grinols (1991), Chandra and Khan (1993) and Gupta (1997) have formalized the urban informal sector as a sector that produces an internationally traded final commodity.

5 Many large industries like carpet weaving, glass manufacturing, leather bag, shoe manufacturing and garment-making have split up into tiny units and shifted the production process to urban slums, in order to utilize the services of children. Some among these industries give subcontracts to enterprises, which produce components of the formal sector output, on an informal basis, hiring child labour. Adult workers can do whatever children do. Hence, these two types of labour are not complementary to each other. These are indeed substitutes. However, the degree of substitutability between these two factors may vary. The assumption that these two factors are perfect substitutes is undoubtedly a very simplifying one. Although Basu (1999) and Chaudhuri (2004) have made this assumption for different purposes, many activities within the informal sector adult labour cannot be substituted by child labour. Hence, if one views the informal sector in a developing economy as a whole, it would be more realistic to assume that these two types of labour are just substitutes.

6 This simplified assumption has been made in Brecher and Alejandro (1977), Khan (1982), Grinols (1991), Chandra and Khan (1993), Gupta (1997) and Chaudhuri (2001a, 2001b, 2005, 2007, 2016) etc. However, in the papers of Beladi and Marjit (1992a, 1992b) and Marjit and Beladi (1996), foreign capital has been treated differently from domestic capital, and these two types of capital are not engaged in the same sector of the economy.

7 An agricultural subsidy policy is an integral part of the poverty eradication programs in the developing countries because most of the poor people directly or indirectly rely on agriculture to earn their livelihoods. On the other hand, these poor people are the potential suppliers of child labour. It is therefore expected that an agricultural subsidy will raise the earning opportunities of the poor households, in turn lowering the supply of child labour through positive income effect. See Dwibedi and Chaudhuri (2014) in this context.

8 This is a simplifying assumption. Because sector 3 uses more than two inputs in production, unless fixed-coefficient technology is assumed, the algebra of the model will be seriously complicated by the presence of partial elasticities of substitutions when one considers the effects of any changes in the price system. However, as the system possesses the decomposition property, the usual CRS production function may be considered when one analyzes the effects of any changes in the output system.

9 Chandra and Khan (1993) and Gupta (1997) have also made this assumption. However, in these papers, the Harris and Todaro (1970) framework has been considered.

10 This aspect has been addressed in chapters 5 and 8, where we recourse to dynamic structures for the purpose of analysis.

11 Assuming that each formal sector firm has a separate trade union, the unionized wage function may be derived as a solution to the Nash bargaining game between the representative firm and the representative union in the competitive formal sector industry. This function has been derived in appendix 3.7.

12 These results have been derived in appendix 4.1.

13 See appendix 4.2.

14 Intuitive explanations have been provided later.

15 See the appendix 4.3 for detailed derivations.

16 It may be an interesting idea to carry out a comparative static exercise with respect to γ. The parameter denoting the degree of altruism on the part of the guardian of a poor working family depends crucially on social values and tradition. Owing to mass literacy and adult education programs and vigorous public campaigns against child labour, social values and tradition may change over time and raise the value of γ. From equation (4.1), it is easy to check that an increase in γ lowers the supply

of child labour from each poor family, l_C. To find out the effect on the aggregate supply of child labour in the economy after differentiating equation (4.2) with respect to γ and using (4.10) and (4.15), we find that

$$(dL_C \ / \ d\gamma) = -(L_C \ / \ \gamma)\left[\frac{\mu\gamma W}{(W - \mu B)l_C \ |\lambda|)}\right]\left[\begin{array}{c}\{\lambda_{L1}(\lambda_{K2} + \lambda_{K3}) - \lambda_{K1}(\lambda_{L2} + \lambda_{L3})\} \\ + l_C\lambda_{L3}\lambda_{K1}(1 - 1 \ / \ \mu)\end{array}\right]$$

From this expression it follows that $(dL_C/d\gamma) > (<)0$ if and only if $|\lambda| < (>)0$. Hence, the incidence of child labour declines iff $|\lambda| > 0$. This result may be intuitively explained in terms of *direct effect* and *adult labour reallocation effect*.

17 We have already pointed out that because child labour and adult labour are substitutes in sector 1 and sector 2, the effective labour force must include child labour subject to a scale correction of μ. Thus, a reduction in the number of child labourers lowers the effective adult labour endowment of the economy.

18 The interpretation of this condition has already been provided.

19 See appendix 4.3.

References

Basu, K. (1999): 'Child labour: Cause, consequence, and cure, with remarks on international labour standards', *Journal of Economic Literature*, 37(September), 1083–1119.

Basu, K. and Van, P.H. (1998): 'The economics of child labour', *American Economic Review*, 88(3), 412–427.

Beladi, H. and Marjit, S. (1992a): 'Foreign capital and protectionism', *Canadian Journal of Economics*, 25, 233–238.

Beladi, H. and Marjit, S. (1992b): 'Foreign capital, unemployment and national welfare', *Japan and the World Economy*, 4, 311–317.

Bose, A.N. (1978): *Calcutta and Rural Bengal: Small Sector Symbiosis*, Minerva Publications, New Delhi.

Brecher, R.A. and Diaz Alejandro, C.F. (1977): 'Tariffs, foreign capital and immiserizing growth', *Journal of International Economics*, 7, 317–322.

Chandra, V. and Khan, M.A. (1993): 'Foreign investment in the presence of an informal sector', *Economica*, 60, 79–103.

Chaudhuri, S. (2001a): 'Foreign capital inflow, technology transfer, and national income', *The Pakistan Development Review*, 40(1), 49–56.

Chaudhuri, S. (2001b): 'Foreign capital inflow, non-traded intermediary, urban unemployment and welfare in a small open economy: A theoretical analysis', *The Pakistan Development Review*, 40(3), 225–235.

Chaudhuri, S. (2004): 'Incidence of child labour, free education policy and trade liberalization in a developing economy', *The Pakistan Development Review*, 43(1), 1–25.

Chaudhuri, S. (2005): 'Labour market distortion, technology transfer and gainful effects of foreign capital', *The Manchester School*, 73(2), 214–227.

Chaudhuri, S. (2007): 'Foreign capital, welfare and unemployment in the presence of agricultural dualism', *Japan and the World Economy*, 19(2), 149–165.

Chaudhuri, S. (2016): 'Trade unionism and welfare consequences of trade and investment reforms in a developing economy', *Metroeconomica*, 67(1), 152–171.

Dwibedi, J.K. and Chaudhuri, S. (2014): 'Agricultural subsidy policies fail to deal with child labour under agricultural dualism: What could be the alternative policies?', *Research in Economics*, 68(3), 277–291.

Grinols, E.L. (1991): 'Unemployment and foreign capital: The relative opportunity cost of domestic labour and welfare', *Economica*, 57, 107–121.

Gupta, M.R. (1997): 'Foreign capital and informal sector: Comments on Chandra and Khan', *Economica*, 64(254), 353–363.

Harris, J.R. and Todaro, M.P. (1970): 'Migration, unemployment and development: A two-sector analysis', *American Economic Review*, 60, 126–142.

ILO (2013): *Marking progress against child labour: Global estimates and trends 2000–2012*. International Labour Office, Geneva.

Joshi, H. and Joshi, V. (1976): *Surplus Labour and the City: A Study of Bombay*, Oxford University Press, New Delhi.

Khan, M.A. (1982): 'Tariffs, foreign capital and immiserizing growth with urban unemployment and specific factors of production', *Journal of Development Economics*, 10, 245–256.

Marjit, S. and Beladi, H. (1996): 'Protection and gainful effects of foreign capital', *Economics Letters*, 53, 311–326.

Papola, T.S. (1981): *Urban Informal Sector in a Developing Economy*, Vikas Publishing House, New Delhi.

PROBE in India. (1999): Oxford University Press, New Delhi, India.

Romatet, E. (1983): 'Calcutta's informal sector: Theory and reality', *Economic and Political Weekly*, 18(50), 2115–2128.

UNICEF. (1997): *The State of the World's Children*, Oxford University Press, Oxford.

5 Is the reduction of poverty a necessity?

5.1 Introduction

The new development strategy with liberalized trade and investment policies, adopted by the developing countries over the last two decades or so, has not so far been an unmixed blessing. In their endeavour to implement such policies, these economies have been facing some adjustment costs, of which increasing skilled–unskilled wage inequality, persistence of poverty and incidence of child labour are worth mentioning. Advocates of economic liberalization with standard trade theoretic models in mind expected the wage inequality to improve in the developing economies. They also believed that economic reforms would take the developing countries into higher growth orbits, the benefits of which would certainly percolate down to the bottom of the society, thereby leading to the reduction of poverty and poverty-driven child labour incidence. However, empirical studies reveal that wage inequality and poverty have increased in many liberalizing economies.[1] Although the problem of child labour has decreased in general, the decline has not been uniform in all regions. ILO (2006) has reported that the number of economically active children in the 5–14 age group declined by 11 per cent in 2004 from the 2000 figure. The decline is the sharpest for Latin America and Caribbean, whereas Asia and Pacific and Sub-Saharan Africa registered very small declines in activity rates.[2]

The supply of child labour in the theoretical literature has largely been attributed to factors like abject poverty and capital market imperfection. Basu and Van (1998) and Basu (1999) have explained child labour, using the poverty argument, while Ranjan (1999, 2001), Baland and Robinson (2000) and Jafarey and Lahiri (2002) emphasize the importance of capital-market imperfection as a contributing factor to inefficient child labour. However, the theoretical literature on how economic reforms can impinge on the incidence of child labour is yet to emerge. The first and foremost task of this theoretical literature would be to identify the different channels through which economic reforms can affect the child labour problem. Empirical studies, such as Cigno et al. (2002) and Neumayer and Soysa (2005), have reported that trade and investment reforms have produced a favourable impact on child labour. However, there are reasons to believe that the incomes of the poorer segments of the working population have decreased in the developing economies during the liberalized regime.[3] It is therefore perplexing how the child labour situation has improved in these economies, especially when poverty has increased[4] following economic reforms inasmuch as it is considered to be the single largest factor behind the child labour problem. Hence, the positive impact on child labour that the liberalized policies have made must have come through channels other than the income effect. The need for identifying these alternative routes has also been recognized by Cigno et al. (2002) and Neumayer and Soysa (2005).

This chapter intends to identify the different ways through which economic reforms can affect the incidence of child labour in a developing economy using a three-sector general equilibrium model.[5] Although the model analyses only the consequence of liberalized investment policies, it may be useful in studying the effects of trade reforms as well. The supply function of child labour of each working family is derived from its intertemporal utility-maximizing behaviour. Sector 1, in the general equilibrium model, is agriculture where child labour is used along with adult unskilled labour and capital. Sector 2 is the low-skill manufacturing sector that uses adult unskilled labour and capital. Finally, sector 3 employs skilled labour and capital to produce a high-skill commodity. In this set-up, the theoretical analysis shows that foreign direct investment (FDI) flow can indeed lower the problem of child labour by raising the return on education and the nonchild income of the working households and by lowering the earning opportunities of children. The analysis demonstrates that a reduction in poverty is not a necessary condition for the problem of child labour to improve in the developing economies in the liberalized regime. There could be other forces strong enough to bring about reduction in the incidence of child labour even without significant improvements in the economic conditions of the households.

5.2　The model

We consider a small open economy with three sectors. Sector 1 produces an agricultural commodity, X_1, using adult unskilled labour (L), child labour (L_C) and capital (K). The capital-output ratio in sector 1, a_{K1}, is assumed to be technologically given.[6] Sector 2 uses unskilled labour and capital to produce a low-skill manufacturing commodity, X_2. This sector does not use child labour as an input of production.[7] Finally, sector 3 produces a high-skill commodity, X_3, with the help of skilled labour (S) and capital. Commodity prices, P_is, are given by the small open economy assumption. Competitive markets, constant returns to scale technologies with positive but diminishing marginal productivities of inputs and full-employment of resources are assumed. Capital endowment of the economy consists of both domestic capital (K_D) and foreign capital (K_F), and these are perfect substitutes.

The usual price-unit cost equality conditions relating to the three sectors are as follows.

$$Wa_{L1} + W_C a_{C1} + Ra_{K1} = P_1 \tag{5.1}$$

$$Wa_{L2} + Ra_{K2} = P_2 \tag{5.2}$$

$$W_S a_{S3} + Ra_{K3} = P_3 \tag{5.3}$$

where a_{ji}s are input–output ratios, and R is the return on capital.

Complete utilization of adult unskilled labour, child labour, capital and skilled labour imply the following four equations, respectively.

$$a_{L1}X_1 + a_{L2}X_2 = L \tag{5.4}$$

$$a_{C1}X_1 = L_C \tag{5.5}$$

$$a_{K1}X_1 + a_{K2}X_2 + a_{K3}X_3 = K_D + K_F = K \tag{5.6}$$

$$a_{S3}X_3 = S \tag{5.7}$$

While endowments of unskilled adult labour, skilled labour and capital are fixed in the economy, the aggregate supply of child labour, L_C, is endogenously determined from the utility-maximizing behaviour of the households.[8] In our model there are two types of families headed by unskilled adult worker and skilled adult worker. We assume that both unskilled and skilled working families are potential suppliers of child labour and that their current wage incomes (W_0) are W and W_S, respectively.[9] Hence, there are L and S numbers of unskilled and skilled working families in the economy, respectively, and each of them makes a working–schooling decision for their children. We use equations (2.24) and (2.25) to get the aggregate child labour supply function of the economy as follows.[10]

$$L_C = \left(\frac{1}{1+\beta}\right)\left[L\left\{\frac{W_S}{(W_S - W)} - \frac{\beta.W}{W_C}\right\} + S\left\{\frac{W_S}{(W_S - W)} - \frac{\beta.W_S}{W_C}\right\}\right] \tag{5.8}$$

5.3   Comparative statics

The general equilibrium structure consists of eight equations ((5.1)–(5.8)) and the same number of variables, namely W, W_C, W_S, R, X_1, X_2, X_3 and L_C. This is an indecomposable system. Hence, factor prices depend on both commodity prices and factor endowments. Given the child wage rate, sectors 1 and 2 together effectively form a miniature Heckscher-Ohlin system as they use both adult unskilled labour and capital. It is sensible to assume that sector 1 is more adult labour–intensive than sector 2 with respect to capital. Totally differentiating equations (5.1)–(5.8) and solving, the following proposition can be established.[11]

Proposition 5.1: FDI inflow leads to (i) increases in both adult unskilled wage and skilled wage, and (ii) a decrease in child wage rate. The skilled–unskilled wage inequality worsens if the high-skill sector is capital-intensive (in a special sense) relative to the low-skill sector.

Proposition 5.1 can be intuitively explained as follows. FDI flow lowers the return on capital, R, as the supply rises given the demand. A Rybczynski effect takes place in the miniature HOS system comprised of sectors 1 and 2, leading to a contraction of sector 1 and an expansion of sector 2 because sector 1 is less capital-intensive relative to the other with respect to adult unskilled labour. Sector 3 also expands as it uses capital but a different type of labour (skilled labour). The demand for child labour falls in sector 1, but the demand for skilled labour rises in sector 3, as these are the two sector-specific inputs. Consequently, the child wage falls while the skilled wage rises. Saving on capital input raises the unskilled wage, W, in sector 2 (see equation (5.2)). What happens to the skilled–unskilled wage inequality depends on the rates of increase in W_S and W. If sector 3 is capital-intensive in a special sense, the saving on capital input in sector 3 is more than that in sector 2, which in turn, implies an increase in the relative wage inequality.[12]

For analyzing the outcome of foreign capital inflows on the supply of child labour in the economy, we use the child labour supply function (equation 5.8). Totally differentiating equation (5.8), the following proposition can be proved.[13]

Proposition 5.2: Inflows of foreign capital lower the incidence of child labour in the economy if the high-skill sector is capital-intensive relative to the low-skill sector.

We explain proposition 5.2 in the following fashion. In proposition 5.1, we have stated how different factor prices and the relative wage inequality respond to inflows of foreign capital. A fall in the child wage rate, W_C, means a decrease in the opportunity cost of education. On the other hand, the return on education rises as the wage inequality rises. Finally, the initial incomes from nonchild sources of both the unskilled and the skilled working families have increased, which lower the supply of child labour by each family via the positive income effect. Hence, under the sufficient condition that the high-skill sector is capital-intensive, all three effects work in the same direction and lower the problem of child labour in the society.

5.4   Concluding remarks

In this chapter, we have explained how foreign capital inflows might produce a favourable effect on the incidence of child labour in a developing economy despite affecting wage inequality adversely. The family supply function of child labour has been derived from the intertemporal utility-maximizing behaviour of the working households, which send some of their children for consumption smoothing owing to the nonexistence of a market for loans against future earnings. Then the aggregate child labour function is derived, and a three-sector general equilibrium model has been developed for analytical purpose. The interesting result is that inflows of foreign capital might exert a downward pressure on the child labour incidence by raising both the return on education (premium on skill) and the initial nonchild incomes of the families and by lowering the child wage (i.e. the opportunity cost of schooling).[14] Hence, the child labour incidence may improve even if nonchild incomes of the families do not increase. There are enough other forces brought about by economic reforms that can overcompensate for decreased parental incomes. Therefore, the reduction of poverty is not a necessary condition for the problem of child labour to improve. These results are consistent with empirical findings that the incidence of child labour has decreased satisfactorily even though the problem of poverty has increased in many of the developing countries.

It should be mentioned that certain assumptions of the model may seem to be restrictive. The model presupposes that the quality of education is good and that the children attending school in the present period will get jobs in the high-skill sector in the future. However, the quality of basic education in the developing countries is generally unsatisfactory, and there is also unemployment of educated workers.[15] Besides, the assumption that child labour is used only in the agricultural sector is simplifying.[16] Finally, the assumption of the nonexistence of any market for loans against future earnings is restrictive but simplifying. In defence, we may note that FDI inflow in the presence of an informal credit market should improve the borrowing terms of the households and lower the cost of education and hence the incidence of child labour in the society.

Appendices

Appendix 5.1 Effects of foreign capital inflows on different endogenous variables

Totally differentiating equations (5.1)–(5.3) and using envelope conditions, the following expressions are obtained.

$$\theta_{L1}\hat{W} + \theta_{C1}\hat{W}_C + \theta_{K1}\hat{R} = 0 \tag{5.A.1}$$

$$\theta_{L2}\hat{W} + \theta_{K2}\hat{R} = 0 \tag{5.A.2}$$

$$\theta_{S3}\hat{W}_S + \theta_{K3}\hat{R} = 0 \tag{5.A.3}$$

where θ_{ji} = distributive share of the jth input in the ith sector, and, '$\wedge$' = proportional change.

Totally differentiating equations (5.4)–(5.8), collecting terms and simplifying, we get the following expressions:

$$\bar{S}_{LL}\hat{W} + \lambda_{L1}S_{LC}^1\hat{W}_C + \bar{S}_{LK}\hat{R} + \lambda_{L1}\hat{X}_1 + \lambda_{L2}\hat{X}_2 = 0 \tag{5.A.4}$$

$$\bar{S}_{KL}\hat{W} + A_2\hat{R} + A_1\hat{W}_S + \lambda_{K1}\hat{X}_1 + \lambda_{K2}\hat{X}_2 = \hat{K} \tag{5.A.5}$$

$$(S_{CL}^1 + A_3)\hat{W} + (S_{CC}^1 - A_4)\hat{W}_C + A_5\hat{W}_S + \hat{X}_1 = 0 \tag{5.A.6}$$

(Note that we have used $\hat{X}_3 = -S_{SS}^3\hat{W}_S - S_{SR}^3\hat{R}$ from (5.7).) where

$$\left.\begin{array}{l}
\bar{S}_{LL} = (\lambda_{L1}S_{LL}^1 + \lambda_{L2}S_{LL}^2) < 0; \bar{S}_{KL} = \lambda_{K2}S_{KL}^2 > 0; \bar{S}_{KK} = (\lambda_{K2}S_{KK}^2 + \lambda_{K3}S_{KK}^3) < 0; \\
\bar{S}_{LK} = \lambda_{L2}S_{LK}^2 > 0; A_1 = \lambda_{K3}(S_{SK}^3 + S_{KS}^3) > 0; A_2 = (\bar{S}_{KK} - \lambda_{K3}S_{SK}^3) < 0; \\
A_3 = (-A(L+S) + BLW); A_4 = B(LW + SW_S) > 0; A_5 = (A(L+S) + BSW_S) > 0; \\
A = \dfrac{W_S.W}{(1+\beta)L_C(W_S - W)^2} > 0; B = \dfrac{\beta}{(1+\beta)L_CW_C} > 0
\end{array}\right\} \tag{5.A.7}$$

S_{ji}^k = the degree of substitution between factors j and i in the kth sector, $j, i = L, S, L_C, K; k = 1,2,3$. $S_{ji}^k > 0$ for $j \neq i$; $S_{jj}^k < 0$; and λ_{ji} = proportion of the jth input employed in the ith sector.

Arranging (5.A.1)–(5.A.6) in matrix notation, we get the following:

$$
\begin{bmatrix}
\theta_{L1} & \theta_{C1} & \theta_{K1} & 0 & 0 & 0 \\
\theta_{L2} & 0 & \theta_{K2} & 0 & 0 & 0 \\
0 & 0 & \theta_{K3} & \theta_{S3} & 0 & 0 \\
\bar{S}_{LL} & \lambda_{L1}S^1_{LC} & \bar{S}_{LK} & 0 & \lambda_{L1} & \lambda_{L2} \\
\bar{S}_{KL} & 0 & A_2 & A_1 & \lambda_{K1} & \lambda_{K2} \\
(S^1_{CL}+A_3) & (S^1_{CC}-A_4) & 0 & A_5 & 1 & 0
\end{bmatrix}
\begin{bmatrix}
\hat{W} \\ \hat{W}_C \\ \hat{R} \\ \hat{W}_S \\ \hat{X}_1 \\ \hat{X}_2
\end{bmatrix}
=
\begin{bmatrix}
0 \\ 0 \\ 0 \\ 0 \\ \hat{K} \\ 0
\end{bmatrix}
\tag{5.A.8}
$$

Solving (5.A.8), the following expressions are obtained:

$$
\hat{W} = -\left(\frac{\theta_{S3}\theta_{C1}\theta_{K2}\lambda_{L2}}{\Delta}\right)\hat{K}
\tag{5.A.9}
$$

$$
\hat{W}_C = \left(\frac{\theta_{S3}|\theta|_{LK}\,\lambda_{L2}}{\Delta}\right)\hat{K}
\tag{5.A.10}
$$

$$
\hat{R} = \left(\frac{\theta_{S3}\theta_{C1}\theta_{L2}\lambda_{L2}}{\Delta}\right)\hat{K}
\tag{5.A.11}
$$

$$
\hat{W}_S = -\left(\frac{\theta_{K3}\theta_{C1}\theta_{L2}\lambda_{L2}}{\Delta}\right)\hat{K}
\tag{5.A.12}
$$

$$
(\hat{W}_S - \hat{W}) = \left(\frac{\theta_{C1}\lambda_{L2}(\theta_{K2}-\theta_{K3})}{\Delta}\right)\hat{K}
\tag{5.A.13}
$$

where

$$
\begin{aligned}
\Delta = &-\theta_{K3}\theta_{C1}\theta_{L2}\{BSW_S|\lambda|_{LK} + A_1\lambda_{L2}\} - \theta_{S3}\theta_{C1}\theta_{L2}(\bar{S}_{LK}\lambda_{K2} - A_2\lambda_{L2}) \\
&+ \theta_{S3}|\theta|_{LK}\{(S^1_{CC}-A_4)|\lambda|_{LK} - \lambda_{K2}\lambda_{L1}S^1_{LC}\} \\
&- \theta_{S3}\theta_{C1}\theta_{K2}\{(S^1_{CL}+BLW)|\lambda|_{LK} - (\lambda_{K2}\bar{S}_{LL} - \lambda_{L2}\bar{S}_{KL})\} \\
&+ A(L+S)\theta_{C1}|\lambda|_{LK}(\theta_{K2}-\theta_{K3})
\end{aligned}
\tag{5.A.14}
$$

with

$$
\left.
\begin{aligned}
|\lambda|_{LK} &= (\lambda_{L1}\lambda_{K2} - \lambda_{K1}\lambda_{L2}) > 0; \\
|\theta|_{LK} &= (\theta_{L1}\theta_{K2} - \theta_{K1}\theta_{L2}) > 0
\end{aligned}
\right\}
\tag{5.A.15}
$$

(Note that $|\lambda|_{LK}$, $|\theta|_{LK} > 0$ because sector 2 is more capital-intensive than sector 1 with respect to adult unskilled labour.)

Using (5.A.7) and (5.A.15), from (5.A.14) it follows that

$$
\Delta < 0 \text{ if } \theta_{K3} > \theta_{K2}
\tag{5.A.16}
$$

However, $\theta_{K3} > \theta_{K2}$ is a sufficient condition only for Δ to be negative.

Using (5.A.7), (5.A.14) and (5.A.15), from (5.A.9) – (5.A.13) we can obtain the following results.

$$
\left.
\begin{aligned}
&\text{(i)} \quad \hat{W} > 0 \text{ when } \hat{K} > 0; \\
&\text{(ii)} \quad \hat{W}_C < 0 \text{ when } \hat{K} > 0; \\
&\text{(iii)} \quad \hat{R} < 0 \text{ when } \hat{K} > 0; \\
&\text{(iv)} \quad \hat{W}_S > 0 \text{ when } \hat{K} > 0; \\
&\text{(v)} \quad (\hat{W}_S - \hat{W}) > 0 \text{ when } \hat{K} > 0 \text{ iff } \theta_{K3} > \theta_{K2}
\end{aligned}
\right\} \qquad (5.A.17)
$$

Appendix 5.2   Effect on the child labour incidence

We use equation (5.8) to examine the impact of foreign capital inflows on the incidence of child labour in the economy. Totally differentiating equation (5.8), we get

$$
\hat{L}_C = -A(L+S)(\hat{W}_S - \hat{W}) - LBW\hat{W} - SBW_S\hat{W}_S + SBW_S\hat{W}_C + LBW\hat{W}_C \quad (5.A.18)
$$

Using (5.A.9)–(5.A.13), the expression (5.A.18) may be rewritten as follows.

$$
\hat{L}_C = \left(\frac{1}{\Delta}\right)\left[\begin{array}{l} -A(L+S)\theta_{C1}\lambda_{L2}(\theta_{K2} - \theta_{K3}) + LBW\theta_{S3}\theta_{C1}\theta_{K2}\lambda_{L2} \\ +SBW_S\theta_{K3}\theta_{C1}\theta_{L2}\lambda_{L2} + (SBW_S + LBW)\theta_{S3}|\theta|_{LK}\,\lambda_{L2} \end{array} \right]\hat{K} \qquad (5.A.19)
$$

From (5.A.19) we find that

$$
\hat{L}_C < 0 \text{ when } \hat{K} > 0 \text{ if } \theta_{K3} > \theta_{K2}
$$

Hence, the incidence of child labour decreases following FDI flow under the sufficient condition $\theta_{K3} > \theta_{K2}$. This implies that sector 3 is capital-intensive relative to sector 2. However, this result may hold under a few other sufficient conditions as well.

Notes

1 Empirical studies of Robbins (1996) and Wood (1997) found that skilled–unskilled wage inequality has, indeed, increased in the developing countries, particularly in the Latin American countries like Mexico, Chile, Costa Rica and Columbia, following liberalized trade and investment policies. Tendulkar et al. (1996) and Khan (1998) also reported widening wage inequality in South Asia.
2 For Asia and Pacific and Sub-Saharan Africa, child labour participation rate (5–14 age group) declined from 19.4 and 28.8 to 18.8 and 26.4, respectively (during 2000 to 2004). For Latin America and Caribbean, activity rate declined from 16.1 per cent in 2000 to 5.1 per cent in 2004.
3 Studies by Wade and Wolf (2002), Riskin (2004), Sen and Himanshu (2004), Wade (2004) and Reddy and Minoiu (2005), among others, reveal that the world poverty might have increased during the liberalized regime. Even the proponents of globalization like the World Bank (2000) have admitted that, despite impressive

growth performance in many large developing countries, absolute poverty world-wide has been still increasing. Tendulkar et al. (1996) and Khan (1998) have also reached the same conclusion.

4 The experience of Latin America and the Caribbean is particularly more puzzling. World Bank (2007) data show that poverty (measured in terms of head count ratio corresponding to a $1 a day poverty line) has increased from 8.46 per cent in 1993 to 8.64 per cent in 2004. Clearly, absolute poverty has increased significantly during this period (see Chen and Ravallion 2007). ILO (2006), on the other hand, estimated that Latin American and Caribbean countries have experienced the most rapid decline in the incidence of child labour during 2000–2004. The number of economically active children fell by two-thirds during this period, and the participation rate by even more.

5 Section 5.2 is based on Dwibedi and Chaudhuri (2010).

6 Although this is a simplifying assumption, it is not completely without basis. Agriculture requires inputs like fertilizers, pesticides, weedicides and the like, which are to be used in recommended doses. Now if capital is used to purchase those inputs, the capital-output ratio becomes constant technologically. However, labour and capital are substitutes, and the production function displays the property of constant returns to scale in these two inputs. However, even if the capital-output ratio is not given, technologically the results of the model still hold under an additional sufficient condition incorporating the partial elasticities of substitution between capital and other inputs in sector 1.

7 See note 16 in this context.

8 The capital endowment of the economy may, however, increase in the presence of either foreign direct investment (K_F) or domestic capital accumulation.

9 One can also assume that the total rental income from domestic capital (RK_D) is equally distributed among the households. In that case, total nonchild labour income of a representative household will be $\left(W_0 + \frac{RK_D}{L+S}\right)$. The qualitative results of our model hold under this assumption as well.

10 This supply function has been derived from the intertemporal utility-maximizing behaviour of each representative working household that supplies child labour (see section 2.2.2). The guardian of each working family in the first period works in the adult labour market and earns a wage, W_0. In this period, the guardian takes the decision about the child's work effort and schooling. Total child time is 1, a part of which (l_C) is sent out to work at the wage rate, W_C. Time not spent on working is spent in school and so ($1 - l_C$) is the child's schooling. The l_C part of the child labour time earns the child wage, W_C, in the first period and the unskilled adult wage, W, in the second period while the ($1 - l_C$) fraction earns nothing in the first period but the skilled wage, W_S, in the second period. In the second period, the guardian earns nothing and lives on the income received from the child, who has become an adult worker by this time. See chapter 2 for details.

11 These results have been proved in appendix 5.1.

12 Here sectors 2 and 3 use two different types of labour. However, there is one intersectorally mobile input, which is capital. Hence, these two sectors cannot be classified in terms of factor intensities, which is usually done in the Hechscher-Ohlin-Samuelson model. Despite this, a special type of factor intensity classification in terms of the relative distributive shares of the mobile factor (i.e. capital) can be made for analytical purposes. The sector in which this share is higher relative to the other may be considered as capital-intensive in a special sense. See Jones and Neary (1984) for details.

13 Derivations are available in appendix 5.2.

14 See Cigno et al. (2002) in this context.

15 If the quality of education is unsatisfactory, the return on education will be low. Nevertheless, so long as the return on education is positive, the same analysis goes through although the force exerting downward pressure on child labour through

this channel becomes weaker. On the other hand, if one considers that the probability of finding a skilled job in future (say, ϕ with $1 > \phi > 0$) is given, the qualitative results of the model do not change.

16 This assumption is partly justified on the grounds that more than 70 per cent of economically active children in the developing countries are engaged in agriculture and allied sectors and less than 9 per cent are involved in manufacturing (ILO (2002) report). However, even if sector 2 uses child labour, the results of this model still hold under different sufficient conditions containing terms of relative intensities in which child labour and the other two inputs are used in the first two sectors.

References

Baland, J. and Robinson, J.A. (2000): 'Is child labour inefficient?', *Journal of Political Economy*, 108(4), 663–679.

Basu, K. (1999): 'Child labour: Cause, consequence, and cure, with remarks on international labour standards', *Journal of Economic Literature*, 37(September), 1083–1119.

Basu, K. and Van, P.H. (1998): 'The economics of child labour', *American Economic Review*, 88(3), 412–427.

Chen, S. and Ravallion, M. (2007): 'Absolute poverty measures for the developing world, 1981–2004', Development Research Group, The World Bank.

Cigno, A., Rosati, F.C. and Guarcello, L. (2002): 'Does globalization increase child labor?', *World Development*, 30, 1579–1589.

Dwibedi, J.K. and Chaudhuri, S. (2010): 'Foreign capital, return to education and child labour', *International Review of Economics and Finance*, 19, 278–286.

ILO. (2002): 'A future without child labour?', International Labour Conference, 90th Session June 2002, International Labour Office, Geneva.

ILO. (2006): 'The end of child labour: Within reach', Global Report Under the Follow-up to the ILO Declaration on Fundamental Principles and Rights at Work 2006. International Labour Office, Geneva.

Jafarey, S. and Lahiri, S. (2002): 'Will trade sanctions reduce child labour? The role of credit markets', *Journal of Development Economics*, 68(1), 137–156.

Jones, R.W. and Neary, P. (1984): 'Positive theory of international trade', in: R.W. Jones and P.B. Kenen (eds.), *Handbook of Development Economics*, Vol. 1, North-Holland, Amsterdam, 1–62.

Khan, A.R. (1998): 'The impact of globalization in South Asia', in: A.S. Bhalla (ed.), *Globalization, Growth and Marginalization*, Macmillan, London, 103–124.

Neumayer, E. and Soysa, I. (2005): 'Trade openness, foreign direct investment and child labour', *World Development*, 33(1), 43–63.

Ranjan, P. (1999): 'An economic analysis of child labour', *Economic Letters*, 64, 99–105.

Ranjan, P. (2001): 'Credit constraints and the phenomenon of child labour', *Journal of Development Economics*, 64, 81–102.

Reddy, S. and Minoiu, C. (2005): 'Chinese poverty: Assessing the impact of alternative assumptions', *Review of Income and Wealth*, 47(3), 283–300.

Riskin, C. (2004): 'The fall in Chinese poverty: Issues of measurement, incidence and cause', mimeo., Columbia University. Available at: https://www.google.co.in/url?sa=t&rct=j&q=&esrc=s&source=web&cd=1&ved=0ahUKEwj8mqW35qDOAhVJso8KHaiwD3UQFggcMAA&url=http%3A%2F%2Fwww.peri.umass.edu%2Ffiledmin%2Fpdf%2Fconference_papers%2FRiskin_paperA.pdf&usg=AFQjCNHOYHpiWrw0cBji2ATVzhXOQgC1Xw&bvm=bv.128617741,d.c2I&cad=rja

Sen, A. and Himanshu (2004): 'Poverty and inequality in India – 1', *Economic and Political Weekly*, 39(38), 4247–4263.

Robbins, D. (1996): 'HOS hits facts: Facts win: Evidence on trade and wages in developing world', DP No. 557, Harvard University.

Tendulkar, S., Sundaram, D.K. and Jain, L.R. (1996): 'Macroeconomic policies and poverty in India 1966–67 to 1993–94', Monograph, ILO, New Delhi.

Wade, R.H. (2004): 'Is globalization reducing poverty and inequality?', *World Development*, 32(4), 567–589.

Wade, R.H. and Wolf, M. (2002): 'Are global poverty and inequality getting worse?', Exchange of Letters Published in Prospect Magazine, UK. Available at: http://www.prospectmagazine

Wood, A. (1997): 'Openness and wage inequality in developing countries: The Latin American challenge to East Asian conventional wisdom', *World Bank Research Observer*, 11(1), 33–57.

World Bank. (2000): *Poverty in an Age of Globalisation*, The World Bank, Washington, DC.

World Bank. (2007): 'Poverty database'. Available at: http://povertydata.worldbank.org/poverty/home/

6 Agricultural dualism, subsidy policies and child labour

6.1 Introduction

The problem of child labour in a developing country can be viewed from two sides: demand and supply. It is the poor working families that supply child labour. On the other hand, the demand for child labour comes from the production units in the agricultural sector, low-skill informal manufacturing and services sectors. The developing countries resort to different poverty-eradication programs designed to increase the earning opportunities of the poor. These policies are expected to produce favourable effect on the incidence of child labour through the supply side of the problem. However, there is now ample empirical evidence suggesting that income prosperity may not always lead to less child labour.[1] A relevant question is why policies that raise the earning opportunities of poor people may sometimes fail to control the poverty-induced child labour problem is perplexing. This calls for theoretical explanation that might be able to show why policy interventions affecting the supply side alone cannot effectively solve the prevalence of the evil in the system. It seems that policies should be designed in such a way so that both the demand and supply sides of the problem are taken care of.

According to ILO (2012), the concentration of child labour is the highest in the rural sector of a developing economy, and child labour is used intensively directly or indirectly in the agricultural sector.[2] Besides, agricultural dualism is a common symptom of the developing countries. The distinction between advanced and backward agriculture can be made on the basis of inputs used, economies of scale, efficiency and elasticity of substitution between different factors of production. In backward agriculture, the production techniques are primitive, the use of capital is very low and child labour can do almost whatever adult labour does. Farming in backward agriculture is mostly done by using bullocks and ploughs, and the cattle-feeding is entirely done by child labour.[3] Besides, during the peak seasons when there is a temporary scarcity of adult labourers, children are often used in the family farms for helping adult members of the family. Use of primitive technology allows the use of child labour in a greater quantity particularly during peak seasons. As the system of agriculture adopts more mechanized and capital-intensive technology, the demand for child labour would fall. The use of modern machines like tractors replaces traditional ploughing done by bullocks and therefore eliminates children's requirement in cattle feeding. It is now well documented that the introduction of good practices in agriculture using more labour-saving technology can reduce and ultimately eliminate the use of child labour in agriculture. Labour- and energy-saving technologies through farm mechanization minimize and eliminate the use of child labour in all farm operations, as well as food storage and utilization. Food and Agriculture Organization's (FAO) intervention in countries like Mali, Malawi, Cambodia and Tanzania has been very successful in this regard.[4]

Agriculture in many countries is supported by government's subsidy policies in the form of price support, export subsidy, credit support and the like. In a developing country like India, farmers in backward agriculture are given price support with a view to protect themselves from sharp falls in their product prices during the times of oversupply in the market. Government's minimum support price (or producers support price) mechanism is a very common form of government subsidy policy that is directed toward improving the economic conditions of the poorer segments of working people who are engaged in backward agriculture and who are the potential suppliers of child labour.[5] It is, therefore, expected that these fiscal measures will raise the earning opportunities of the poor households, which in turn will lower the supply of child labour by these families through positive income effect. However, the matter is not as straightforward as it appears to be at the first sight. This is because, apart from their impact on adult wages, these policies affect the output composition of different sectors and the demand for child labour and therefore earning opportunities by children as well. An expansion of backward agriculture resulting from an increase in producers support price, for example, will result in a higher demand for child labour and raise the use of child labour in the economy. Even if there is a positive income effect due to an increase in adult wages, the net effect on child labour might be perverse. On the contrary, a policy of subsidizing advanced agriculture, in the form of a credit or price subsidy, leads to a contraction (an expansion) of backward (advanced) agriculture, lowers the demand for child labour in the economy and is expected to mitigate the child labour incidence through the demand side effect. Any policy effect on the child labour incidence should therefore be carried out in a multisector general equilibrium framework so as to capture various *demand and supply* linkages that may exist in the system.

The existing theoretical literature on child labour, however, has not so far paid sufficient attention to identify both the demand and supply side effects of the poverty alleviation programs on the problem of child labour in a developing economy with agricultural dualism.[6] The focus of the present chapter is to examine how the supply side measures, through different agricultural subsidies that are primarily designed to eradicate poverty, affect the incidence of child labour in the society. We also analyze how these policies impinge on the welfare of the child labour–supplying families. A three-sector full-employment general equilibrium model with child labour and agricultural dualism has been considered for the analytical purpose.[7] The economy is divided into two agricultural and one manufacturing sectors. One of the two agricultural sectors is backward agriculture (sector 2) that uses child labour. In this set-up we have examined the consequence of a price subsidy policy (in the form of increasing the minimum support price) designed to benefit backward agriculture and the poorer segment of the working population on the aggregate supply of child labour in the economy. Our analysis finds that a price subsidy to backward agriculture is most likely to produce a perverse effect on the child labour incidence even though it raises the nonchild labour income and welfare of the child labour–supplying families. A policy of directly subsidizing advanced agriculture, on the other hand, might be effective in lessening the child labour incidence but at the cost of lowering adult income and family welfare. Moreover, these agricultural subsidy policies have serious distortionary effects on the economy as a whole and therefore should not ideally be recommended for eliminating child labour and improving the welfare of the poor working families. As an alternative policy, we have also studied the efficacy of a direct cash transfer policy to poor working households on the problem of child labour and family welfare. Our results suggest that a direct cash transfer policy, which impinges on the incidence of child labour through the supply side and at the same time does not disturb the demand side adversely, will be effective not only in mitigating the problem but also in improving family welfare. We advocate in favour of nondistortionay policies like a direct cash transfer to the poor, which are expected to work from both the demand and the supply sides of the problem.

6.2   The model

Our model economy is a small open economy with three sectors: two agricultural and one manufacturing. The two agricultural sectors produce two different exportable commodities or different varieties (or qualities) of the same agricultural commodity with different prices at the international markets. Sector 1 is the advanced agricultural sector that produces its output, X_1, by means of adult labour (L), land (N) and capital (K). Capital used in this sector includes both physical capital like tractors and harvesters and working capital required for purchasing material inputs like fertilizers, pesticides, weedicides and the like. The other agricultural sector, namely the backward agriculture (sector 2), produces its output, X_2, using adult labour, child labour (L_C) and land. Because the backward agriculture uses primitive production techniques, we assume that sector 2 does not require capital in its production. The land-output ratios in sectors 1 and 2 (a_{N1} and a_{N2}) are assumed to be technologically given. This assumption not only simplifies the algebra but also can be defended as follows. In one hectare of land, the number of saplings that can be sown is given. There should be a minimum gap between two saplings, and land cannot be substituted by other factors of production.

The backward agricultural sector is assumed to be more adult labour–intensive relative to the advanced agricultural sector with respect to land. This implies that $\frac{a_{L2}}{a_{N2}} > \frac{a_{L1}}{a_{N1}}$, where a_{ji}s are input–output ratios. Available empirical evidence suggests that in developing economies, child labour is used intensively directly or indirectly in backward agriculture that uses primitive production techniques. The advanced agricultural sector, on the other hand, uses mechanized techniques of production that require the strength of adult males, and so we can safely assume that it does not require child labour in its production process. Child labour is therefore specific to backward agriculture. In the two agricultural sectors, adult workers receive the competitive wage, W. Sector 3 is the import-competing sector that produces a manufacturing commodity, X_3, with the help of adult labour and capital. Child labour is not used in the manufacturing sector because it is a formal sector where the use of child labour is prohibited due to government laws.[8] It faces a unionized labour market where workers receive a contractual wage, $\bar{W}$ with $\bar{W} > W$. The adult labour allocation mechanism is as follows. Adult workers first try to find employment in the manufacturing sector that offers the higher wage, and those who are unable to find employment in the said sector are automatically absorbed into the two agricultural sectors, since the wage rate there is perfectly flexible.[9] Because we are considering the case of a small open economy with no nontraded goods, prices of all of the commodities are given internationally. Competitive markets, except the formal sector labour market, constant returns to scale (CRS) technologies with positive and diminishing marginal productivities of factors of production and full-employment of resources are assumed.[10] Finally, commodity 1 is chosen as the numeraire.

Given the competitive product markets, the usual price-unit cost equality conditions relating to the three sectors of the economy are as follows.

$$Wa_{L1} + Ra_{N1} + ra_{K1} = 1 \tag{6.1}$$

$$Wa_{L2} + W_C a_{C2} + Ra_{N2} = P_2 \tag{6.2}$$

$$\bar{W}a_{L3} + ra_{K3} = P_3 \tag{6.3}$$

where R, r and W_C stand for return to land, return to capital and child wage rate, respectively.

Complete utilization of adult labour, capital, land and child labour implies the following four equations, respectively.

$$a_{L1}X_1 + a_{L2}X_2 + a_{L3}X_3 = L \tag{6.4}$$

$$a_{K1}X_1 + a_{K3}X_3 = K \tag{6.5}$$

$$a_{N1}X_1 + a_{N2}X_2 = N \tag{6.6}$$

$$a_{C2}X_2 = L_C \tag{6.7}$$

While endowments of adult labour, land and capital are fixed in the economy, the aggregate supply of child labour, L_C, is endogenously determined from the utility-maximizing behaviour of the poor working households.

In our model, we assume that workers who are engaged in the two agricultural sectors constitute the poorer segment of the economy, and they are the potential child labour suppliers.[11] Adult workers belonging to this segment consider themselves as poor because of their low incomes from nonchild sources (competitive adult wage) and decide to send many of their children to the job market to supplement low family income (luxury axiom of Basu and Van 1998). We then derive the child labour supply by each working household my maximizing the family utility function as given by equation 2.2 in chapter 2. The supply function of child labour by each poor working family is given by the following.[12]

$$l_C = \{(1 - \gamma)n - \gamma(W/W_C)\} \tag{6.8}$$

In our model, there are L_I $(= L - a_{L3}X_3)$ number of adult workers engaged in the two agricultural sectors, and each of them sends l_C number of children to the workplace. Thus, the aggregate supply function of child labour in the economy is given by

$$L_C = [(1 - \gamma)n - \gamma(W/W_C)](L - a_{L3}X_3) \tag{6.9}$$

Now using (6.9), equation (6.7) can be rewritten as

$$a_{C2}X_2 = [(1 - \gamma)n - \gamma(W/W_C)](L - a_{L3}X_3) \tag{6.7.1}$$

The general equilibrium structure of the economy is represented by equations (6.1)–(6.6), (6.7.1) and (6.9). There are eight endogenous variables in the system: W, W_C, R, r, X_1, X_2, X_3 and L_C and the same number of independent equations (namely equations (6.1)–(6.6), (6.7.1) and (6.9)). The parameters in the system are P_2, P_3, L, K, N, $\bar{W}$, α, β, ρ, γ and n. Equations (6.1)–(6.3) constitute the price system. This is an indecomposable system with three price equations and four factor prices: W, W_C, r and R. So factor prices depend on both commodity prices and factor endowments. Given the child wage rate, sectors 1 and 2 together effectively form a modified Heckscher-Ohlin system because they use both adult unskilled labour and land in their production. Given the price and the unionized wage , $\bar{W}$, r is determined from equation (6.3). Now W, W_C, R, X_1, X_2 and X_3 are simultaneously obtained from equations (6.1), (6.2), (6.4)–(6.6) and (6.7.1). Finally, L_C is determined from (6.9).

6.3   Comparative statics

Agriculture in many countries, irrespective of whether backward or advanced, is supported by different government subsidies. The primary objective of such a fiscal support in a developing economy is poverty alleviation. As these policies are designed to benefit the poorer segment of the working population, conventional wisdom suggests that these measures will raise the adult income of the poor households, which in turn will put a brake on the problem of child labour in the society. This section is aimed at examining the efficacy of a price subsidy policy either to backward or to advanced agriculture in mitigating the child labour problem and in improving the welfare of the child labour–supplying families.

To examine the consequences of a price subsidy policy on backward agriculture, captured through an increase in P_2, on factor prices and output composition of the economy, we totally differentiate equations (6.1), (6.2), (6.4)–(6.6) and (6.7.1). Solving and rearranging terms, we can establish the following proposition.[13]

Proposition 6.1: A price subsidy to backward agriculture leads to (i) increases in both adult wage, W, and child wage, W_C; (ii) a fall in the (W/W_C) ratio and an expansion (a contraction) of backward (advanced) agriculture. The manufacturing sector contracts if $\left\{ S_{KL}^1 |\lambda|_{NL}^{12} + \lambda_{N2}\lambda_{L1}S_{LL}^1 \right\} \geq 0$.[14]

We can explain proposition 1 in the following way. As r is determined from the zero-profit condition for sector 3 (equation (6.3)) it remains fixed despite an increase in P_2. Sector 1 and sector 2 together can effectively be regarded as a *Modified Hechscher-Ohlin subsystem* (*MHOSS*) because they use two common inputs: adult labour and land. The modification is due to the fact that apart from adult labour and land, sector 2 uses child labour, and sector 1 uses capital as inputs. An increase in P_2 lowers the rate of return to land, R, and raises the adult wage, W, following a *Stolper-Samuelson type effect*, as sector 2 is more adult labour-intensive than sector 1 with respect to land. Producers in sector 1 substitute adult labour by capital while their counterparts in sector 2 substitute adult labour by child labour. As the adult labour-output ratios (a_{L1} and a_{L2}) in the two agricultural sectors fall, the availability of adult labour to the *MHOSS* rises, in turn producing an expansionary (a contractionary) effect on sector 2 (sector 1) following a *Rybczynski type effect*. As backward agriculture expands, the demand for child labour increases because child labour is specific to that sector. This raises the child wage rate (W_C). As both W and W_C increase, there would be two opposite effects on the supply of child labour by each family. It is easy to check that the proportionate increase in child wage rate is greater than that in adult wage so that (W/W_C) falls.[15] What happens to sector 3 will be determined by the movement of capital between sector 1 and sector 3. As adult wage rate increases, with a given rate of interest and constant land coefficient, the wage-rental ratio in the advanced agricultural sector increases, and therefore producers substitute adult labour by capital, resulting in an increase in a_{K1}. But as sector 1 has contracted, the net effect on the use of capital in this sector is ambiguous. However, it can be proved that the use of capital increases (decreases) in sector 1 (sector 3) under the sufficient condition that $\left\{ S_{KL}^1 |\lambda|_{NL}^{12} + \lambda_{N2}\lambda_{L1}S_{LL}^1 \right\} \geq 0$. Consequently, sector 3 contracts.[16]

6.3.1   *Price subsidy to backward agriculture, incidence of child labour and family welfare*

To examine the impact of a price subsidy given to backward agriculture on the incidence of child labour in the economy, we use the aggregate child labour supply function given by equation (6.9). Note that any policy affects the supply of child labour in two ways: (i) through a change in the size of the adult labour force employed in the two agricultural sectors, ($L_I = L - a_{L3}X_3$), as these families are considered to be the potential suppliers of child labour; and (ii) through a change in l_C (the number of child workers supplied by each poor family), which results from a change in the (W/W_C) ratio. Differentiating equation (6.9), the following proposition can be proved.[17]

Proposition 6.2: A price subsidy policy directed towards backward agriculture worsens the problem of child labour in the economy either if $\left\{ S_{KL}^1 |\lambda|_{NL}^{12} + \lambda_{N2}\lambda_{L1}S_{LL}^1 \right\} \geq 0$ or if $S_{LC}^2 S_{KL}^1 \geq S_{CC}^2 S_{LL}^1$.

As explained earlier, a price subsidy policy to backward agriculture lowers the (W/W_C) ratio, which in turn increases the supply of child labour from each poor working family. As the formal sector contracts in terms of output and employment (under the sufficient condition mentioned earlier), the number of poor working families, which are considered to be the suppliers of child labour, $(L - a_{L3}X_3)$, increases. Hence, we have a situation where there are more poor families each supplying an increased number of child workers. Therefore, a price subsidy to backward agriculture aggravates the problem of child labour in the society.

We now turn our attention to examine the implications of a price subsidy policy to backward agriculture on the welfare of the child labour–supplying families. We capture this in terms of the family utility function (see equation 2.2). After substituting the optimum values of consumption of commodities, $(C_1, C_2$ and $C_3)$, and children's leisure, $(n - l_C)$, in the family utility function, totally differentiating and rearranging terms, the following proposition can be established.[18]

Proposition 6.3: A price subsidy policy to backward agriculture unambiguously improves the welfare of each child labour–supplying family.

A price subsidy to backward agriculture raises both the adult wage, W, and child wage, W_C. This generates an income effect that leads to increased consumption of all the physical commodities $(C_1, C_2$ and $C_3)$. The children's leisure, $(n - l_C)$, also increases due to the positive income effect. But, as the opportunity cost of leisure (W_C) has increased, children's leisure falls due to a negative price effect. As the (W/W_C) ratio falls, the price effect dominates over the income effect. The net outcome would be a decrease in children's leisure and hence an increase in the supply of child labour (l_C) by each family. This works negatively on the welfare of the family. However, our analysis shows that the increase in family welfare caused due to increases in physical commodities dominates over the decrease in household utility resulting from a fall in children's leisure. Hence, family welfare unambiguously improves.

6.3.2   Price subsidy to advanced agriculture, incidence of child labour and family welfare

A policy of directly subsidizing advanced agriculture in the form of a price and/ or a credit subsidy will be effective in lessening the magnitude of the child labour problem but at the cost of lowering the adult wage rate and family welfare. This can be explained intuitively in the following way. A price and/or a credit subsidy to advanced agriculture effectively raises (lowers) the relative price of commodity 1 (commodity 2). This produces a *Stolper-Samuelson effect* in the *MHOSS* that results in an increase in the return to land, R, and a decrease in the adult wage, W, because sector 1 is more land-intensive relative to sector 2 with respect to adult labour. This produces an expansionary (a contractionary) effect on sector 1 (sector 2). As sector 2 contracts, the demand for child labour goes down because it is specific to this sector. Consequently, the child wage rate falls. From the standard trade-theoretic result, it follows that the return to the specific factor (child labour) falls at a higher rate relative to that of the intersectorally mobile factor (adult labour). Consequently, the (W/W_C) ratio rises. This lowers the supply of child labour by each poor working family, l_C (equation (6.8)). It can be shown that there could be a few other sufficient conditions as well, in any one of which sector 3 expands.[19] Hence, we have a situation where there are a fewer families with each of them supplying a lower number of child workers. Consequently, the aggregate supply of child labour falls. On the other hand, we have found that both

W and W_C fall due to this policy. Hence, the aggregate income of each family unequivocally plummets as l_C falls too. As family welfare is a positive function of aggregate income, the well-being of each child labour–supplying family worsens, although children's leisure rises due to price effect.

This establishes the following proposition.

Proposition 6.4: A price and/or a credit subsidy to advanced agriculture succeeds in bringing down the prevalence of child labour in the society under the sufficient condition that $\left\{ S_{KL}^1 \left| \lambda \right|_{NL}^{12} + \lambda_{N2} \lambda_{L1} S_{LL}^1 \right\} \geq 0$. However, this policy lowers the family welfare of the child labour–supplying families.

Therefore, our results indicate that a subsidy policy, either to backward agriculture or to advanced agriculture, cannot simultaneously mitigate the incidence of child labour and improve welfare of the poor families.[20]

6.4 Quest for an alternative policy

An important question at this juncture is what alternative policy(ies) we can recommend that would simultaneously be effective in combating the problem of child labour and in improving the welfare of the poor families, especially when the conventional subsidy policies fail to deliver the goods. In this section we examine the efficacy of a policy in the form of a direct cash transfer to poor families. We examine its implication for the family child labour decision, as well as family welfare.

6.4.1 Direct cash transfer to poor households

The recent trend worldwide has been to move away from the distortionary market intervention mechanism by a welfare state through traditional subsidies towards decoupled income support, preferably in the form of direct cash transfer for a more egalitarian distribution of income. The preference for a direct cash transfer is implicit in the rules of the WTO agreement as well. The reason for this is that in economic theory, market interventions through subsidies distort trade and production, whereas such effects are minimal for decoupled income support. India, for example, has started implementing direct cash transfer for some of its subsidy programs to target groups through the Aadhar scheme.[21]

We analyze the effect of a direct cash transfer given to poor households by introducing a lump-sum cash transfer to each poor family of the amount $G > 0$. This per-capita cash transfer, G, will be added to family income from nonchild labour sources. This will lead to a family child labour supply function as follows.[22]

$$l_C = [(1 - \gamma)n - \gamma\{(W + G)/W_C\}] \tag{6.10}$$

Apart from its usual properties, family child labour is now influenced by the amount of the direct cash transfer, G, by the government. A rise in G produces a positive income effect so that adult workers choose more leisure for their children and therefore decides to send a fewer number of children to the workplace. This is the direct effect of cash transfer on child labour.

The modified aggregate supply function of child labour would be

$$L_C = [(1 - \gamma)n - \gamma\{(W + G)/W_C\}](L - a_{L3}X_3) \tag{6.9.1}$$

For determining the consequences of the cash transfer policy on factor prices, output composition, aggregate supply of child labour and family welfare, we totally differentiate equations (6.1), (6.2), (6.4)–(6.7), (2.2) and (6.9.1) to establish the following proposition.[23]

Proposition 6.5: An increase in direct cash transfer to poor families leads to (i) a fall in adult wage (W); (ii) an increase in aggregate income from nonchild sources ($W + G$); (iii) a fall in child wage (W_C); (iv) a contraction of the formal manufacturing sector; (v) a lower incidence of child labour (L_C); and (vi) an improvement in the welfare of each child labour–supplying family.

We now interpret these results in economic terms. An increase in direct cash transfer lowers the supply of child labour by each poor family through a direct positive income effect at a given W and W_C. This lowers the aggregate supply of child labour given the output composition of the economy. However, W, W_C and the output composition would remain unchanged. This is because of the following reasons. Backward agriculture being the only sector that uses child labour contracts and releases adult labour and land that would expand the advanced agricultural sector. Because advanced agriculture is less adult labour–intensive relative to backward agriculture, both W and W_C would fall. Although W falls, the aggregate income of every poor family from nonchild labour sources, including the cash transfer (i.e. ($W + G$)) rises.[24] Hence, the supply of child labour by each family, l_C, indeed falls due to both income and price effects.[25] On the other hand, the expanding advanced agriculture draws capital from the formal manufacturing sector (sector 3), causing the latter sector to contract in terms of both output and employment. So a larger number of adult workers are now absorbed in the two agricultural sectors, each of them sending a lower number of children to the job market. The effect on the aggregate child labour supply at this stage remains inconclusive. However, our analysis shows that the net effect will be an unambiguous fall in the aggregate supply of child labour in the society.[26] A recent empirical study by Hoop and Rosati (2014) also supports our theoretical findings. They have found that cash transfers as an antipoverty strategy seems to be effective in reducing child labour incidence.

The welfare effect of the direct cash transfer policy also works in favour of the child labour–supplying families.[27] As the aggregate nonchild income of each family increases, it would be able to consume higher amounts of all commodities including children's leisure due to positive income effect. Besides, as W_C has fallen, it would enable the family to consume some more children's leisure. Hence, the welfare of the family improves due to both income and price effects.

6.5 Concluding remarks

In this chapter, we have provided a theoretical explanation of why subsidy policies to agriculture especially designed to benefit the poorer segment of the working population in the agricultural sector of the economy are not capable of mitigating the incidence of child labour and simultaneously improving the welfare of the poor families that supply child labour. It is a common belief that agriculture should be subsidized because poorer groups of the working population are employed in this sector who send many of their children out to work to supplement low family incomes. If the economic conditions of these people can be improved, the social menace of child labour could automatically be mitigated. The analysis of this chapter has challenged this populist belief by using a three-sector general equilibrium model with child labour and agricultural dualism. Advanced agriculture is distinguished from backward agriculture as follows. The former uses capital in the form of agricultural machineries that prevent child labour to work in these farms. On the contrary, backward agriculture uses primitive techniques of cultivation and employs child labour in significant numbers. Apart from this, backward agriculture uses more labour-intensive (adult labour) technique vis-à-vis advanced agriculture with respect to land. In this set-up, we have shown that a price subsidy policy designed to benefit the poorer segment of the working population affecting the child labour problem only through the supply side cannot ultimately be able to deliver the goods. Although the policy exerts a downward pressure on the child labour incidence through the supply side, by raising adult wage income it increases the demand for child labour through an expansion of backward agriculture. But as the demand side effect dominates over the supply side effect, the incidence of child labour gets a boost, even though the welfare of poor families improves. On the contrary, a subsidy policy to benefit advanced agriculture mitigates the child labour problem only at the cost of the welfare of the poorer group of the working families. So our analysis clearly demonstrates that the indirect poverty alleviation programs through subsidies to agriculture, irrespective of whether advanced or backward, would not be able to achieve both the targets concurrently. As a possible alternative policy, we have analyzed the efficacy of a direct cash transfer program to poor families. We have found that this policy can tackle the problem of child labour through both demand and supply sides. It increases incomes from nonchild labour source(s), raise the consumption of children's leisure and hence lower the supply of child labour by these altruistic poor families. These automatically improve their family welfare. All these effects take place through the supply side of the problem. On the demand side, the demand for child labour decreases as advanced agriculture expands that does not use child labour and backward agriculture contracts. This is how both demand and supply side effects work together to lessen the gravity of the child labour incidence.

Finally, it should be pointed out that certain assumptions of the model may seem to be restrictive. For example, child labour is used only in backward agriculture; nothing has been said about how the subsidies are financed, and the effects of the policies on national welfare have not been studied. However, these may be defended as follows. One may quite easily introduce an informal sector (say, sector M) that either produces a nontraded intermediate good for the formal sector (sector 3) by means of adult labour, child labour and capital or a nontraded final good/services with the help of two types of labour that is consumed by the richer segment of the population consisting of adult workers employed in sector 3 earning a high unionized wage, landowners and capitalists. However, it may intuitively be checked that most of the important results of the model hold under different sufficient conditions containing terms of relative intensities in which child labour and the other input(s) are used in the two child labour–using sectors.[28] Furthermore, considering national income at domestic or international prices as the measure of social welfare, it would not be difficult to analyze the effects of different policies on social welfare. Finally, despite abstraction and simplicity, the results of this model are important because these can at least question the appropriateness of the indirect poverty alleviation programs through distortionary agricultural subsidies and suggest alternative policies that can successfully eradicate the menace of child labour and improve the welfare of the poorer segment of the working population.

Appendices

Appendix 6.1   Changes in factor prices

As r is determined from equation (6.3), it is independent of any changes in P_2 and K. In other words, we have $\hat{r} = 0$.

Now we totally differentiate equations (6.1), (6.2), (6.4)–(6.6) and (6.7.1). Then, collecting terms and arranging in matrix notation, we get the following expression.

$$
\begin{bmatrix}
\theta_{L1} & \theta_{N1} & 0 & 0 & 0 & 0 \\
\theta_{L2} & \theta_{N2} & \theta_{C2} & 0 & 0 & 0 \\
\bar{S}_{LL} & 0 & \lambda_{L2}S^2_{LC} & \lambda_{L1} & \lambda_{L2} & \lambda_{L3} \\
\lambda_{K1}S^1_{KL} & 0 & 0 & \lambda_{K1} & 0 & \lambda_{K3} \\
0 & 0 & 0 & \lambda_{N1} & \lambda_{N2} & 0 \\
\left(S^2_{CL} + \dfrac{\gamma W}{l_C W_C}\right) & 0 & \left(S^2_{CC} - \dfrac{\gamma W}{l_C W_C}\right) & 0 & 1 & \dfrac{\lambda_{L3}}{(1-\lambda_{L3})}
\end{bmatrix}
\begin{bmatrix}
\hat{W} \\ \hat{R} \\ \hat{W}_C \\ \hat{X}_1 \\ \hat{X}_2 \\ \hat{X}_3
\end{bmatrix}
=
\begin{bmatrix}
0 \\ \hat{P}_2 \\ 0 \\ 0 \\ 0 \\ 0
\end{bmatrix}
\quad (6.A.1)
$$

where

$$
\bar{S}_{LL} = (\lambda_{L1}S^1_{LL} + \lambda_{L2}S^2_{LL}) < 0
$$

$$
\Delta = \left[
\begin{aligned}
&\left\{\lambda_{L2}S^2_{LC}A_1 - \left(S^2_{CC} - \frac{\gamma W}{l_C W_C}\right)A_2\right\}(\theta_{L1}\theta_{N2} - \theta_{N1}\theta_{L2}) \\
&+ \theta_{N1}\theta_{C2}\left\{\bar{S}_{LL}A_1 - \lambda_{K1}S^1_{KL}A_3 - \left(S^2_{CL} + \frac{\gamma W}{l_C W_C}\right)A_2\right\}
\end{aligned}
\right] < 0
$$

$$
A_1 = \lambda_{K1}\left(\lambda_{N2}\frac{\lambda_{L3}}{1-\lambda_{L3}}\right) + \lambda_{N1}\lambda_{K3} > 0
$$

$$
A_2 = \lambda_{K3}(\lambda_{N1}\lambda_{L2} - \lambda_{L1}\lambda_{N2}) + \lambda_{K1}\lambda_{L3}\lambda_{N2} > 0
$$

$$
A_3 = \frac{1}{1-\lambda_{L3}}(\lambda_{N2}\lambda_{L3}\lambda_{L1} + \lambda_{N1}\lambda_{L3}\lambda_{L1}) = \frac{\lambda_{L3}\lambda_{L1}}{1-\lambda_{L3}} > 0
$$

$$
(6.A.2)
$$

$|\lambda|^{12}_{NL} = (\lambda_{N1}\lambda_{L2} - \lambda_{L1}\lambda_{N2}) > 0$ as we have assumed that the backward agricultural sector is more adult labour-intensive vis-à-vis the advanced agricultural sector with respect to land both in physical and value sense. The latter implies that $(\theta_{L1}\theta_{N2} - \theta_{N1}\theta_{L2}) < 0$ which in turn shows that $\Delta < 0$.

Solving (6.A.1) by Cramer's rule the following expressions are obtained.

$$\hat{W} = -\frac{1}{\Delta}\left\{\lambda_{L2}S_{LC}^2 A_1 - \left(S_{CC}^2 - \frac{\gamma W}{l_C W_C}\right)A_2\right\}\theta_{N1}\hat{P}_2$$

$$\quad\quad (-)\quad\quad\quad (+)\quad\quad\quad (-)\quad\quad (+)\quad\quad (+)$$

$$\tag{6.A.3}$$

$$\hat{W}_C = \frac{1}{\Delta}\left\{\bar{S}_{LL}A_1 - \lambda_{K1}S_{KL}^1 A_3 - \left(S_{CL}^2 + \frac{\gamma W}{l_C W_C}\right)A_2\right\}\theta_{N1}\hat{P}_2$$

$$\quad (-)\;(-)\;(+)\quad\quad\quad (+)\quad\quad\quad (+)\quad\quad\quad (+)\quad\quad (+)$$

$$\tag{6.A.4}$$

$$\hat{R} = \frac{1}{\Delta}\left\{\lambda_{L2}S_{LC}^2 A_1 - \left(S_{CC}^2 - \frac{\gamma W}{l_C W_C}\right)A_2\right\}\theta_{L1}\hat{P}_2$$

$$\quad\quad (-)\quad\quad\quad (+)\quad\quad\quad (-)\quad\quad (+)\quad (+)$$

$$\tag{6.A.5}$$

Now subtraction of (6.A.4) from (6.A.3) yields

$$(\hat{W} - \hat{W}_C) = -\frac{1}{\Delta}\left[A_1\left(\lambda_{L2}S_{LC}^2 + \bar{S}_{LL}\right) - A_2\left(S_{CC}^2 + S_{CL}^2\right) - \left(\lambda_{K1}S_{KL}^1 A_3\right)\right]\theta_{N1}\hat{P}_2$$

Using the expression of $\bar{S}_{LL}$ from (6.A.2), we can further simplify the expression of $(\hat{W} - \hat{W}_C)$ as follows.

$$(\hat{W} - \hat{W}_C) = -\frac{1}{\Delta}\left[A_1\lambda_{L1}S_{LL}^1 - \lambda_{K1}S_{KL}^1 A_3\right]\theta_{N1}\hat{P}_2$$

$$\quad\quad\quad (-)\;(+)\;(-)\quad\quad\quad (+)\quad\quad (+)$$

$$\tag{6.A.6}$$

(Note that $(S_{CC}^2 + S_{CL}^2) = 0$ and $(S_{LL}^2 + S_{LC}^2) = 0$, Also, as a_{N2} is constant, $S_{CN}^2 = 0$ and $S_{LN}^2 = 0$.)

Using (6.A.2), from (6.A.3)–(6.A.5) and (6.A.6) we can obtain the following results.

$$\left.\begin{array}{l} (i)\,\hat{W} > 0,\,\hat{R} < 0 \quad\text{and}\quad \hat{W}_C > 0 \quad\text{when}\quad \hat{P}_2 >;0 \\[2mm] (ii)\,(\hat{W} - \hat{W}_C) < 0 \quad\text{when}\quad \hat{P}_2 > 0 \end{array}\right\} \tag{6.A.7}$$

Appendix 6.2   Changes in output composition

Solving (6.A.1) by Cramer's rule we can derive the following expressions as well.

$$\hat{X}_1 = -\frac{1}{\Delta}\left[\left(S_{CL}^2 + \frac{\gamma W}{l_C W_C}\right)\lambda_{L2}S_{LC}^2\lambda_{K3} - \left(S_{CC}^2 - \frac{\gamma W}{l_C W_C}\right)(\bar{S}_{LL}\lambda_{K3} - \lambda_{K1}S_{KL}^1\lambda_{L3})\right.$$

$$\left. - \frac{\lambda_{L3}}{(1-\lambda_{L3})}\lambda_{L2}S_{LC}^2\lambda_{K1}S_{KL}^1\right]\theta_{N1}\lambda_{N2}\hat{P}_2$$

or

$$\hat{X}_1 = -\frac{1}{\Delta}\left[-\left(S_{CC}^2 - \frac{\gamma W}{l_C W_C}\right)(\lambda_{L1}S_{LL}^1\lambda_{K3} - \lambda_{K1}S_{KL}^1\lambda_{L3}) - \frac{\lambda_{L3}}{(1-\lambda_{L3})}\right.$$

$$\underset{(-)}{}\qquad\underset{(-)}{}\qquad\qquad\underset{(-)}{}$$

$$\left.\lambda_{L2}S_{LC}^2\lambda_{K1}S_{KL}^1\right]\theta_{N1}\lambda_{N2}\hat{P}_2 \tag{6.A.8}$$

$$\underset{(+)}{}\qquad\qquad\underset{(+)}{}$$

$$\hat{X}_2 = \frac{1}{\Delta}\left[-\left(S_{CC}^2 - \frac{\gamma W}{l_C W_C}\right)(\lambda_{L1}S_{LL}^1\lambda_{K3} - \lambda_{K1}S_{KL}^1\lambda_{L3}) - \frac{\lambda_{L3}}{(1-\lambda_{L3})}\right.$$

$$\underset{(-)}{}\qquad\underset{(-)}{}\qquad\qquad\underset{(-)}{}\qquad\underset{(+)}{}$$

$$\left.\lambda_{L2}S_{LC}^2\lambda_{K1}S_{KL}^1\right]\theta_{N1}\lambda_{N1}\hat{P}_2 \tag{6.A.9}$$

$$\underset{(+)}{}\qquad\qquad\underset{(+)}{}$$

(We have used the expression of $\bar{S}_{LL}$, and note that $S_{LC}^2 + S_{LL}^2 = 0$ and $S_{CC}^2 + S_{CL}^2 = 0$.)

$$\hat{X}_3 = -\frac{1}{\Delta}\left[\begin{array}{l}\left\{\left(S_{CC}^2 - \frac{\gamma W}{l_C W_C}\right)\lambda_{L2}\lambda_{K1}S_{KL}^1 - \lambda_{L2}S_{LC}^2\lambda_{K1}S_{KL}^1\right\}\lambda_{N1}\\[2mm] -\left\{\left(S_{LC}^2 + \frac{\gamma W}{l_C W_C}\right)\lambda_{L2}S_{LC}^2\lambda_{K1} - \left(S_{CC}^2 - \frac{\gamma W}{l_C W_C}\right)(\bar{S}_{LL}\lambda_{K1} - \lambda_{L1}\lambda_{K1}S_{KL}^1)\right\}\lambda_{N2}\end{array}\right]\theta_{N1}\hat{P}_2$$

or

$$\hat{X}_3 = -\frac{1}{\Delta}\left[-\lambda_{L2}S_{LC}^2S_{KL}^1\lambda_{N1} + \left(S_{CC}^2 - \frac{\gamma W}{l_C W_C}\right)\left\{S_{KL}^1|\lambda|_{NL}^{12} + \lambda_{N2}\lambda_{L1}S_{LL}^1\right\}\right]\lambda_{K1}\theta_{N1}\hat{P}_2 \tag{6.A.10}$$

$$\underset{(-)}{}\qquad\underset{(+)}{}\qquad\underset{(-)}{}\qquad\quad\underset{(+)}{}\qquad\quad\underset{(-)}{}\qquad\underset{(+)}{}$$

From (6.A.8)–(6.A.10), we get the following

(iii) $\hat{X}_1 < 0, \hat{X}_2 > 0$ when $\hat{P}_2 > 0$;

(iv) $\hat{X}_3 < 0$ when $\hat{P}_2 > 0$

under the sufficient condition that $\left\{S_{KL}^1|\lambda|_{NL}^{12} + \lambda_{N2}\lambda_{L1}S_{LL}^1\right\} \geq 0$ $\qquad$ (6.A.11)

Also note that $\hat{K}_3 = \hat{X}_3$ where $K_3 = a_{K3}X_3$ (this is because $\hat{a}_{K3} = 0$). So

(v) $\hat{K}_3 < 0$ when $\hat{P}_2 > 0$; and $\qquad\qquad\qquad$ (6.A.12)

Appendix 6.3   Proof of proposition 6.2

Totally differentiating equation (6.9), we get the following.

$$\hat{L}_C = -\frac{\gamma W}{l_C W_C}(\hat{W} - \hat{W}_C) - \frac{\lambda_{L3}}{(1-\lambda_{L3})}\hat{X}_3$$

We now substitute the expressions of $\hat{X}_3$ and $(\hat{W} - \hat{W}_C)$ from (A.10) and (A.6), respectively, to get the following expression.

$$\hat{L}_C = -\frac{1}{\Delta}\left[-\frac{\gamma W}{l_C W_C}\underset{(-)}{(A_1\lambda_{L1}\underset{(-)}{S_{LL}^1} - \lambda_{K1}\underset{(+)}{S_{KL}^1}A_3)} \right.$$

$$\left. -\frac{\lambda_{L3}}{(1-\lambda_{L3})}\left\{ -\lambda_{L2}\underset{(+)}{S_{LC}^2}S_{KL}^1\lambda_{N1} + \left[\underset{(-)}{S_{CC}^2} -\frac{\gamma W}{l_C W_C}\right]\underset{(+)}{(S_{KL}^1|\lambda|_{NL}^{12}} + \lambda_{N2}\lambda_{L1}\underset{(-)}{S_{LL}^1})\right\}\lambda_{K1} \right]\underset{(+)}{\theta_{N1}\hat{P}_2} \quad\text{(6.A.13)}$$

From (6.A.13), we get the following results.

$\hat{L}_C > 0$ when $\hat{P}_2 > 0$ under the sufficient condition $\{S_{KL}^1|\lambda|_{NL}^{12} + \lambda_{N2}\lambda_{L1}S_{LL}^1\} \geq 0$

Rewriting (6.A.13) in a different way, it can be shown that the above result also holds under the sufficient condition that $S_{LC}^2 S_{KL}^1 \geq S_{CC}^2 S_{LL}^1$.

Appendix 6.4   Effects on family welfare

We substitute the optimum values of consumption of commodities (C_1, C_2 and C_3) (from equations (2.7.1)–(2.7.3)) and children's leisure ($n - l_C$) (from equation (6.8)) into the utility function (equation (2.8)) to get the following expression.

$$V = H\frac{(nW_C + W)}{(W_C)^\gamma} \quad\text{(6.A.14)}$$

where V stands for family welfare and $H = \gamma A\left(\frac{\alpha}{\gamma}\right)^\alpha\left(\frac{\beta}{\gamma P_2}\right)^\beta\left(\frac{\rho}{\gamma P_3}\right)^\rho > 0$.

Totally differentiating the preceding expression, we get the following.

$$\hat{V} = \frac{(l_C W_C\hat{W}_C + W\hat{W})}{(nW_C + W)} \quad\text{(6.A.15)}$$

From this expression, it is clear that family welfare is an increasing function of both W and W_C.

We now substitute $\hat{W}$ and $\hat{W}_C$ from (6.A.3) and (6.A.4) into (6.A.15) to get the following.

$$\hat{V} = \frac{1}{\underset{(-)}{\Delta(nW_C + W)}}\left| \begin{array}{l} -W\left\{ \lambda_{L2}\underset{(+)}{S_{LC}^2}A_1 - \left[\underset{(-)}{S_{CC}^2} -\frac{\gamma W}{l_C W_C}\right]\underset{(+)}{A_2}\right\} \\ \\ +\left\{ \underset{(-)}{\overline{S}_{LL}^1 A_1} - \lambda_{K1}\underset{(+)}{S_{KL}^1}A_3 - \left[\underset{(+)}{S_{CL}^2} +\frac{\gamma W}{l_C W_C}\right]\underset{(+)}{A_2}\right\} \end{array}\right|\theta_{N1}\hat{P}_2 \quad\text{(6.A.16)}$$

From (6.A.16), we can obtain the following result.

$$\hat{V} > 0 \text{ when } \hat{P}_2 > 0$$

Appendix 6.5 Effects of a change in G on child labour incidence

As we introduce direct cash transfer in our model, this modifies the family child labour supply function (equation (6.9)). This will modify equation (6.7.1), and its modified form would be as follows.

$$a_{C2}X_2 = [(1-\gamma)n - \gamma\{(W+G)/W_C\}](L - a_{L3}X_3) \tag{6.7.2}$$

Thus, the aggregate supply function of child labour in the economy is now given by

$$L_C = [(1-\gamma)n - \gamma\{(W+G)/W_C\}](L - a_{L3}X_3) \tag{6.9.1}$$

Now totally differentiate equations (6.1), (6.2), (6.4)–(6.6) and (6.7.2) and then solving by Cramer's rule, the following expressions are obtained.

$$\hat{W} = \frac{1}{\Delta}\theta_{N1}\theta_{C2}A_2\frac{\gamma G}{l_CW_C}\hat{G} \tag{6.A.17}$$
$$\quad (-) \qquad\qquad (+)$$

$$\hat{W}_C = -\frac{1}{\Delta}(\theta_{L1}\theta_{N2} - \theta_{N1}\theta_{L2})A_2\frac{\gamma G}{l_CW_C}\hat{G} \tag{6.A.18}$$
$$\quad (-) \qquad\quad (-) \qquad\quad (+)$$

$$\hat{X}_3 = \frac{1}{\Delta}\big[\theta_{N1}\theta_{C2}\lambda_{L1}\lambda_{K1}S^1_{KL} - \lambda_{L2}S^2_{LC}\lambda_{K1}\lambda_{N2}(\theta_{L1}\theta_{N2} - \theta_{N1}\theta_{L2})$$
$$\qquad (-) \qquad\qquad (+) \qquad\qquad\qquad (+) \qquad\qquad\qquad (-)$$
$$\qquad\quad -\theta_{N1}\theta_{C2}\overline{S}_{LL}\lambda_{K1}\lambda_{N2}\big]\frac{\gamma G}{l_CW_C}\hat{G} \tag{6.A.19}$$
$$\qquad\qquad (-)$$

where

$$\Delta = \left|\begin{array}{l}\left[\left\{\lambda_{L2}S^2_{LC}A_1 - \left(S^2_{CC} - \frac{\gamma(W+G)}{l_CW_C}\right)A_2\right\}(\theta_{L1}\theta_{N2} - \theta_{N1}\theta_{L2})\right] \\ +\theta_{N1}\theta_{C2}\left\{\overline{S}_{LL}A_1 - \lambda_{K1}S^1_{KL}A_3 - \left(S^2_{CL} + \frac{\gamma W}{l_CW_C}\right)A_2\right\}\end{array}\right| < 0 \tag{6.A.20}$$

Now, let the family income from nonchild labour sources be denoted by $M = W + G$. So

$$\hat{M} = W\hat{W} + G\hat{G} \tag{6.A.21}$$

Substituting (6.A.17) in (6.A.21) and simplifying, we can obtain the following expression.

$$\hat{M} = \frac{1}{\Delta}\Big[\{\lambda_{L2}S_{LC}^2 A_1 - (S_{CC}^2 - \frac{\gamma(W+G)}{l_C W_C})A_2\}(\theta_{L1}\theta_{N2} - \theta_{N1}\theta_{L2})$$

$$\quad (-) \qquad\quad (+) \qquad\quad (-) \qquad\qquad\qquad (-) \tag{6.A.22}$$

$$+\theta_{N1}\theta_{C2}\{\bar{S}_{LL}A_1 - \lambda_{K1}S_{KL}^1 A_3 - S_{CL}^2 A_2\}\Big]G\hat{G}$$

$$\quad (-) \qquad\qquad (+) \qquad (+)$$

From (6.A.22), one can easily check that $\hat{M} > 0$ when $\hat{G} > 0$.

Using (6.A.17)–(6.A.19) and (6.A.22), we get the following results.

(i) $\hat{W} < 0$ and $\hat{W}_C < 0$ when $\hat{G} > 0$

(ii) $\hat{X}_3 < 0$ when $\hat{G} > 0$

(iii) $M > 0$ when $G > 0$

To examine the effect of a change in G on the aggregate child labour supply, we totally differentiate equation (6.9.1) and obtain the following expression.

$$\hat{L}_C = -\frac{\gamma G}{l_C W_C}\hat{G} - \frac{\gamma W}{l_C W_C}\hat{W} + \frac{\gamma(W+G)}{l_C W_C}\hat{W}_C - \frac{\lambda_{L3}}{(1-\lambda_{L3})}\hat{X}_3 \tag{6.A.23}$$

Using (6.A.17)–(6.A.19) in (6.A.23) and simplifying, the following expression can be obtained.

$$\hat{L}_C = -\frac{1}{\Delta}\Big[-(S_{CC}^2 - \frac{\gamma(W+G)}{l_C W_C})A_2(\theta_{L1}\theta_{N2} - \theta_{N1}\theta_{L2})$$

$$\quad (-) \qquad\quad (-) \qquad\qquad (+) \qquad (-) \tag{6.A.24}$$

$$-\theta_{N1}\theta_{C2}S_{CL}^2 A_2 + \frac{\gamma(W+G)}{l_C W_C}(\theta_{L1}\theta_{N2} - \theta_{N1}\theta_{L2})\Big]\frac{\gamma G}{l_C W_C}\hat{G}$$

$$\quad (+) \qquad\quad (+) \qquad\qquad\quad (-)$$

From (6.A.24), we get the following results.

$$\hat{L}_C < 0 \text{ when } \hat{G} > 0$$

Appendix 6.6   Effect of a change in G on family welfare

Introduction of cash transfer in the model will alter equation (6.A.15) as follows.

$$\hat{V} = \frac{(G\hat{G} + l_C W_C \hat{W}_C + W\hat{W})}{(G + nW_C + W)} \tag{6.A.25}$$

After substituting $\hat{W}$ and $\hat{W}_C$ from (6.A.17) and (6.A.18) in (6.A.25) and simplifying, we find

$$\hat{V} = \frac{1}{\Delta(G + nW_C + W)}$$
$$\underset{(-)}{}$$

$$\begin{bmatrix} \left\{ \lambda_{L2} S_{LC}^2 A_1 - \left(S_{CC}^2 - \frac{\gamma(W + G)}{l_C W_C} \right) A_2 \right\} (\theta_{L1}\theta_{N2} - \theta_{N1}\theta_{L2}) \\ \underset{(+)}{} \quad \underset{(-)}{} \quad \underset{(-)}{} \\ +\theta_{N1}\theta_{C2} \{ \bar{S}_{LL} A_1 - \lambda_{K1} S_{KL}^1 A_3 \} G - \gamma G A_2 \theta_{L1}\theta_{N2} + G A_2 \theta_{N1} (\gamma\theta_{L2} - \theta_{C2} S_{CL}^2) \\ \underset{(-)}{} \quad \underset{(+)}{} \quad \underset{(+)}{} \quad \underset{(+)}{} \end{bmatrix} \hat{G}$$

(6.A.26)

From (6.A.26), we get the following result.

$\hat{V} > 0$ when $\hat{G} > 0$ under the sufficient condition $(\gamma\theta_{L2} - \theta_{C2} S_{CL}^2) \leq 0$

Notes

1 See, for example, Barros et al. (1994), Jensen and Nielsen (1997), Swaminathan (1998), Cartwright (1999), Edmonds and Turk (2002), Bhalotra and Heady (2003), Duryea and Arends-Kuenning (2003) and Kruger (2007).
2 According to the ILO (2012), more than 59 per cent of economically active children in the developing countries are engaged in agriculture and allied sectors. In the case of India, this figure is as high as 68 per cent (National Sample Survey Organization 2004–2005).
3 See Gupta (2000) in this context.
4 See FAO (2012) and Mwamadi and Seiffert (2012) for details.
5 In a developing country, like India, for protecting the interests of the small and marginal farmers and the poorer segment of the consumers, the government often tinkers with market mechanism by its procurement and distribution activities. It declares in advance the minimum support prices (MSPs) for essential crops at which public agencies procure foodgrains and other essential crops from farmers. On the other hand, it distributes foodgrains among the weaker segments of consumers at subsidized issue prices through its public distribution system. Another important objective of these operations is to maintain satisfactory levels of operational and buffer stocks of foodgrains in order to ensure National Food Security. All these practices are being followed in a country like India. See http://fciweb. nic.in/ for more details.
6 See Basu an Van (1998), Basu (1999, 2000), Ranjan (1999, 2001), Baland and Robinson (2000), Gupta (2000, 2002), Jafarey and Lahiri (2002), Chaudhuri and Dwibedi (2006, 2007), Chaudhuri (2010) and Dwibedi and Chaudhuri (2010) among others. In the literature the supply of child labour has been attributed to factors such as abject poverty, lack of educational facilities and poor quality of schooling, capital market imperfection, parental attitudes including the objectives to maximize present income etc.
7 The model described in section 6.2 is based on Dwibedi and Chaudhuri (2014).
8 It has been mentioned earlier that more than 59 per cent of economically active children in the developing countries are engaged in agriculture and allied sectors and less than 8 per cent are involved in manufacturing and nearly 32 per cent in

services (ILO (2012)). Apart from agriculture, child workers are mainly used in the informal manufacturing sector, which constitutes unregistered units that produce mainly intermediate goods for the formal manufacturing sector. Child labour is also often used in nontraded services like domestic help and prostitution, which are consumed primarily by the richer segment of the population. Chaudhuri and Dwibedi (2007) dealt with this type of child labour in their analysis. Because our objective is to focus on child labour in dualistic agriculture, we have not separately considered an informal manufacturing sector with child labour. However, even if one introduces an informal manufacturing sector where child labour, adult labour and capital are used to produce a nontraded input for the formal sector, the basic results of this model still hold under different sufficient conditions containing terms of relative intensities in which child labour and the other two inputs are used in the two child labour–using sectors.

9 A relevant question in this context is what mechanism stops the entire labour force being employed in the higher paid formal sector (sector 3), especially when we are considering a small open economy that is a price-taker at the international market. If we look at the price system of the model we find that capital is used by sector 1 and sector 3. The return to capital, r, is determined from equation (6.3) because $\overline{W}$ and P_3 are exogenously given. Once r is determined the factor coefficients in sector 3 i.e. a_{L3} and a_{K3} are also determined. Sector 1 uses $a_{K1}X_1$ units of capital. All other factor prices and factor coefficients are determined from the remaining two price equations and the factor endowments equations. As commodity prices and factor endowments are given all other factor prices and factor coefficients are also given. Now sector 3 actually gets $(K - a_{K1}X_1)$ amount of capital which in turn can produce $\left(\dfrac{K - a_{K1}X_1}{a_{K3}}\right)$ units of good 3 and can at best employ $\left(\dfrac{K - a_{K1}X_1}{a_{K3}}\right)a_{L3}$ number of worker. For a wide range of parameter values the labour endowment, L, is greater than $\left(\dfrac{K - a_{K1}X_1}{a_{K3}}\right)a_{L3}$. This is the case which we are considering. Therefore, owing to scarcity of capital all workers are not employed in sector 3. However, the employment level in this sector rises if the capital stock of the economy goes up.

10 The land-output ratios in the two agricultural sectors (a_{N1} and a_{N2}) have been assumed to be technologically given. However, the other inputs exhibit CRS between themselves.

11 For a detailed discussion on household behaviour see chapter 2.

12 This supply function has been derived from the welfare-maximizing behaviour of each representative poor working household that supplies child labour (see equation 2.8).

13 See appendices 6.1 and 6.2 for detailed derivations.

14 Here S_{ji}^k is the degree of substitution between factors j and i in the kth sector with $S_{ji}^k > 0$ for $j \neq i$; and $S_{jj}^k < 0$ while λ_{ji} is the allocative share of jth input in the ith sector. Besides, $|\lambda|_{NL}^{12} = (\lambda_{N1}\lambda_{L2} - \lambda_{L1}\lambda_{N2}) > 0$ inasmuch as backward agriculture (sector 2) is more adult labour–intensive vis-à-vis advanced agriculture (sector 1) with respect to land.

15 This result is consistent with specific factor models. For an understanding of how returns to intersectorally mobile factors and specific factors react to changes in relative commodity prices, one can go through Jones (1971). See appendix 6.1 for mathematical proof.

16 Note that the capital-output ratio in sector 3 (a_{K3}) remains unchanged since r does not change.

17 This has been mathematically proved in appendix 6.3

18 For mathematical derivation, see appendix 6.4.
19 Interested readers can easily check this after going through appendix 6.3.
20 Additionally, different subsidies distort the relative prices of commodities and consequently lead to the misallocation of economic resources between the sectors that would affect the social welfare of the economy adversely.
21 It is a centralized electronic benefit transfer system to undertake the transfer of benefits (like old age pension, social security pension etc.) and subsidies directly to the beneficiaries, by way of crediting to their bank accounts. See http://www.npci.org.in/AEPSOverview.aspx.
22 From equation (6.10), it is evident that $l_C = 0$ if $(W + G) \geq \dfrac{n(1-\gamma)W_C}{\gamma}$.
23 See appendix 6.3 for mathematical derivations.
24 See appendices 6.5 and 6.6.
25 Note that the opportunity cost of children's leisure, W_C, has decreased.
26 See appendix 6.5 for mathematical derivations.
27 See appendix 6.6 for mathematical proofs of this result.
28 See also note 8 in this context.

References

Baland, J. and Robinson, J.A. (2000): 'Is child labour inefficient?', *Journal of Political Economy*, 108(4), 663–679.

Barros, R., Mendonca, R. and Velazco, T. (1994): 'Is poverty the main cause of child work in urban Brazil?', Texto Para Discussao No. 351, Servico Editorial.

Basu, K. (1999): 'Child labour: Cause, consequence, and cure, with remarks on international labour standards', *Journal of Economic Literature*, 37(September), 1083–1119.

Basu, K. (2000): 'The intriguing relationship between adult minimum wage and child labour', *The Economic Journal*, 110(462), C50–C61.

Basu, K. and Van, P.H. (1998): 'The economics of child labour', *American Economic Review*, 88(3), 412–427.

Bhalotra, S. and Heady, C. (2003): 'Child farm labor: The wealth paradox', *World Bank Econ Review*, 17, 197–227.

Cartwright, K. (1999): 'Child labor in Colombia', in: Christiaan Grootaert and Harry Anthony Patrinos (eds.), *The Policy Analysis of Child Labor, a Comparative Study*, World Bank, Washington, DC, 63–102.

Chaudhuri, S. (2010): 'Mid-day meal program and incidence of child labour in a developing economy', *Japanese Economic Review*, 61(2), 252–265.

Chaudhuri, S. and Dwibedi, J.K. (2006): 'Trade liberalization in agriculture in developed nations and incidence of child labour in a developing economy', *Bulletin of Economic Research*, 58(2), 129–150.

Chaudhuri, S. and Dwibedi, J.K. (2007): 'Foreign capital inflow, fiscal policies and incidence of child labour in a developing economy', *The Manchester School*, 75(1), 17–46.

Duryea, S. and Arends-Kuenning, M.P. (2003): 'School attendance, child labor, and local labor markets in urban Brazil', *World Development*, 31, 1165–1178.

Dwibedi, J.K. and Chaudhuri, S. (2010): 'Foreign capital, return to education and child labour', *International Review of Economics and Finance*, 19(2), 278–286.

Dwibedi, J.K. and Chaudhuri, S. (2014): 'Agricultural subsidy policies fail to deal with child labour under agricultural dualism: What could be the alternative policies?', *Research in Economics*, 68(3), 277–291.

Edmonds, E. and Turk, C. (2002): 'Child labor in transition in Vietnam', World Bank Policy Research Paper No. 2774.

FAO. (2012): 'FAO's contribution to reducing and preventing child labour in agriculture 2007–11'. Available at: http://www.fao.org/docrep/015/md090e/md090e00.pdf

Gupta, M.R. (2000): 'Wage determination of a child worker: A theoretical analysis', *Review of Development Economics*, 4(2), 219–228.

Gupta, M.R. (2002): 'Trade sanctions, adult unemployment and the supply of child labour: A theoretical analysis', *Development Policy Review*, 20(3), 317–332.

Hoop, J. and Rosati, F.C. (2014): 'Cash transfers and child labor', Policy Research Working Paper No. 6826, The World Bank.

ILO. (2012): 'Making progress against child labour: Global estimates and trends 2000–2012', International Labour Office, Geneva.

Jafarey, S. and Lahiri, S. (2002): 'Will trade sanctions reduce child labour? The role of credit markets', *Journal of Development Economics*, 68(1), 137–156.

Jensen, P. and Nielsen, H.S. (1997): 'Child labor or school attendance? Evidence from Zambia', *Journal of Population Economics*, 10, 407–424.

Jones, R.W. (1971): 'A three factor model in theory, trade, and history', Ch. 1 in: J. Bhagwati, R.W. Jones, R.A. Mundell and J. Vanek (eds.), *Trade, Balance of Payments and Growth*, North-Holland, Amsterdam (reprinted as Ch. 3 in Neary, J.P. (ed.). (1995): *International Trade*, Vol. II, Edward Elgar, Cheltenham.

Kruger, D.I. (2007): 'Coffee production effects on child labor and schooling in rural Brazil', *Journal of Development Economics*, 82, 448–463.

Mwamadi, N. and Seiffert, B. (2012): 'Reducing child labour in agriculture through good agricultural practices: FAO experiences'. Available at: www.fao.org/.../fao.../Safer-Agricultural-Practices-FAO-experiences.pdf

National Sample Survey Organization. (2004–05): 'Employment and unemployment situation in India 2004–05', Report No. 515(61/10/1), Government of India.

Ranjan, P. (1999): 'An economic analysis of child labour', *Economic Letters*, 64, 99–105.

Ranjan, P. (2001): 'Credit constraints and the phenomenon of child labour', *Journal of Development Economic*, 64, 81–102.

Swaminathan, M. (1998): 'Economic growth and the persistence of child labor: Evidence from an Indian city', *World Development*, 26, 1513–1528.

7 Child labour, human capital formation and the possibility of failure of incentive-based schemes

7.1 Introduction

Governments all over the world, irrespective of whether developed or developing, devote substantial resources to their education sector with an eye to promoting human capital formation. Education through positive externalities promotes human capital formation, which is conducive to economic growth and the prosperity of an economy as well as having an egalitarian effect because it is likely to lower the difference in wages between the various groups of workers that are differentiated with respect to their skills. In 1995, public spending on education accounted for 15.7 per cent of total government expenditure in developing countries (see Bedi and Garg 2000). Furthermore, the majority of students in developing countries are educated in publicly funded and publicly managed educational institutions. According to Jimenez and Lockheed (1995), almost 90 per cent of all primary and 70 per cent of all secondary enrollments in developing countries are in public schools. In the public education system in the developing economies, policies like stipends, free educational goods and free midday meals have been designed to pull and retain children in school. These are likely to stimulate school attendance and retention and mitigate the problem of child labour by keeping them in school.

In recent times, there have been many randomized evaluations of incentive-based educational programs in the developing countries, including programs to increase school participation, provide educational inputs and reform education. School participation can be bolstered substantially by health programs, the reduction of costs of school to households or the provision of meals. Schultz (2004) has found that in Mexico cash grants to families, conditional on sending their children to school, raised an average increase in enrolment by 3.4 per cent for all students. However, school meals may provide a stronger incentive to attend school than take-home rations conditioned on school attendance (Sen 2002). Vermeersch (2002) has found that school participation was 30 per cent higher in 25 Kenyan preschools where a free breakfast was introduced than in 25 comparison schools. Besides, Kremer et al. (2002) have found that due to the provision of school uniforms, textbooks and classroom construction, the dropout rate has fallen considerably in some randomly selected schools in Kenya and that many students from nearby schools transferred into program schools, raising class size by 50 per cent. Poor health may also result in lower school participation. On the other hand, Miguel and Kremer (2004) have found that a treatment with inexpensive deworming drugs in many primary schools in Kenya has produced a significant improvement in school participation not only at program schools but also at nearby schools, owing to reduced disease transmission. The existence of strong external effects among untreated students of nearby schools alone justifies full subsidization of this program. Although randomized evaluations are labour-intensive and no more costly than other types of surveys, these cannot be completely relied upon to mitigate a nationwide problem like child labour.

ILO (1999) and later ILO (2006) have viewed that incentive schemes are extremely important in raising education levels and retaining children in school and ought to be employed in the developing countries with child labour, since they are likely to lower the incidence of child labour by lessening the forgone effective child wage income, in addition to raising the future earning potential of the children attending school through human capital formation. But before introducing these policies it is necessary to theoretically analyse how these incentive schemes work and whether they deliver the goods at all. Unfortunately, trade and development economists have not paid adequate attention[1] in analyzing the effects of midday meal programs and/or cash stipend schemes on the problem of child labour using a general equilibrium framework with due emphasis on human capital formation.

The present chapter intends to examine the consequences of midday meal programs and/or the provision of cash stipends to school-attending children with respect to the incidence of child labour in a developing economy using a three-sector general equilibrium model.[2] The supply function of child labour of each working family is derived from its intertemporal utility-maximizing behaviour. Sector 1 is the agricultural sector where child labour is used along with adult unskilled labour and capital. Sector 2 is the low-skill manufacturing sector that uses adult unskilled labour and capital. Finally, sector 3 employs skilled labour and capital to produce a high-skill commodity. In this set-up, we examine the consequence of the midday meal program or cash stipend scheme on the aggregate supply of child labour in the society. We identify the different channels through which the policy affects the prevalence of child labour in the system. It is found that the policy may be counterproductive as it lowers both the initial incomes of the working families and the return to education. Direct cash payments to the working families instead of a midday meal program are likely to be effective in eradicating the problem of child labour.

7.2 Household behaviour and the derivation of the supply function of child labour

In the small open economy, we consider there are two types of adult labour (and hence working households) differentiated with respect to their level of skills. These are skilled labour and unskilled labour. Because the level of skills of a skilled worker is higher than that of an unskilled worker, the skilled wage, W_S, is greater than that of the unskilled worker, W.[3] Each working household, irrespective of whether skilled or unskilled, consists of one adult member (guardian) and one child. The total child time is assumed unity. Let us make the simplifying assumption that child labour is supplied by the unskilled working families only.[4] The supply function of child labour by each unskilled working family is determined from its intertemporal utility-maximizing behaviour. Staying in line with the traditional model of the household (Becker 1964), we consider each household as a single decision-making unit.[5] On behalf of the family, the guardian unilaterally takes the decision regarding the allocation of consumption in the two periods and the labour supply of the available child time. The guardian in the first period works in the adult unskilled labour market and earns the unskilled wage W. In this period, he decides on the allocation of the total child labour time between work effort (l_C) and schooling, $(1 - l_C)$. Because a market for loans against future earnings does not exist, the parent is compelled to use income from child work to smooth out the family consumption.[6] There are provisions for midday meals and cash stipends for children attending school, the monetary value of which is b per unit of child time attending school. Hence, l_C is the amount of time the child works at the child wage, (W_C), in the first period and then works at the adult unskilled wage (W) in the second period, while during the remaining time $(1 - l_C)$ the child earns b in the first period and the skilled wage (W_S) in the second period. Because we do not consider unemployment of either type of adult labour, the child time spent in school in the current period would have no difficulty in finding skilled jobs in future. It is also assumed that $W_C > b$; otherwise the supply of child labour would be zero. In the second period, the guardian earns nothing and lives on the income received from the child (children) who has (have) become adult worker(s) by this time.

We assume that the parent cares only about the lifetime family consumption. Maximizing the lifetime family consumption with respect to l_C, we derive the following supply function of child labour by each unskilled working family.

$$l_C = \left[\frac{W_S}{(1+\beta)(W_S - W)} - \frac{\beta(W + b)}{(1+\beta)(W_C - b)} \right] \tag{7.1}$$

This is the same child labour supply function (2.24.1) as derived in chapter 2 with slight modifications. Here the family does not receive any part of the economy's capital income because it has been assumed that workers are not the owners of domestic capital. Besides, the supply of child labour comes only from the unskilled working families. The properties of this function have already been discussed in chapter 2.

Because there are L number of unskilled working families in the economy, the aggregate supply of child labour is given by the following.

$$L_C = \left[\frac{W_S}{(1+\beta)(W_S - W)} - \frac{\beta(W + b)}{(1+\beta)(W_C - b)} \right] L \tag{7.2}$$

7.3 The general equilibrium model

We have already stated that in our small open economy there are three sectors. Sector 1 produces an agricultural commodity, X_1, using adult unskilled labour (L), child labour (L_C) and capital (K). The capital-output ratio in sector 1, a_{K1}, is assumed to be technologically given.[7] Sector 2 uses unskilled labour and capital to produce a low-skill commodity, X_2. Finally, sector 3 produces a high-skill commodity, X_3, with the help of skilled labour (S) and capital. Hence, child labour is used in the agricultural sector only while skilled labour is specific to sector 3.[8] Commodity prices, P_is, are given by the small open economy assumption. We assume competitive markets, constant returns to scale technologies with positive but diminishing marginal productivities of inputs and full employment of resources.

The usual zero-profit conditions relating to the three sectors are given by the following.

$$Wa_{L1} + W_c a_{C1} + Ra_{K1} = P_1 \qquad (7.3)$$

$$Wa_{L2} + Ra_{K2} = P_2 \qquad (7.4)$$

$$W_s a_{S3} + Ra_{K3} = P_3 \qquad (7.5)$$

where a_{ji}s are input–output ratios, and R is the return to capital.

The full employment of adult unskilled labour, child labour, capital and skilled labour implies the following four equations, respectively.

$$a_{L1}X_1 + a_{L2}X_2 = L \qquad (7.6)$$

$$a_{C1}X_1 = L_C \qquad (7.7)$$

$$a_{K1}X_1 + a_{K2}X_2 + a_{K3}X_3 = K \qquad (7.8)$$

$$a_{S3}X_3 = S \qquad (7.9)$$

Here L, K and S denote the endowments of adult unskilled labour, capital and skilled labour, respectively, which are given exogenously. Finally, L_C denotes the endowment of child labour, which is endogenously determined.

7.4   Comparative statics

The general equilibrium structure consists of eight equations ((7.2)–(7.9)) and the same number of endogenous variables: W, W_C, W_S, R, X_1, X_2, X_3 and L_C. The price system of the model consists of equations (7.3)–(7.5) and involves four unknown factor prices: W, W_C, W_S and R. Hence, factor prices cannot be solved from the price system only, which means that it is an indecomposable production structure. Therefore, factor prices and the composition of output need to be simultaneously determined from the entire system, and by that process the aggregate supply of child labour is determined.

Given the child wage rate, W_C, sectors 1 and 2 together can effectively be regarded as a *Modified Hechscher-Ohlin subsystem (MHOSS)* because these sectors use two common inputs, adult labour and capital. The modification is due to the fact that sector 1, apart from adult unskilled labour and capital, also uses child labour. It is sensible to assume that sector 1 is more adult labour–intensive than sector 2 with respect to capital. Child labour is specific to sector 1, and its aggregate supply is endogenously determined. Totally differentiating equations (7.2)–(7.9) and solving, the following proposition can be established.[9]

Proposition 7.1: A midday meal program and/or cash stipend to school-attending children lead to (i) a fall in the adult wage; (ii) an increase in the child wage; and (iii) a decrease in the skilled wage rate. The policy improves the skilled–unskilled wage inequality iff the high-skill sector is capital-intensive relative to the low-skill sector in a special sense.[10]

Proposition 7.1 can be explained in the following fashion. An increase in the pecuniary value of midday meals and/or cash stipends, *ceteris paribus*, lowers the effective child wage, ($W_C - b$), which in turn initially lowers the aggregate supply of child labour in the economy. This raises the child wage rate, W_C. Because the child wage rate rises, the effective price of commodity 1, net of cost on child labour, falls. This produces a Stolper-Samuelson type effect in the *Modified Heckscher-Ohlin subsystem* (*MHOSS*). The return to capital, R, rises while the adult unskilled wage, W, falls because sector 1 is more adult labour-intensive vis-à-vis sector 2 with respect to capital. The Stolper-Samuelson type effect is followed by a Rybczynski type effect that leads to a contraction of sector 1 and an expansion of sector 2.[11] The amount of capital released by sector 1 is inadequate for the expansion of sector 2. Hence, sector 3 also has to release capital to the expanding sector 2. Thus, sector 3 contracts for scarcity of capital. The demand for skilled labour falls and lowers the skilled wage, W_S. What happens to the skilled–unskilled wage inequality depends on the rates of decrease in W_S and W, which in turn depends on the distributive shares of capital in the two sectors. If the high-skill sector (sector 3) is capital-intensive in a special sense, the increase in cost on capital input in sector 3 is higher relative to that in the low-skill sector (sector 2), which in turn, implies a decrease in the relative wage inequality.

We now analyze the consequence of the midday meal program/cash stipend scheme on the incidence of child labour in the society. Totally differentiating equation (7.2) and using the results of proposition 7.1, the following proposition can be proved.[12]

Proposition 7.2: The midday meal program and/or cash stipend scheme for the school-attending children will increase the supply of child labour in the economy if (i) sector 3 is capital-intensive (in a special sense) and (ii) the effective child wage does not fall.

We explain proposition 7.2 in the following way. In this model, the supply of child labour comes solely from families of the unskilled workers. From equation (7.2), it is evident that the aggregate supply of child labour in the economy depends negatively on the initial income of each family from nonchild sources, which is here equal to the adult unskilled wage, as well as on the return to education. On the contrary, it depends positively on the effective child wage and the endowment of unskilled labour. As stated in proposition 8.1, although the midday meal program lowers both the skilled wage, W_S, and the adult unskilled wage, W, the policy raises the child wage rate, W_C. However, the outcome on the effective child wage, ($W_C - b$), is uncertain. All of these factors affect the supply of child labour in different ways. First, the supply of child labour by each family rises due to the negative income effect because the initial income from nonchild sources has decreased. Second, the supply of child labour increases if the return to education falls. Nonetheless, the wage inequality and hence the return to education will fall if sector 3 is capital-intensive in the Jones and Neary (1984) sense. Finally, the consequence of a change in the effective child wage on the supply of child labour is ambiguous. However, if the effective wage of child labour, $(W_C - b)$, does not fall, the incidence of child labour in the economy rises because all of the three effects work together to raise the supply of child labour. It is, of course, possible for the incidence of child labour to increase even when $(W_C - b)$ falls if the sum of the first two effects outweighs the outcome on the effective child wage.

7.5   Effect on family welfare

The effect of the midday meal program on the welfare of the working households that supply child labour can be intuitively discussed by inspecting equations (2.20.2), (2.21.1) and (2.22). Note that in the present case $n = 1$, $W_0 = W$ and $R_H = 0$. Although the midday meal program directly raises the first period's consumption, C_1, of each household, the policy lowers the initial adult wage income and raises the child wage rate (see proposition 7.1). Thus, the net effect on C_1 is uncertain. The second period's consumption, C_2, unambiguously falls since both the skilled and unskilled wages fall. Thus, the overall effect on the welfare of each family is ambiguous. This establishes the following proposition.

Proposition 7.3: The consequence of the midday meal program and/or cash stipend scheme on the welfare of the families that supply child labour is ambiguous.

7.6   Concluding remarks

This chapter explains how economic incentive schemes designed to keep children in school might fail in arresting the child labour problem in the society although child schooling leads to skill formation and increases their future earning opportunities. The supply of child labour comes from the families of unskilled workers, and the family supply function of child labour is derived from the intertemporal utility maximizing behaviour of each family. The family decides to send some of their children to the job market for consumption smoothing because of non-existence of a market for loans against future earnings. A three-sector general equilibrium model has been developed for the purpose of analysis. The interesting result that emerges from our exercise is that economic incentive schemes like the midday meal program and provision for cash stipend might exert an upward pressure on the incidence of child labour by lowering both the return to education and the initial incomes of the unskilled working population from non-child sources. Therefore, the gravity of the problem may intensify due to both a negative income effect and a reduction in the return to education even if the effective child wage falls. Moreover, the welfare of the working families may worsen due to this policy unless the increase in the child wage rate is sufficiently high.[13]

Certain assumptions of the model may seem to be restrictive. The model presupposes that the quality of education is good and that the children attending school in the present period will get jobs in the high-skill sector in future. However, the quality of basic education in the developing countries is generally unsatisfactory, and there is also unemployment of educated workers.[14,15,16] Besides, the assumption that child labour is used only in the agricultural sector is simplifying.[17] Despite the simplicity and abstraction, the theoretical analysis presented in this chapter may be of some interest because its results question the desirability of the midday meal program and/or the provision of cash stipends in eliminating the problem of child labour in the developing countries.

Appendices

Appendix 7.1 Policy effects on factor prices and output composition

Totally differentiating equations (7.3)–(7.5) and using envelope conditions, the following expressions are obtained.

$$\theta_{L1}\hat{W} + \theta_{C1}\hat{W}_C + \theta_{K1}\hat{R} = 0 \tag{7.A.1}$$

$$\theta_{L2}\hat{W} + \theta_{K2}\hat{R} = 0 \tag{7.A.2}$$

$$\theta_{S3}\hat{W}_S + \theta_{K3}\hat{R} = 0 \tag{7.A.3}$$

where θ_{ji} = distributive share of the jth input in the ith sector, and '∧' = proportional change.

Totally differentiating equations (7.2) and (7.6)–(7.9), collecting terms and simplifying, we get the following expressions.

$$\bar{S}_{LL}\hat{W} + \lambda_{L1}S^1_{LC}\hat{W}_C + \bar{S}_{LK}\hat{R} + \lambda_{L1}\hat{X}_1 + \lambda_{L2}\hat{X}_2 = 0 \tag{7.A.4}$$

$$\bar{S}_{KL}\hat{W} + A_2\hat{R} + A_1\hat{W}_S + \lambda_{K1}\hat{X}_1 + \lambda_{K2}\hat{X}_2 = 0 \tag{7.A.5}$$

$$(S^1_{CL} + E)\hat{W} + (S^1_{CC} - F)\hat{W}_C + G\hat{W}_S + \hat{X}_1 = -H\hat{b} \tag{7.A.6}$$

(Note that we have used $\hat{X}_3 = -S^3_{SS}\hat{W}_S - S^3_{SK}\hat{R}$ from equation (7.9))
where

$$\left.\begin{aligned}
&\bar{S}_{LL} = (\lambda_{L1}S^1_{LL} + \lambda_{L2}S^2_{LL}) < 0, \bar{S}_{KL} = \lambda_{K2}S^2_{KL} > 0,\\
&\bar{S}_{KK} = (\lambda_{K2}S^2_{KK} + \lambda_{K3}S^3_{KK}) < 0; \bar{S}_{LK} = \lambda_{L2}S^2_{LK} > 0;\\
&A_1 = \lambda_{K3}(S^3_{SK} + S^3_{KS}) > 0; A_2 = (\bar{S}_{KK} - \lambda_{K3}S^3_{SK}) < 0,\\
&A = \frac{W_S.W}{(1+\beta)L_C(W_S - W)^2} > 0, B = \frac{\beta}{(1+\beta)L_C(W_C - b)} > 0;\\
&D = \frac{\beta}{(1+\beta)L_C(W_C - b)^2} > 0; E = L(BW - A);\\
&F = [DW_C(WL + bL)] > 0; G = AL > 0;\\
&H = [DbL(W_C + W)] > 0
\end{aligned}\right\} \tag{7.A.7}$$

S_{ji}^k = the degree of substitutability between factors j and i in the kth sector, j; i = L, L_C, K, S; and k = 1,2,3. For example, $S_{LC}^1 \equiv (W_C/a_{L1})(\partial a_{L1}/\partial W_C)$, $S_{LL}^1 \equiv (W/a_{L1})(\partial a_{L1}/\partial W)$ etc. $S_{ji}^k > 0$ for $j \neq i$; $S_{jj}^k < 0$; $(S_{LL}^1 + S_{LC}^1) = 0 \Rightarrow$ $S_{LL}^1 = -S_{LC}^1$; and $(S_{LL}^2 + S_{LK}^2) = 0$; $(S_{SS}^3 + S_{SK}^3) = 0$ etc. λ_{ji} = proportion of the jth input employed in the ith sector.

Equations (7.A.1)–(7.A.6) are arranged in the following matrix form.

$$
\begin{bmatrix}
\theta_{L1} & \theta_{C1} & \theta_{K1} & 0 & 0 & 0 \\
\theta_{L2} & 0 & \theta_{K2} & 0 & 0 & 0 \\
0 & 0 & \theta_{K3} & \theta_{S3} & 0 & 0 \\
\overline{S}_{LL} & \lambda_{L1}S_{LC}^1 & \overline{S}_{LK} & 0 & \lambda_{L1} & \lambda_{L2} \\
\overline{S}_{KL} & 0 & A_2 & A_1 & \lambda_{K1} & \lambda_{K2} \\
(S_{CL}^1 + E) & (S_{CC}^1 - F) & 0 & G & 1 & 0
\end{bmatrix}
\begin{bmatrix}
\hat{W} \\
\hat{W}_C \\
\hat{R} \\
\hat{W}_S \\
\hat{X}_1 \\
\hat{X}_2
\end{bmatrix}
=
\begin{bmatrix}
0 \\
0 \\
0 \\
0 \\
0 \\
-H\hat{b}
\end{bmatrix}
\qquad (7.A.8)
$$

Solving (7.A.8), we get the following expressions.

$$
\hat{W} = \left(\frac{\hat{b}}{\Delta}\right)(\theta_{S3}\theta_{C1}\theta_{K2}|\lambda|_{LK} H)
\qquad (7.A.9)
$$

$$
\hat{W}_C = -\left(\frac{\hat{b}}{\Delta}\right)(\theta_{S3}|\theta|_{LK}|\lambda|_{LK} H)
\qquad (7.A.10)
$$

$$
\hat{R} = -\left(\frac{\hat{b}}{\Delta}\right)(\theta_{S3}\theta_{C1}\theta_{L2}|\lambda|_{LK} H)
\qquad (7.A.11)
$$

$$
\hat{W}_S = \left(\frac{\hat{b}}{\Delta}\right)(\theta_{K3}\theta_{C1}\theta_{L2}|\lambda|_{LK} H)
\qquad (7.A.12)
$$

and

$$
(\hat{W}_S - \hat{W}) = \left(\frac{\hat{b}H\theta_{C1}|\lambda|_{LK}}{\Delta}\right)(\theta_{K3} - \theta_{K2})
\qquad (7.A.13)
$$

$$
\hat{X}_1 = \left(\frac{H\hat{b}}{\Delta}\right)[\lambda_{L1}\lambda_{K2}|\theta|_{LK} S_{LC}^1 + \theta_{C1}\theta_{L2}\theta_{K3}\lambda_{L2}A_1 + \theta_{C1}\theta_{S3}\{\theta_{L2}(\overline{S}_{LK}\lambda_{K2} - \lambda_{L2}A_2)
$$
$$
\qquad\qquad\qquad\qquad - \theta_{K2}(\overline{S}_{LL}\lambda_{K2} - \lambda_{L2}\overline{S}_{KL})\}]
\qquad (7.A.14)
$$

$$
\hat{X}_2 = -\left(\frac{H\hat{b}}{\Delta}\right)[\lambda_{L1}\lambda_{K1}\theta_{S3}|\theta|_{LK} S_{LC}^1 + \theta_{C1}\theta_{L2}\theta_{K3}\lambda_{L1}A_1
$$
$$
\qquad\qquad + \theta_{C1}\theta_{S3}\{\theta_{L2}(\overline{S}_{LK}\lambda_{K1} - \lambda_{L1}A_2) - \theta_{K2}(\overline{S}_{LL}\lambda_{K1} - \lambda_{L1}\overline{S}_{KL})\}]
\qquad (7.A.15)
$$

where

$$\Delta = -[\theta_{C1}\theta_{L2}(\theta_{K3}A_1\lambda_{L2}) + \theta_{S3}(\bar{S}_{LK}\lambda_{K2} - A_2\lambda_{L2})]$$
$$+ \theta_{S3}|\theta|_{LK}\{(S^1_{CC} - F)|\lambda|_{LK} - \lambda_{K2}\lambda_{L1}S^1_{LC}\}$$
$$- \theta_{S3}\theta_{C1}\theta_{K2}\{(S^1_{CL} + BLW)|\lambda|_{LK} - (\lambda_{K2}\bar{S}_{LL} - \lambda_{L2}\bar{S}_{KL})\}$$
$$+ AL\theta_{C1}|\lambda|_{LK}(\theta_{K2} - \theta_{K3}) \tag{7.A.16}$$

$$\left.\begin{array}{l}|\lambda|_{LK} = (\lambda_{L1}\lambda_{K2} - \lambda_{K1}\lambda_{L2}) > 0; \text{and} \\ |\theta|_{LK} = (\theta_{L1}\theta_{K2} - \theta_{K1}\theta_{L2}) > 0\end{array}\right\} \tag{7.A.17}$$

(Note that $|\lambda|_{LK}, |\theta|_{LK} > 0$ since sector 2 is more capital-intensive than sector 1 with respect to adult unskilled labour.)

Using (7.A.7) and (7.A.17), from (7.A.16) it follows that

$$\Delta < 0 \text{ if } \theta_{K3} > \theta_{K2} \tag{7.A.18}$$

However, $\theta_{K3} > \theta_{K2}$ is only a sufficient condition for Δ to be negative.

Using (7.A.7), (7.A.16) and (7.A.17), from (7.A.9)–(7.A.15) we can obtain the following results.

$$\left.\begin{array}{l}\text{(i)}\,\hat{W} < 0 \quad \text{when} \quad \hat{b} > 0; \\ \text{(ii)}\,\hat{W}_C > 0 \quad \text{when} \quad \hat{b} > 0; \\ \text{(iii)}\,\hat{R} > 0 \quad \text{when} \quad \hat{b} > 0; \\ \text{(iv)}\,\hat{W}_S < 0 \quad \text{when} \quad \hat{b} > 0; \\ \text{(v)}\,\hat{X}_1 < 0 \quad \text{when} \quad \hat{b} > 0; \\ \text{(vi)}\,\hat{X}_2 > 0 \quad \text{when} \quad \hat{b} > 0; \\ \text{(vii)}\,(\hat{W}_S - \hat{W}) < 0 \quad \text{when} \quad \hat{b} > 0; \text{iff } \theta_{K3} > \theta_{K2}\end{array}\right] \tag{7.A.19}$$

Appendix 7.2   Policy consequences on child labour incidence

We use equation (7.2) to examine the impact of the midday meal program on the incidence of child labour in the economy. Totally differentiating equation (7.2), the following expression is obtained.

$$\hat{L}_C = L[(A - BW)\hat{W} - A\hat{W}_S + DW_C(W + b)\hat{W}_C] - H\hat{b}$$

A little manipulation yields

$$\hat{L}_C = -L[A(\hat{W}_S - \hat{W}) - BW\hat{W}] + \hat{W}_C DW_C(W + b)L - H\hat{b} \tag{7.A.20}$$

Using (7.A.9), (7.A.10), (7.A.12) and (7.A.13), the expression (7.A.20) may be rewritten as follows.

$$\hat{L}_C = -\left(\frac{\theta_{C1}H|\lambda|_{LK}}{\Delta}\right)[(\theta_{K3} - \theta_{K2})A + BW\theta_{S3}\theta_{K2}]$$

$$L\hat{b} - H\hat{b}\left[1 + \left(\frac{\theta_{S3}|\theta|_{LK}|\lambda|_{LK}F}{\Delta}\right)\right]$$

(7.A.21)

From (7.A.21), it follows that $\hat{L}_C > 0$ when $b > 0$ if (i) $\theta_{K3} > \theta_{K2}$, and (ii) $\left[1 + \left(\frac{\theta_{S3}|\theta|_{LK}|\lambda|_{LK}F}{\Delta}\right)\right] \leq 0.$

Hence, the incidence of child labour increases owing to the midday meal program and/or school enrollment subsidy under the following two sufficient conditions.

(i) $\theta_{K3} > \theta_{K2}$ and   (ii) $\left[1 + \left(\frac{\theta_{S3}|\theta|_{LK}|\lambda|_{LK}F}{\Delta}\right)\right] \leq 0$

Condition (i) implies that sector 3 is capital-intensive relative to sector 2 (in the Jones-Neary sense), while condition (ii) suggests that the effective child wage does not fall. However, it is not difficult to check that the aggregate supply of child labour may increase even if the effective child wage falls because condition (ii) is only a sufficient but not a necessary one.

Notes

1   Although Chaudhuri and Dwibedi (2007) analyze the effect of a free education policy on the incidence of child labour in a developing economy, their primary concern is to explain the puzzling empirical finding as to why economic growth with foreign capital produces dissimilar results under different circumstances. They consider education subsidy schemes only with the view to recommending the policy in those cases where economic growth fails to combat the child labour problem. Besides, they have used a static general equilibrium framework and hence ignored the aspect of skill formation.
2   The model that has been developed in this chapter is based on Chaudhuri (2010).
3   If we consider that skill formation takes place only through education, the skilled–unskilled wage differential has to be explained in terms of return to education.
4   This assumption eases the algebra a lot. However, someone who goes through Chaudhuri (2010) will find that the qualitative results of the model remains unaffected although the sufficient conditions that are required for the results to hold may change somewhat.
5   It may be noted that in the developing countries most of the children below a certain age, say 10–12, have very negligible bargaining power in the households. The guardian takes the decision about the supply of labour by the children. The guardian may either be altruistically concerned about the welfare of the offspring, as considered in the works of Basu and Van (1998), Ranjan (1999, 2001), Baland and Robinson (2000), Jafarey and Lahiri (2002, 2005) and Chaudhuri and Dwibedi (2006, 2007), among others, or behave selfishly and maximize his own consumption as found in the work of Gupta (2000). However, there is empirical evidence (see, for example, Andvig (2000) and Yasuyuki et al. (2006)) in support

of the fact that teenage workers do have significant intrahousehold bargaining power in determining their labour supply and consumption decision. One has to recourse to collective models like those of Bourguignon and Chiappori (1994) and Moehling (1995) for analyzing intrahousehold bargaining. However, this case has not been considered in the analysis of this chapter. An interesting extension of the present analysis would be to investigate the consequences of the incentive-based schemes on the incidence of child labour in the case where at least some of the children have significant bargaining power in the family regarding their labour supply and schooling decisions.

6 Although informal credit markets as a substitute to missing formal credit markets in the developing countries exist, they mainly deal with short-term loans. Poor households need long-term credit to be able to substitute for the foregone earnings of their children, which is in general not available in the developing countries. In this connection, one may go through Ranjan (1999, 2001), Baland and Robinson (2000) and Jafarey and Lahiri (2002, 2005) etc. The crucial role of credit constraint in explaining inefficient child labour has been empirically verified by Beegle et al. (2003) and Dehejia and Gatti (2003), among others.

7 Although this is a simplifying assumption, it is not completely unrealistic. Agriculture requires material inputs like fertilizers, pesticides, weedicides and the like, which are to be used in recommended doses. Now if capital is used to purchase those inputs, the capital-output ratio becomes constant technologically. However, labour and capital are substitutes, and the production function displays the property of constant returns to scale in these two inputs.

8 This assumption may be justified on the grounds that, as per the ILO (2012) report, more than 59 per cent of economically active children in the developing countries are engaged in agriculture and allied sectors and less than 8 per cent are involved in manufacturing. Nevertheless, even if sector 2 uses child labour, the results of this model hold under different sufficient conditions.

9 This has been proved in appendix 7.1.

10 Here, sectors 2 and 3 use two different types of labour, and there is one intersectorally mobile input, capital. So these two sectors cannot be classified in terms of factor intensities, which is usually done in the Hechscher-Ohlin-Samuelson model. However, a special type of factor intensity classification in terms of the relative distributive shares of the mobile factor (i.e. capital) can be made for analytical purposes. The sector in which this share is higher relative to the other may be considered as capital-intensive in a special sense. See Jones and Neary (1984) for details.

11 See appendix 7.1 for detailed mathematical proof.

12 This has been proved in appendix 7.2.

13 The policy conclusion, however, might be different if incentive programs create strong spillover effects on the people who have not themselves been directly benefited. Vermeersch (2002) has reported that provision of school meals in Kenya led competing local schools to reduce school fees. If the magnitude of externalities created by incentive programs is sufficiently high, these schemes might produce the desired effects in keeping children in school and in producing a favourable impact on the incidence of child labour in the system.

14 That the quality of basic education in India is abysmally poor has been reported in a study of India by the PROBE team (1999). They have also observed that even though parents valued education in its own right, they believed that their children were unlikely to benefit from education in its current state.

15 The introduction of uncertainty in securing a skilled job in the second period would be an interesting theoretical exercise. It may, however, be checked that the results of the model hold if the probability in finding a high-skill job is given exogenously.

16 It may be worthwhile to mention a work by Jafarey and Lahiri (2005) that has examined the relative efficacy of two different policies, 'food subsidy on education'

and 'investment in education quality', for reducing child labour under credit constraint. They have found that the result crucially hinges on the elasticity of the supply of credit.

17 See note 8 in this context.

References

Andvig, J.C. (2000): 'An essay on child labour in Sub-Saharan Africa – A bargaining approach', Norwegian Institute of International Affairs Working Paper No. 613.

Baland, J. and Robinson, J.A. (2000): 'Is child labour inefficient?', *Journal of Political Economy*, 108(4), 663–679.

Basu, K. and Van, P.H. (1998): 'The economics of child labour', *American Economic Review*, 88(3), 412–427.

Becker, G.S. (1964): *Human Capital*, Columbia University Press, New York.

Bedi, A.S. and Garg, A. (2000): 'The effectiveness of private versus public schools: The case of Indonesia', *Journal of Development Economics*, 61, 463–494.

Beegle, K., Dehejia, R.H. and Gatti, R. (2003): 'Child labour, crop shocks, and credit constraints', NBER Working Paper No. W10088.

Bourguignon, F. and Chiappori, P.A. (1994): 'The collective approach to household behaviour', in: R. Blundell, I. Preston and I. Walker (eds.), *The Measurement of Household Welfare*, Cambridge University Press, Cambridge, UK, 70–85.

Chaudhuri, S. (2010): 'Mid-day meal program and incidence of child labour in a developing economy', *Japanese Economic Review*, 61(2), 252–265.

Chaudhuri, S. and Dwibedi, J.K. (2006): 'Trade liberalization in agriculture in developed nations and incidence of child labour in a developing economy', *Bulletin of Economic Research*, 58(2), 129–150.

Chaudhuri, S. and Dwibedi, J.K. (2007): 'Foreign capital inflow, fiscal policies and incidence of child labour in a developing economy', *The Manchester School*, 75(1), 17–46.

Dehejia, R.H. and Gatti, R. (2003): 'Child labour: The role of income variability and credit constraints across countries', NBER Working Paper No. 9018.

Gupta, M.R. (2000): 'Wage determination of a child worker: A theoretical analysis', *Review of Development Economics*, 4(2), 219–228.

ILO. (1999): 'Worst forms of child labour convention', International Labour Office, Geneva.

ILO. (2006): 'The end of child labour: Within reach', International Labour Conference, 95th Session 2006, Report I (B), International Labour Office, Geneva.

ILO. (2012): 'Making progress against child labour: Global estimates and trends 2000–2012', International Labour Office, Geneva.

Jafarey, S. and Lahiri, S. (2002): 'Will trade sanctions reduce child labour? The role of credit markets', *Journal of Development Economics*, 68(1), 137–156.

Jafarey, S. and Lahiri, S. (2005): 'Food for education versus school quality: A comparison of policy options to reduce child labour', *Canadian Journal of Economics*, 38(2), 394–419.

Jimenez, E. and Lockheed, M. (1995): 'Public and private secondary education in developing countries: A comparative study', World Bank Discussion Paper No. 309, The World Bank, Washington, DC.

Jones, R.W. and Neary, P. (1984): 'Positive theory of international trade', in: R.W. Jones and P.B. Kenen (eds.), *Handbook of Development Economics*, Vol. 1, North-Holland, Amsterdam, 1–62.

Kremer, M., Moulin, S. and Namunyu, R. (2002): 'Unbalanced decentralization', Mimeograph, Harvard University.

Miguel, E. and Kremer, M. (2004): 'Worms: Identifying impacts on education and health in the presence of treatment externalities', *Econometrica*, 72(1), 159–217.

Moehling, C.M. (1995): 'The intra-household allocation of resources and the participation of children in household decision-making: Evidence from early twentieth century America', Mimeograph, Northwestern University.

PROBE. (1999): *Public Report on Basic Education in India*, Oxford University Press, New Delhi.

Ranjan, P. (1999): 'An economic analysis of child labour', *Economic Letters*, 64, 99–105.

Ranjan, P. (2001): 'Credit constraints and the phenomenon of child labour', *Journal of Development Economics*, 64, 81–102.

Schultz, T.P. (2004): 'School subsidies for the poor: Evaluating the Mexican Progresa poverty program', *Journal of Development Economics*, 74(1), 199–250.

Sen, A. (2002): 'The Pratichi report', Pratichi India Trust.

Vermeersch, C. (2002): 'School meals, educational achievement and school competition: Evidence from a randomized experiment', Mimeograph, Harvard University.

Yasuyuki, S., Kensuke, K., Nobuhiko, F., Seiro, I. and Kurosaki, T. (2006): 'On the mother and the child labour nexus under credit constraints: Findings from rural', *Developing Economies*, 44(4), 465–499.

8 Economic growth and domestic child labour

8.1 Introduction

The incidence of child labour worldwide has decreased over the last few years, in both absolute and percentage terms. As mentioned in chapter 3, the ILO (2002) reports that one in every six children aged between 5 and 17 – or 246 million children – were involved in child labour. Of those, about 170 million child workers were found in different hazardous and illegal activities. However, revised ILO (2013a) estimates show that 168 million children aged 5–17 years were involved in child labour in 2012 (10.6 per cent), compared to 215 million in 2008 (13.6 per cent)—47 million fewer than in 2008. Compared with the figures in 2002 in absolute terms, the magnitude of decrease has been 78 million. Interestingly, the ILO reports (2013a, 2013b) highlighted some new important dimensions of the problem. There has been an increase in the relative importance of child labour in services in recent years. The share of child labour in services has increased from 26 per cent in 2008 to 32 per cent in 2012. More specifically, among different services rendered by children, the incidence of child labour in domestic work has increased significantly from 10.57 million (4.9 per cent) in 2008 to 11.53 million (6.9 per cent) in 2012.[1]

Why child labour in services like domestic work has increased significantly both in absolute number as well as in terms of activity rate, especially when the incidence of child labour in both counts has appreciably fallen across the globe, is the question of the hour. This kind of child labour falls under the category of the worst form of child labour and is quite exploitative, seriously affecting the mental and proper physical growth of the hapless children who are employed as domestic help. This calls for urgent theoretical explanation(s) so that appropriate corrective measures can be undertaken to get rid of the problem.

The reduction in child labour at a satisfactory rate can largely be attributed to the liberalized economic policies that the developing countries have been pursuing for the last two decades or so.[2] The pace of economic reforms has particularly gathered momentum in the last decade. Barring a couple of years of economic recession, these countries have achieved high rates of economic growth relying mostly on abundant inflows of foreign capital. It is now well-accepted that abject poverty is the root cause behind the incidence of child labour.[3] Economic growth through foreign direct investment (FDI) is believed to work on poverty primarily through the so-called percolation effects. Higher economic growth means higher economic activities, which in turn would lead to higher employment and wages and hence less poverty and poverty-induced child labour. Nevertheless, why FDI-led growth has increasingly pushed children to various services including domestic help is the prime question that needs to be answered.

Under the circumstances, the present chapter is devoted to explore how policies like investment liberalization in the form of increased FDI affects the intersectoral composition of child labour in a developing economy in terms of a four-sector general equilibrium model with a nontraded services sector producing services that are consumed by the richer sector of the population.[4] We also examine the consequences of the policy on the overall incidence of child labour in the economy and on the welfare of the poor child labour–supplying families. Finally, we verbally explained the effectiveness of a supplementary composite public policy that can successfully deal with child labour in the nontraded sector without adversely affecting the overall child labour situation and welfare of the poor families.

8.2 The model

The economy we consider is a small open developing economy, which is divided into two informal sectors and two formal sectors. Three types of labour are available in the economy: adult unskilled labour (L), child labour (L_C) and skilled labour (S). Sector 1 (an informal sector) produces an exportable agricultural commodity, X_1, with the help of adult unskilled labour, child labour and capital (K). The per-unit requirement of capital to produce one unit of output of commodity 1, a_{K1}, is assumed to be technologically given.[5] Sector 2 is a low-skill formal manufacturing sector that uses adult unskilled labour and capital as inputs. This is also the import-competing sector of the economy. Adult unskilled workers in sector 2 earn a high exogenously given wage, W^*, while their counterparts in sector 1 earn a competitive wage, W with $W^* > W$.[6] Because of this intersectoral wage differential, there is distortion in the market for adult unskilled labour in sector 2. The other formal sector (sector 3) produces a high-skill commodity (e.g. computer software) by means of skilled labour and capital. The country exports goods 1 (agricultural commodity) and goods 3 (high-skill commodity), while it is a net importer of the low-skill goods (commodity 2). This diversified trade pattern is suitable to a country like India, which exports both high-skill and primary agricultural commodities.[7] The second informal sector (sector C) produces a nontraded final commodity (domestic services), X_C, using child labour only. This goes without saying that the use of child labour as domestic help is highly exploitative in nature because in most cases the children are subjected too much physical and mental harassment.[8] Generally, the services provided by child workers as domestic help are used by the richer segment of the population consisting of adult unskilled workers employed in the highly paid sector 2, skilled workers and the capitalists.[9]

While skilled labour is specific to sector 3, capital is perfectly mobile between the first three sectors, and its economy-wide return is r. Besides, there is also complete mobility of child labour between sectors 1 and C that leads to the uniform child wage, W_C, in those two sectors. However, adult labour is imperfectly mobile between sector 1 and sector 2. The allocation mechanism of unskilled labour between sector 1 and sector 2 in this model is the following.

Adult unskilled workers first compete for jobs in sector 2, where the wage rate is high because of institutional factors. However, those who cannot get employment in that sector are automatically absorbed into sector 1 providing the competitive wage. Hence, there remains no unemployment in the adult unskilled labour market equilibrium. Besides, workers employed in sector 2 do not have any restrictions to move to sector 1. Nevertheless, they will not move because of the high wage. On the contrary, workers absorbed in sector 1 cannot switch over to sector 2 despite their willingness because the number of jobs in the latter sector is limited. Hence, we have imperfect labour mobility between the two sectors of the economy. However, an exogenous shock can affect the output composition and the employment levels that would lead to reallocation of labour between the two sectors of the economy.

The exogenously given endowments of skilled labour, adult unskilled labour and capital in the economy are S, L and K, respectively, while the endowment of child labour, L_C is endogenously determined.[10] The aggregate stock of capital in the economy consists of both domestic capital (K_D) and foreign capital (K_F), which are perfect substitutes. All foreign capital income is repatriated. All the factors of production are fully employed. All markets, except the adult labour market in sector 2, are perfectly competitive. Production functions exhibit constant returns to scale with diminishing marginal productivity to each factor.[11] The prices of the three traded commodities, P_is or $i = 1, 2, 3$, are internationally given because of the small open economy assumption. Since the commodity (services) produced by the child labour is produced and consumed domestically, its price is determined within the country by the demand–supply mechanism.

Because sector 1 and sector 2 use two common factors, adult unskilled labour and capital, these two can be classified in terms of factor intensities. It is quite natural to assume that sector 2 is more capital-intensive vis-à-vis sector 1 with respect to adult unskilled labour in value terms, which means $\dfrac{a_{K2}}{W^* a_{L2}} > \dfrac{a_{K1}}{Wa_{L1}}$ where a_{ji} is the amount of the jth input required to produce 1 unit of output in the ith sector for $j = L, K$ and $i = 1,2$.

8.2.1 *The equational structure*

As previously stated, the aggregate supply of child labour in the economy is endogenously determined from the optimizing behaviour of the altruistic poor unskilled working households who send out some of their children to the job market due to utter poverty.

The aggregate supply function of child labour in the economy is given as follows.

$$L_C = l_C a_{L1} X_1 = [(1-\gamma)n - \gamma(W/W_C)]a_{L1}X_1 \tag{8.1}$$

The supply of child labour comes only from the families of the unskilled workers employed in sector 1. Each family consists of one adult member (guardian) and n

number of children. The adult member takes all of the decisions on behalf of the family. The supply of child labour by each family, l_c, is determined by maximizing the family welfare function, $U = \bar{A}(C_1)^\alpha (C_2)^\beta (n - l_c)^\gamma$ with $\bar{A} > 0$, $1 > \alpha$, β, $\gamma > 0$ and $(\alpha + \beta + \gamma) = 1$. Here C_i denotes family consumption of the ith good for $i = 1, 2$, and $(n - l_c)$ denotes children's leisure. These families consume neither the nontraded commodity, C, nor the high-skill commodity, X_3. The family welfare function is maximized with respect to C_1, C_2 and l_c and subject to the family budget constraint, $C_1 + P_2 C_2 = (W_C l_C + W)$. The detailed derivation of this function has been provided in chapter 2.

Given the assumption of perfectly competitive commodity markets, the usual zero-profit conditions relating to the four sectors of the economy are given by the following four equations, respectively.

$$a_{L1}W + a_{C1}W_C + a_{K1}r = P_1 \tag{8.2}$$
$$a_{L2}W^* + a_{K2}r = P_2 \tag{8.3}$$
$$a_{S3}W_S + a_{K3}r = P_3 \tag{8.4}$$
$$a_{CC}W_C = P_C \tag{8.5}$$

Complete utilization of adult unskilled labour, capital, skilled labour and child labour imply the following four equations, respectively.

$$a_{L1}X_1 + a_{L2}X_2 = L \tag{8.6}$$
$$a_{K1}X_1 + a_{K2}X_2 + a_{K3}X_3 = K_D + K_F = K \tag{8.7}$$
$$a_{S3}X_3 = S \tag{8.8}$$
$$a_{C1}X_1 + a_{CC}X_C = L_C \tag{8.9}$$

The richer segment of the society consumes the goods (services) produced (rendered) by child labour in sector C. In this model, the richer segment of the economy consists of skilled workers, unskilled workers employed in the high wage–paying sector (sector 2) and the capitalists.[12] We assume that a fixed fraction, α, of the aggregate income of the affluent people, Y, is spent on this commodity. Therefore, the demand function for commodity C is written as follows.

$$D = \alpha \left(\frac{Y}{P_C} \right) = \alpha \left(\frac{W^* a_{L3}X_3 + W_S S + rK_D}{P_C} \right); 1 > \alpha > 0 \tag{8.10}$$

where

$$Y = W^* a_{L2}X_2 + W_S S + rK_D \tag{8.11}$$

Note that the entire foreign capital income is repatriated and hence is not included in the aggregate income of the rich people, Y.

It is quite evident from equation (8.10) that the income elasticity $\left(E_Y = \left(\frac{\partial D}{\partial Y} \frac{Y}{D} \right) \right)$ and the own price elasticity $\left(E_Y = \left(\frac{\partial D}{\partial Y} \frac{Y}{D} \right) \right)$ of demand for goods (services) C are equal to 1 and –1, respectively. The cross-price elasticities are equal to zero.[13]

The demand for the nontraded final commodity (services) must be equal to its supply, in equilibrium. Hence, the equilibrium condition in the market for commodity C is as follows.

$$\alpha \left(\frac{W^* a_{L3} X_3 + W_S S + r K_D}{P_C} \right) = X_C \tag{8.12}$$

Using (8.1), one may rewrite equation (8.9).

$$a_{C1} X_1 + a_{CC} X_C = [(1 - \gamma)n - \gamma(W / W_C)](a_{L1} X_1) \tag{8.9.1}$$

Furthermore, with the help of (8.8), one can rewrite equation (8.7) as follows.

$$a_{K1} X_1 + a_{K2} X_2 + \left(\frac{a_{K3}}{a_{S3}} S \right) = K_D + K_F = K \tag{8.7.1}$$

In this general equilibrium structure, there are 12 endogenous variables (W, W_C, W_S, r, P_C, D, Y, X_1, X_2, X_3, X_C, and L_C) and same number of independent equations (equations (8.1)–(8.8), (8.9.1) and (8.10)–(8.12). Equations (8.2)–(8.5) together constitute the price system with five endogenous variables: W, W_C, W_S, r and P_C. This implies that the system does not satisfy the decomposition property. Hence, at least some of these variables depend not only on commodity prices but also on factor endowments. How all of the endogenous variables in this system are determined is described as follows.

The return to capital, r, is determined from equation (8.3) because W^* is exogenously given. The skilled wage, W_S, is then found from (8.4). Hence, r and W_S depend only on commodity prices. Any changes in factor endowments cannot affect them. Because r has already been obtained, W and W_C can be obtained from equations (8.2) and (8.5) as functions of P_C. Since the factor-coefficients, a_{ji} s, are functions of factor prices, these are automatically known. Then, solving equations (8.6), (8.7.1) and (8.9.1) simultaneously, one can find out X_1, X_2 and X_C as functions of P_C. L_C and Y are found from equations (8.1) and (8.11), respectively. Then D is found from (8.10). Finally, the equilibrium value of P_C can be obtained from (8.12). Once P_C is found, the equilibrium values of all other variables are determined. Note that we have already determined the equilibrium value of X_3 from equation (8.8).

8.3 Comparative statics

Because poverty is considered to be the main factor responsible for the prevalence of child labour, it can be expected that high economic growth with inflows of foreign capital via its so-called trickle-down effects would lower poverty, thereby putting a significant brake on the problem. We have already pointed out that although the global incidence of child labour has decreased over time, in some sectors where children are involved in hazardous activities, the incidence has been on the rise. Therefore, it is quite important to examine the consequence of economic growth on the sectoral allocation of child labour using a general equilibrium structure. Hence, this section of the chapter is devoted to studying the outcomes of FDI-led economic growth on both the magnitude of child labour and its sectoral allocation in this small open developing economy.

The aggregate supply of child labour is the number of children sent out to work per poor working family, l_C, multiplied by the number of poor families, $L_1 = \alpha_{L1}X_1$ (see equation (8.1)). The family supply of child labour is a negative function of the (W/W_C) ratio. Therefore, to know what happens to W/W_C and L_1 is of extreme importance. On the other hand, to see whether the use of child labour in activities like domestic help has relatively increased, we need to analyze the change in the proportion of aggregate number of child labour employed in sector C (i.e. λ_{CC}). Both of these issues crucially hinge on the effect of FDI flow on the price of the nontraded goods produced by children (i.e. P_C).

To examine the effects of FDI on W/W_C, L_1 and P_C, we totally differentiate equations (8.2)–(8.8), (8.9.1) and (8.10)–(8.12) and obtain some important results that are stated in terms of the following proposition.[14]

Proposition 8.1: FDI flow leads to (i) an increase in P_C; (ii) a decrease in the competitive unskilled wage W; (ii) an increase in the child wage, W_C; (iv) a decrease in the (W/W_C) ratio; (v) an increase (a decrease) in the output of sector 2 (sector 1); and (vi) an increase (a decrease in) in adult unskilled employment in sector 2, $L_2 = \alpha_{L2}X_2$ (in sector 1, $L_1 = \alpha_{L1}X_1$). The high-skill sector (sector 3), the skilled wage, W_S and the return to capital, r, however, remain unaffected.

Proposition 8.1 is verbally explained in the following manner. FDI flow raises the aggregate capital stock of the economy, K, and leads to changes in all the endogenous variables except the skilled wage and the return to capital, r. The return to capital, r, does not change as the high adult unskilled wage in sector 2, W^*, is exogenously given (see equation 8.3). Because of this, the skilled wage, W_S, also remains unaffected (see equation 8.4). FDI flow affects the factor prices and the output levels of different sectors both directly and indirectly. The indirect effects take place through the change in P_C. Owing to an increase in K, a Rybczynski effect takes place that leads to an expansion of sector 2 and a contraction of sector 1 because the former sector is more capital-intensive (with respect to adult unskilled labour) vis-à-vis sector 1. For the expansion of sector 2, more adult unskilled labour is required that comes from sector 1. Because the higher wage-paying sector 2 is now employing more adult unskilled workers than previously, the aggregate income of the richer segment of the population, Y, rises (see equation 8.11), and that increases the demand for commodity (services) C given its price, P_C (see equation 8.10). Whether the output level, X_C, increases or not depends on the availability of child labour to this sector. However, we find that P_C must increase in the stable equilibrium since its demand has increased.[15] Nonetheless, the direction of change in the supply, X_C, determines the magnitude of increase in P_C. If the supply falls (rises), the increase in P_C would be relatively high (low).

Since, the child wage, W_C, is positively related to P_C (see equation 8.5), an increase in P_C raises W_C. In order to maintain zero-profit in sector 1, the competitive adult unskilled wage, W, must fall (see equation 8.2). Note that the international price of commodity 1 is exogenously given by the small open economy assumption and that the return to capital, r, does not change due to FDI flow. This means that the (W/W_C) ratio decreases.

Apart from the direct impacts of FDI flow on X_1 and X_2 that take place through the Rybczynski effect, there would also be induced effects that occur through an increase in P_C. We have seen that an increase in P_C lowers both (W/W_C) and X_1, which in turn affects the supply of child labour (see equation 8.1). Our analysis finds that sector 1 contracts further and releases some amount of capital that goes to sector 2, causing it to expand further. Therefore, both the direct and the indirect effects work together and lead to an unequivocal expansion of sector 2 and a contraction of sector 1.

Because W^* is exogenously given and r does not change due to FDI flow, the unskilled labour-output ratio in sector 2, α_{12}, remains unaffected. Therefore, the level of employment of adult unskilled labour in sector 2, $L_2(= a_{12}X_2)$ unambiguously increases. Since this is a full-employment model, an increase in L_2 implies a decrease in employment of adult unskilled labour in sector 1, $L_1(= a_{L1}X_1)$.

Let us now study the outcome of FDI flow on the incidence of child labour in the economy. For this purpose, we use the aggregate child labour supply function, which is given by equation (8.1). We note that FDI flow affects the supply of child labour in two ways: (i) through a change in the size of the adult unskilled labour force employed in sector 1 (i.e. $a_{L1}X_1$), since these families are considered to be the suppliers of child labour; and (ii) through a change in l_e (the number of child workers supplied by each poor family), which results from a change in the (W/W_C) ratio. Differentiating equations (8.1)–(8.5), (8.9.1) and (8.12) and using the stability condition in the market for commodity C, we can derive the following expression.[16]

$$\left(\frac{\hat{L}_C}{\hat{K}}\right) = -\left(\frac{L_2\lambda_{L1}}{L_1|\lambda|^{LK}}\right) - \left(\frac{\theta_{C1}+\theta_{L1}}{\theta_{L1}}\right)\Theta\left[\left(\frac{L_2}{L_1}\right)\left(\frac{\lambda_{K1}\lambda_{L1}S_{LC}^1}{|\lambda|^{LK}}\right) - \left(\frac{\gamma W}{W_C l_c}\right)\right] \quad (8.13)$$

Here, θ_{ji} is the distributive share of the jth factor in sector 1 for $j = L, L_C$; λ_{j1} is the allocative share of the jth input in sector 1 for $j = L, K$; and $|\lambda|^{LK}$, S_{LC}^1, Θ and γ are positive terms defined in the Appendices. Others symbols have been defined previously.

It is evident from equation (8.13) that $\left(\frac{\hat{L}_C}{\hat{K}}\right) < 0$ if $\left(\frac{\lambda_{K1}\lambda_{L1}S_{LC}^1}{|\lambda|^{LK}}\right) \geq \left(\frac{\gamma W}{W_C l_c}\right)$. This condition is satisfied if γ is sufficiently low and/or income from child labour in a family relative to adult unskilled income is sufficiently high.

However, from (8.13), it is also clear that there could be a couple of other sufficient conditions subject to any one of which the incidence of child labour in the society falls following FDI flow. Hence, the following proposition can now be established.

Proposition 8.2: Inflows of foreign capital lower the incidence of child labour in the economy if $\left(\frac{\lambda_{K1}\lambda_{L1}S_{LC}^1}{|\lambda|^{LK}}\right) \geq \left(\frac{\gamma W}{W_C l_c}\right)$.

We have already explained how FDI flow lowers both the (W/W_C) ratio and the employment level of unskilled labour in sector 1, $a_{L1}X_1$. As (W/W_C) falls, the supply of child labour by each poor family, l_e, rises given $a_{L1}X_1$. Note that $a_{L1}X_1$ is the number of poor unskilled working families that supply child labour. This pushes up the aggregate supply of child labour (see equation 8.1). We call it the *relative wage effect*. On the other hand, as $a_{L1}X_1$ falls, the aggregate supply of child labour falls at the given (W/W_C) ratio. This may be termed as the *adult unskilled labour reallocation effect*. Thus, we find that there are two opposite effects on the aggregate supply of child labour. The net outcome would depend on the relative strengths of the two effects. Our analysis finds that the latter effect dominates over the former under the sufficient condition as provided in proposition 8.2.

We now proceed to investigate the result of inflows of foreign capital on the sectoral allocation of child labour. The proportion of the child labour force employed in sector 1, denoted λ_{C1}, is given by the following.

$$\lambda_{C1} = \frac{a_{C1}X_1}{L_C} = \frac{a_{C1}X_1}{l_C X_1} = \frac{a_{C1}}{l_C a_{L1}} \tag{8.14}$$

From proposition 8.1, we note that FDI flow raises W_C, although the policy lowers W, $\left(\dfrac{W}{W_C}\right)$ and X_1. The supply of child labour by each poor working family, l_c, increases as $\left(\dfrac{W}{W_C}\right)$ falls. On the other hand, producers in sector 1 would substitute child labour by adult unskilled labour because the adult unskilled wage relative to child wage has fallen. This raises the adult unskilled labour-output ratio, a_{L1}, and lowers the child labour-output ratio, a_{C1}. From equation (8.14), it is evident that λ_{C1} falls. Note that $\hat{\lambda}_{CC} = -\left(\dfrac{\lambda_{C1}}{\lambda_{CC}}\right)\hat{\lambda}_{C1}$ because $(\lambda_{C1} + \lambda_{CC}) = 1$. Therefore, a decrease in λ_{C1} means an increase in λ_{CC}. This establishes the following proposition.

Proposition 8.3: FDI flow unequivocally drives child workers to domestic work in an increasing proportion.

Finally, we intend to study the impact of FDI flow on the welfare of the child labour–supplying families. We capture this in terms of the family utility function as presented in section 8.2.1. The optimum utility of the family depends on both the competitive adult unskilled wage and the child wage. Differentiating the indirect utility function, the following proposition can be proved.[17]

Proposition 8.4: Inflows of foreign capital unambiguously improve the welfare of each child labour–supplying family.

FDI flow lowers the competitive adult unskilled wage worker, W, although it raises the child wage rate, W_C. Since the family income from nonchild sources falls and the opportunity cost of children's leisure (the child wage) rises, the guardian will send more children to the job market to supplement low family income. Hence, l_C and $W_C l_C$ increase, which would outweigh the fall in W. Consequently, the aggregate family income unambiguously rises. The positive income effect leads to increases in the consumption of all of the commodities including children's leisure. On the other hand, because the opportunity cost of children's leisure (child wage) has increased, there would be a downward pressure on the consumption of children's leisure due to a negative price effect. Our analysis finds that the price effect would outweigh the income effect. Therefore, the net effect would be a decrease in the household's consumption of children's leisure, ($n - l_C$), and hence an increase in l_C. Although this works negatively on the welfare of the family, the increase in family welfare caused due to increases in material goods outweighs the decrease in household utility resulting from a decrease in children's leisure. Hence, family welfare unambiguously improves.

8.4 Role of a supplementary composite policy

It is understood that the incidence of child labour in the developing economies cannot be completely mitigated and that its complete elimination may not be desirable, particularly because the use of child labour after a certain age in some nonhazardous activities leads to on-the-job training that raises their future earning possibilities. Because of the very pathetic condition of primary education, the rate of return to education in these countries is extremely poor (see PROBE report 1999). Hence, a free education policy of the government cannot keep children in school. When the poor guardians find that sending children to school does not lead to skill formation to the extent that could increase their children's future job prospects, they find it worthwhile to send them out to the job market for some immediate gains and increase their family income, at least in the short run. It seems that no outside interventions to eliminate child labour are desirable unless the quality of free primary education can be improved. Nonetheless, the authorities should take the necessary steps to control, to the extent possible, the use of children in hazardous and exploitative activities that badly affect their proper mental and physical growth and that lower their future earning opportunities.

In the model that we have considered in this chapter, FDI-led growth indeed lowers the incidence of child labour, although it drives the children to hazardous and exploitative services in an increasing proportion. In order to take care of the latter undesirable effect of FDI flow, there is urgent need on the part of the regulatory authority to resort to certain supplementary measures. We are now going to explore the consequences of certain composite supplementary policies that should accompany the liberalized investment policy that could mitigate not only the problem of child labour but also at the same time ensure that the hapless working children do not move to the hazardous sector. In the existing set-up, the problem crops up due to an increase in the demand for the hazardous services rendered by child labour originating from the increase in the resulting aggregate income of the richer segment of the population due to FDI-led growth. Hence, the supplementary policies should contain an instrument ensuring that the demand for goods/ services involving hazardous child labour must decrease and another instrument raises the aggregate income of each poor family from nonchild sources.

Such a supplementary composite policy could be a program of direct cash transfer to poor people the cost of which may be financed through the imposition of lump-sum taxes on the richer segment of the population.[18] Let us suppose that the government decides to transfer a fixed amount of money, M, to each of the poor people (unskilled families) engaged in sector 1. Thus, the amount of funds that the government would require is $Ma_{L1}X_1$, where $a_{L1}X_1$ is the number of poor adult unskilled workers (families) employed in sector 1. This amount of money is financed through the imposition of a lump-sum tax on the richer people, T, consisting of capitalists, skilled workers and unskilled workers employed in sector 2. The cash transfer program is expected to increase the aggregate income of each family from its nonchild sources (i.e. $(W + M)$), while the tax on the richer people would decrease their income and hence the aggregate demand for the nontraded services rendered by child labour. Although the budget of the government always remains balanced, T has to be necessarily adjusted with a change in $a_{L1}X_1$ so that the authority can indeed transfer the amount of money, M, to each of the poor people.

Thus, the balanced-budget condition of the government is written as follows.

$$T = Ma_{L1}X_1 \tag{8.15}$$

Note that in (8.15), T and M comprise the supplementary composite policy that the government may undertake along with the liberalized investment policy that brings more foreign capital into the host country. Then the task of the government would be to carefully determine the values of these two policy variables so that favourable outcomes always take place.

The aggregate income of the richer segment of the population given by equation (8.11) has to be rewritten as follows.

$$Y = W * a_{L2}X_2 + W_sS + rK_D - T \tag{8.11.1}$$

The supply function of child labour by each poor family and the aggregate child labour function are then, respectively rewritten as follows.

$$l_C = \left[(1 - \gamma)n - \gamma\{(W + M)/W_C\}\right] \tag{8.16}$$

and

$$L_C = l_C a_{L1}X_1 = \left[(1 - \gamma)n - \gamma\{(W + M)/W_C\}\right]a_{L1}X_1 \tag{8.17}$$

In a static model like this, it is not possible to mathematically find out the net effect of all of the policies if carried out simultaneously. However, it is possible to give some rough ideas about their overall effects on the endogenous variables intuitively.

Inflows of foreign capital produce a Rybczynski effect and leads to an expansion (a contraction) of sector 2 (sector 1), in terms of both output and employment of unskilled labour. More adult unskilled workers are now employed in sector 2 that offers a high wage. This leads to an increase in Y, raising the demand for services, C, rendered by child labour. Nevertheless, this time by increasing T, the government can mop up the additional income of the richer segment of the population so that the demand for C and consequently its price, P_C, cannot increase.

Since some adult unskilled workers move from sector 1 to sector 2, the competitive adult unskilled wage, W, should increase, and the child wage, W_C, should decrease to satisfy the price-unit cost equality condition in sector 1. Since $\{(W + M)/W_C\}$ rises, the supply of child labour by each poor family, l_C, falls. From equation (8.1), it then follows that the aggregate number of child labour in the society, L_C, must also fall because the number of child labour–supplying families, $a_{L1}X_1$, has fallen. On the other hand, family welfare definitely improves because an increase in nonchild income, $(W + M)$, makes it possible for the family to increase the consumption levels of all of commodities including children's leisure. Finally, because the (W/W_C) ratio rises, the producers in sector 1 would substitute adult labour by child labour that lowers a_{L1} and raises a_{C1}. From equation (8.14), it follows that λ_{C1} unquestionably rises. Consequently, the proportion of child labour employed in sector C, λ_{CC}, unambiguously falls.

8.5 Concluding remarks

It is quite puzzling as to why the use of child labour as domestic help has significantly increased in recent times in both absolute and percentage terms even though the overall incidence of child labour in the developing countries has satisfactorily decreased. Because domestic child labour is hazardous and exploitative, the problem should draw the attention of economists and policy makers. Given that no attempt has so far been made to explain this peculiar empirical finding theoretically and to suggest measures to tackle the problem, the theoretical exercise in this chapter purports to address this problem in terms of a four-sector general equilibrium model with a nontraded sector that produces a final commodity (services) for the richer segment of the society with the help of child labour only. Sector 1 is an informal sector (agriculture) that uses adult unskilled labour, child labour and capital, while sector 2 is the formal import-competing sector that produces a low-skill manufacturing commodity by means of adult unskilled labour and capital. Adult unskilled workers in sector 2 earn a high institutionally given wage vis-à-vis their counterparts in sector 1. Sector 3 (another formal sector) produces a high-skill commodity using skilled labour and capital. The supply of child labour solely comes from the families of the poor unskilled workers employed in sector 1. Child labour and capital are perfectly mobile intersectorally, while adult labour is imperfectly mobile between sector 1 and sector 2. Skilled labour is specific to sector 3. The price of the nontraded services provided by child labour is determined domestically by the demand–supply mechanism. In this scenario, we have analyzed the consequences of FDI-led economic growth on the overall incidence of child labour and its sectoral allocation and on the welfare of the child labour–supplying families. Our analysis has found that the proportion of children employed as domestic help and family welfare unambiguously increases while the aggregate supply (hence incidence) decreases subject to any one of the few meaningful sufficient conditions. Then we have proceeded to recommend a supplementary composite policy in the form of the imposition of a lump-sum tax on the richer segment of the population comprised of capitalists, skilled workers and higher-earning unskilled workers and the redistribution of the tax proceeds to the poor families through the direct cash transfer scheme. Without resorting to mathematics, we have intuitively explained why such a composite policy would be successful not only in reducing the use of child labour as domestic help but also in bringing down the overall incidence of child labour in the economy and in improving the welfare of poor families. Finally, despite abstraction and simplicity, this work deserves some attention because it addresses a new dimension of the child labour problem and suggests measures to deal with the situation.

Appendices

Appendix 8.1   Some useful expressions

Totally differentiating equations (8.2)–(8.5), we can derive the following expressions.

$$
\left.
\begin{aligned}
\hat{r} &= 0 \\
\hat{W}_S &= 0 \\
\hat{W}_C &= \hat{P}_C \\
\hat{W} &= -\frac{\theta_{C1}}{\theta_{L1}}\hat{P}_C
\end{aligned}
\right\}
\tag{8.A.1}
$$

where $'\wedge'$ = proportional change (e.g. $\hat{P}_C \equiv \dfrac{dP_C}{P_C}$).

Totally differentiating equation (8.8) and using (8.A.1), it is easy to show that

$$
\hat{X}_3 = 0 \tag{8.A.2}
$$

Now totally differentiating equations (8.6), (8.7.1) and (8.9.1), using (8.A.1) and simplifying, we can find the following expressions, respectively.

$$
\left.
\begin{aligned}
\lambda_{L1}\hat{X}_1 + \lambda_{L2}\hat{X}_2 &= -B_1\hat{P}_C \\
\lambda_{K1}\hat{X}_1 + \lambda_{K2}\hat{X}_2 &= \hat{K} \\
-\lambda_{CC}\hat{X}_1 + \lambda_{CC}\hat{X}_C &= B_2\hat{P}_C
\end{aligned}
\right\}
\tag{8.A.3}
$$

where

$$
\left.
\begin{aligned}
B_1 &= \lambda_{L1}S_{LC}^1\left(\frac{\theta_{C1}+\theta_{L1}}{\theta_{L1}}\right) > 0 \\
B_2 &= \left[\left(\lambda_{C1}S_{CL}^1 + S_{LC}^1 + \frac{\gamma W}{l_C W_C}\right)\left(\frac{\theta_{C1}+\theta_{L1}}{\theta_{L1}}\right)\right] > 0
\end{aligned}
\right\}
\tag{8.A.4}
$$

where S_{ji}^1 = the degree of substitution between factors j and i in sector 1 for j,i = L, L_C. For example, $S_{CL}^1 \equiv (\partial a_{C1}/\partial W)(W/a_{C1})$, $S_{CC}^1 \equiv (\partial a_{C1}/\partial W_C)(W_C/a_{C1})$

and so on. $S_{ji}^1 > 0$ for $j \neq i$; and $S_{jj}^1 < 0$. Besides, $\left(S_{ji}^1 + S_{jj}^1\right) = 0$ because factor-coefficients, a_{ji}s, are homogeneous of degree zero in factor prices.

Arranging the expressions of (8.A.3) in matrix notation, we write the following.

$$
\begin{bmatrix}
\lambda_{L1} & \lambda_{L2} & 0 \\
\lambda_{K1} & \lambda_{K2} & 0 \\
-\lambda_{C1} & 0 & \lambda_{CC}
\end{bmatrix}
\begin{bmatrix}
\hat{X}_1 \\
\hat{X}_2 \\
\hat{X}_C
\end{bmatrix}
=
\begin{bmatrix}
-B_1 \hat{P}_C \\
\hat{K} \\
B_2 \hat{P}_C
\end{bmatrix}
\tag{8.A.5}
$$

Solving (8.A.5) and simplifying, we can obtain the following expressions.

$$
\hat{X}_1 = -\left(\frac{\lambda_{CC}\lambda_{L2}}{|\lambda|}\right)\hat{K} - \left(\frac{A_1}{|\lambda|}\right)\hat{P}_C
\tag{8.A.6}
$$

$$
\hat{X}_2 = \left(\frac{\lambda_{CC}\lambda_{L1}}{|\lambda|}\right)\hat{K} + \left(\frac{A_2}{|\lambda|}\right)\hat{P}_C
\tag{8.A.7}
$$

$$
\hat{X}_C = -\left(\frac{\lambda_{CC}\lambda_{L2}}{|\lambda|}\right)\hat{K} + \left(\frac{A_3}{|\lambda|}\right)\hat{P}_C
\tag{8.A.8}
$$

where

$$
\left.
\begin{aligned}
&|\lambda| = \lambda_{CC}(\lambda_{L1}\lambda_{K2} - \lambda_{K1}\lambda_{L2}) > 0 \quad \text{(because sector 2 is more capital-intensive} \\
&\hspace{5.5cm}\text{vis-à-vis sector 1 with respect to adult} \\
&\hspace{5.5cm}\text{unskilled labour)} \\
&A_1 = \lambda_{CC}\lambda_{K2}B_1 > 0 \\
&A_2 = \lambda_{CC}\lambda_{K1}B_1 > 0 \\
&A_3 = (|\lambda_{LK}|B_2 - B_1\lambda_{CC}\lambda_{K2}) \\
&|\lambda|^{LK} = (\lambda_{L1}\lambda_{K2} - \lambda_{K1}\lambda_{L2}) > 0
\end{aligned}
\right\}
\tag{8.A.9}
$$

Using (8.A.4) and (8.A.9) and simplifying, we can rewrite the expression for A_3 as follows.

$$
A_3 = \left(\frac{\theta_{C1} + \theta_{L1}}{\theta_{L1}}\right)\left[\begin{array}{l}(\lambda_{L1}\lambda_{K2} - \lambda_{K1}\lambda_{L2})\left(\lambda_{C1}S_{CL}^1 + \dfrac{\gamma W}{l_C W_C}\right) \\ + (\lambda_{C1}\lambda_{K2}\lambda_{L1} - \lambda_{K1}\lambda_{L2})S_{LC}^1\end{array}\right] > 0 \text{ if } (\lambda_{C1}\lambda_{K2}\lambda_{L1} \geq \lambda_{K1}\lambda_{L2})
\tag{8.A.10}
$$

Appendix 8.2 Stability condition of the market for good C

Because commodity C is nontraded, its market must clear domestically. The stability condition in the market for commodity C requires that $(d(D - X_C)/dP_C) < 0$. This implies around equilibrium, initially, $D = X_C$. Thus, $((\hat{D}/\hat{P}_C) - (\hat{X}_C/\hat{P}_C)) < 0$.

Differentiating the demand function for commodity C given by equation (8.10), the following expression can be derived.

$$
\hat{D} = \left(\frac{W^* a_{L2} X_2}{Y}\right)\hat{X}_2 - \hat{P}_C
\tag{8.A.11}
$$

Substituting $\hat{X}_2$ from (8.A.7) in (8.A.11), collecting terms and simplifying, we obtain the following expression.

$$\hat{D} = M\hat{P}_C + \Upsilon_L\left(\frac{\lambda_{CC}\lambda_{L1}}{|\lambda|}\right)\hat{K} \tag{8.A.12}$$

where

$$M = \left[\Upsilon_L\left(\frac{A_2}{|\lambda|}\right) - 1\right]$$

and Υ_L is the share of adult unskilled labour income in Υ (i.e. $\Upsilon_L = \dfrac{W^* a_{L2} X_2}{\Upsilon}$).

Allowing only P_C to change and keeping all parameters unchanged from (8.A.12), we find that

$$\left(\frac{\hat{D}}{\hat{P}_C}\right) = M \tag{8.A.13}$$

Now, turning back to the supply side of commodity C, from equation (8.A.8) we get the following.

$$\left(\frac{\hat{X}_C}{\hat{P}_C}\right) = \left(\frac{A_3}{|\lambda|}\right) \tag{8.A.14}$$

Therefore, using (8.A.13) and (8.A.14), we find that for stability in the market for commodity C, one requires the following.

$$\left(\frac{\hat{D}}{\hat{P}_C} - \frac{\hat{X}_C}{\hat{P}_C}\right) = \left[M - \left(\frac{A_3}{|\lambda|}\right)\right] = \Psi < 0 \tag{8.A.15}$$

Appendix 8.3   Effect of FDI flow on P_C

In equilibrium, in the market for commodity C, we have $\hat{X}_C^D = \hat{X}_C$. Now using (8.A.8) and (8.A.12), we can write

$$M\hat{P}_C + \Upsilon_L\left(\frac{\lambda_{CC}\lambda_{L1}}{|\lambda|}\right)\hat{K} = -\left(\frac{\lambda_{CC}\lambda_{L2}}{|\lambda|}\right)\hat{K} + \left(\frac{A_3}{|\lambda|}\right)\hat{P}_C$$

or

$$\left[M - \left(\frac{A_3}{|\lambda|}\right)\right]\hat{P}_C = -\left[\frac{\lambda_{CC}(\Upsilon_L\lambda_{L1} + \lambda_{L2})}{|\lambda|}\right]\hat{K}$$

Using (8.A.15), the preceding expression may be rewritten as follows.

$$\left(\frac{\hat{P}_C}{\hat{K}}\right) = \Theta > 0 \tag{8.A.16}$$

where

$$\Theta = -\left[\frac{\lambda_{CC}(\Upsilon_L \lambda_{L1} + \lambda_{L2})}{\Psi|\lambda|}\right] > 0 \tag{8.A.17}$$

Hence, inflows of foreign capital raise the price of the commodity (services) produced (rendered) by child labour in sector C.

Appendix 8.4   Effects of FDI flow on factor prices and output composition

Using (8.A.16) and simplifying from equation (8.A.1), we obtain the following results.

$$\left.\begin{array}{l} \left(\dfrac{\hat{r}}{\hat{K}}\right) = 0 \\[2ex] \left(\dfrac{\hat{W}_S}{\hat{K}}\right) = 0 \\[2ex] \left(\dfrac{\hat{W}_C}{\hat{K}}\right) = \Theta > 0 \\[2ex] \left(\dfrac{\hat{W}}{\hat{K}}\right) = -\dfrac{\theta_{C1}}{\theta_{L1}}\Theta < 0 \end{array}\right\} \tag{8.A.18}$$

Hence, while FDI raises the child wage, W_C, it lowers the competitive unskilled adult wage, W. The return to capital (r) and the skilled wage (W_S), however, do not change.

Using (8.A.16), (8.A.17) and (8.A.18) and simplifying from expressions (8.A.6)–(8.A.8), we finally arrive at the following results.

$$\left(\frac{\hat{X}_1}{\hat{K}}\right) = -\left[\frac{\lambda_{L2} + \lambda_{K2}B_1\Theta}{|\lambda|^{LK}}\right] < 0 \Bigg\} \tag{8.A.6.1}$$

$$\left(\frac{\hat{X}_2}{\hat{K}}\right) = \left[\frac{\lambda_{L1} + \lambda_{K1}B_1\Theta}{|\lambda|^{LK}}\right] > 0 \Bigg\} \tag{8.A.7.1}$$

However, the effect of a change in K on X_C is ambiguous.

Using (8.A.9), (8.A.10), (8.A.16) and (8.A.17) and simplifying, from (8.A.8) one finds the following.

$$\left(\frac{\hat{X}_C}{\hat{K}}\right) = \frac{1}{\Psi(|\lambda|)^2}[\lambda_{CC}\lambda_{L2}|\lambda| - \lambda_{CC}\lambda_{L2}A_2\Upsilon_L - A_3\lambda_{CC}\Upsilon_L\lambda_{L1}] \tag{8.A.8.1}$$

Note that $\left(\dfrac{\hat{X}_C}{\hat{K}}\right) > 0$ if $[\lambda_{CC}\lambda_{l2}|\lambda| - \lambda_{CC}\lambda_{l2}A_2\Upsilon_L - A_3\lambda_{CC}\Upsilon_L\lambda_{L1}] < 0$ (8.A.8.2)

because from the stability condition, we know $\psi < 0$ (see 8.A.15).

From (8.A.8.2), it follows that

$$\left(\frac{\hat{X}_C}{\hat{K}}\right) > 0 \text{ if } 1 \geq \frac{|\lambda|}{\Upsilon_L A_2} \tag{8.A.8.3}$$

Appendix 8.5   Effect of FDI flow on aggregate child labour supply

Using (8.6), equation (8.1) can be rewritten as follows.

$$L_C = l_C L_1 = l_C (L - L_2) \tag{8.A.19}$$

Here, l_C is the supply of child labour by each poor unskilled working family and is equal to $[(1 - \gamma)n - \gamma(W/W_C)]$. The level of adult unskilled employment in sector 1 is $L_1 = a_{L1}X_1 = (L - L_2)$, where $L_2 = a_{L2}X_2$ is the adult unskilled employment in sector 2.

Differentiating equations (8.A.19), and $L_2 (= a_{L2}X_2)$, we can, respectively, write

$$\hat{L}_C = -\left[\left(\frac{\gamma W}{l_C W_C}\right)(\hat{W} - \hat{W}_C) + \left(\frac{L_2}{L_1}\right)\hat{L}_2\right] \tag{8.A.20}$$

and

$$\hat{L}_2 = \hat{a}_{L2} + \hat{X}_2 = \hat{X}_2 \tag{8.A.21}$$

Note that $\hat{a}_{L2} = 0$ because W^* is exogenously given and $\hat{r} = 0$ (see 7.A.1). We also note that

$$\hat{l}_C = -\left(\frac{\gamma W}{l_C W_C}\right)(\hat{W} - \hat{W}_C) \tag{8.A.22}$$

Now, using (8.A.15), (8.A.17), (8.A.18), (8.A.7.1), (8.A.21) and (8.A.22) and simplifying, from equation (8.A.20) the following expression can be obtained.

$$\left(\frac{\hat{L}_C}{\hat{K}}\right) = -\left(\frac{L_2 \lambda_{L1}}{L_1 |\lambda|^{LK}}\right) - \left(\frac{\theta_{C1} + \theta_{L1}}{\theta_{L1}}\right)\Theta\left[\left(\frac{L_2}{L_1}\right)\left(\frac{\lambda_{K1}\lambda_{L1}S_{LC}^1}{|\lambda|^{LK}}\right) - \left(\frac{\gamma W}{W_C l_C}\right)\right] \tag{8.A.23}$$

$$(+)(+)(+)$$

From (8.A.23), it follows that

$$\left(\frac{\hat{L}_C}{\hat{K}}\right) < 0 \text{ if } \left(\frac{\lambda_{K1}\lambda_{L1}S_{LC}^1}{|\lambda|^{LK}}\right) \geq \left(\frac{\gamma W}{W_C l_C}\right) \tag{8.A.24}$$

However, one can derive a couple of other sufficient conditions under any one of which $\left|\dfrac{\hat{L}_C}{\hat{K}}\right| < 0$.

It is to be noted from the condition as presented in (8.A.24) that it is satisfied if (i) γ is sufficiently low, and/or (ii) income from child labour in a family relative to adult unskilled income is sufficiently high.

Appendix 8.6   Effect of FDI on sectoral allocation of child labour

The proportions of child labour allocated to sector 1 and sector C are

$$\lambda_{C1}\left(=\frac{a_{C1}X_1}{L_C}\right) \quad \text{and} \quad \lambda_{CC}\left(=\frac{a_{CC}X_C}{L_C}\right), \text{respectively and } (\lambda_{C1}+\lambda_{CC})=1.$$

Now

$$\hat{\lambda}_{C1}=\hat{a}_{C1}+\hat{X}_1-\hat{L}_C=(\hat{a}_{C1}+\hat{X}_1)-(\hat{l}_C+\hat{a}_{L1}+\hat{X}_1)$$

Hence, finally we have

$$\hat{\lambda}_{C1}=(\hat{a}_{C1}-\hat{a}_{L1})-\hat{l}_C \tag{8.A.25}$$

Using (8.A.22) and simplifying, from (8.A.25) we get

$$\hat{\lambda}_{C1}=\left(S_{CL}^1+S_{LC}^1+\frac{\gamma W}{l_C W_C}\right)(\hat{W}-\hat{W}_C)$$

With the help of (8.A.18), from the preceding expression it is easy to derive the following result.

$$\left(\frac{\hat{\lambda}_{C1}}{\hat{K}}\right)=-\left[\left(\frac{\theta_{C1}+\theta_{L1}}{\theta_{L1}}\right)\left(S_{CL}^1+S_{LC}^1+\frac{\gamma W}{l_C W_C}\right)\right]\Theta<0 \tag{8.A.26}$$
$$\qquad\qquad (+)\qquad\qquad (+)\qquad\qquad (+)$$

Because $(\lambda_{C1}+\lambda_{CC})=1$. from (8.A.26) it follows that

$$\left(\frac{\hat{\lambda}_{CC}}{\hat{K}}\right)=-\left[\left(\frac{\lambda_{C1}}{\lambda_{CC}}\right)\left(\frac{\hat{\lambda}_{C1}}{\hat{K}}\right)\right]=\left(\frac{\lambda_{C1}}{\lambda_{CC}}\right)\left[\left(\frac{\theta_{C1}+\theta_{L1}}{\theta_{L1}}\right)\left(S_{CL}^1+S_{LC}^1+\frac{\gamma W}{l_C W_C}\right)\right]\Theta>0 \tag{8.A.27}$$

Hence, inflows of foreign capital unequivocally raise the proportion of child labour employed in sector C.

Appendix 8.7   The consequence of FDI flow on the welfare of the child labour–supplying families

Substituting the optimum values of consumption of commodities (C_1 and C_2) and children's leisure ($n-l_c$) obtained from equations (2.7.1), (2.8.1) and (2.8.2) in the family's utility function (equation (2.2), we get the optimum welfare of each child labour–supplying family as follows.

$$U^*=J\left[\frac{(nW_C+W)}{(W_C)^\gamma}\right] \tag{8.A.28}$$

where U^* stands for the optimum family welfare and $J = \left[\gamma A \left(\dfrac{\alpha}{\gamma} \right)^{\alpha} \left(\dfrac{\beta}{\gamma P_2} \right)^{\beta} \right] > 0$.

Totally differentiating this expression, we get the following.

$$\hat{U}^* = \frac{(l_C W_C \hat{W}_C + W \hat{W})}{(n W_C + W)} \tag{8.A.29}$$

From this expression, it is clear that family welfare is an increasing function of both W and W_C.

Substituting $\hat{W}$ and $\hat{W}_C$ from (8.A.18) in (8.A.29) and simplifying, we get the following.

$$\hat{U}^* = \left(\frac{W W_C}{P_1 X_1} \right) \left(\frac{1}{n W_C + W} \right) [l_C a_{L1} X_1 - a_{C1} X_1] \Theta \hat{K} \tag{8.A.30}$$

Using equations (8.1) and (8.9), from (8.A.30) we finally obtain

$$\left(\frac{\hat{U}^*}{\hat{K}} \right) = \left(\frac{W W_C}{P_1 X_1} \right) \left(\frac{a_{C2} X_2}{n W_C + W} \right) \Theta > 0 \tag{8.A.31}$$

Hence, inflows of foreign capital improve the welfare of each child labour-supplying family.

Notes

1 As per ILO (2013b), the term 'child domestic work' refers to the situation where children aged 5 to 17 years perform domestic tasks in the home of a third party or employer (with or without remuneration).
2 There is no gainsaying that expansion of primary education and incentive schemes like the midday meal program to attract children to school also might have contributed to the reduction in the problem of child labour.
3 See World Development Report (1995), Basu and Van (1998) and Basu (1999, 2000), among others.
4 Certain portions of this chapter have been borrowed from Chaudhuri and Dwibedi (2016, forthcoming).
5 Although this is a simplifying assumption, it is not completely without basis. Agriculture requires inputs like fertilizers, pesticides, weedicides and the like, which are to be used in recommended doses. Now if capital is used to purchase those inputs, the capital-output ratio becomes constant technologically. However, adult labour and child labour are substitutes, and the production function displays the property of constant returns to scale in these two inputs. However, even if the capital-output ratio is not given technologically, the results of the model still hold under an additional sufficient condition incorporating the partial elasticities of substitution between capital and other inputs in sector 1.
6 The existence of high wage in the formal sector can be explained in different ways. However, in the literature on trade and development, it has most commonly been explained either in terms of strict implementation of the minimum wage law of the government or collective bargaining on the part of labour unions with their employers or in terms of efficiency wage considerations of the employers in this sector. See Khan (2007) for more details.

7   The results of the model, however, do not depend on the trade pattern of the country in question.

8   For more information on different aspects of domestic child labour, one can go through ILO (2001).

9   According to an ILO study on domestic child labour in Nepal, more affluent and high-cast households are more likely to employ child workers as domestic help. For more on the employers' profiles of domestic child labour, one can go through ILO (2001).

10   The endogenous determination of the supply function of child labour has been provided in chapter 2.

11   There are two points to be noted here. First, the capital-output ratio in sector 1 (a_{K1}) has been assumed to be technologically given. However, the other two inputs, adult labour and child labour, exhibit CRS between themselves. Second, in sector C child labour is the only input. This implies that a_{CC} is given.

12   The assumption that the poor people do not consume either commodity 3 or commodity C is a simplifying one. However, it may be checked that the qualitative results of this model hold under different sufficient conditions even if this assumption is dropped.

13   It may be checked that the results of the model hold even if one considers a more general form of the demand function. However, the sufficient conditions subject to which some of the results hold would contain terms denoting different elasticities of demand for commodity C.

14   These results have been proved in appendices 8.3 and 8.4.

15   See appendix 8.3.

16   See appendix 8.3.

17   For mathematical derivation see appendix 8.7.

18   See appendix 8.3.

References

Basu, K. (1999): 'Child labour: Cause, consequence, and cure, with remarks on international labour standards', *Journal of Economic Literature*, 37(September), 1083–1119.

Basu, K. (2000): 'The intriguing relationship between adult minimum wage and child labour', *The Economic Journal*, 110(462), C50–C61.

Basu, K. and Van, P.H. (1998): 'The economics of child labour', *American Economic Review*, 88(3), 412–427.

Chaudhuri, S. and Dwibedi, J.K. (2016): 'Foreign direct investment and domestic child labour', *Review of Development Economics* (forthcoming). DOI: 10.1111/rode.12263

ILO. (2001): *Situation of Domestic Child Labourers in Kathmandu: A Rapid Assessment*, International Labour Office, Geneva.

ILO. (2002): 'A future without child labour?', International Labour Conference, 90th Session June 2002, International Labour Office, Geneva.

ILO. (2013a): 'Global child labour trends 2008 to 2012', International Labour Office, International Programme on the Elimination of Child Labour (IPEC), Geneva.

ILO. (2013b): *Making Progress Against Child Labour: Global Estimates and Trends 2000–2012*, International Labour Office, Geneva.

Khan, M.A. (2007): 'The Harris-Todaro hypothesis', PIDE-Working Paper No. 16, Pakistan Institute of Development Economics.

World Development Report. (1995): Published by Oxford University Press for The World Bank.

9 Policy implications of results and sketching the future path of research on child labour

9.1 Introduction

Child labour is a slur on the fair face of the globalized world. Although the magnitude of the problem has decreased in the recent times, the absolute number of child workers continues to be a matter of serious concern for economists, policy makers and social activists, among others.

Poverty has been considered the single largest factor behind the problem of child labour. If we consider the situation up to 2008, we find that antipoverty measures, free primary education policy with different incentive schemes (e.g. provisions for midday meals, enrollment subsidies and distribution of bicycles, school uniforms, shoes etc.) for keeping children in school and other purposes have failed to deliver the goods. Besides, liberalized economic policies like achieving higher rates of growth primarily relying on FDI were believed to work positively on poverty and its allied problems like poverty-induced child labour. These policies were supposed to alter the employment patterns and adult wages, thereby affecting the incidence of child labour and their wages. Unfortunately, despite achieving decent rates of economic growth resulting from abundant inflows of foreign capital in a developing country like India, the gravity of the problem of child labour did not change much at least up to 2008.[1]

In the circumstances, in this volume we have tried to discuss the different facets of the problem of child labour in the developing nations. Our primary focus has been on policy issues. Using several simple general equilibrium models, we have attempted to pinpoint the reasons why the economic liberalism that the developing economies have been pursuing for the last two and a half decades with various domestic policies has not been achieved in any big way. In this context, an important point to be kept in mind is that a policy cannot be called successful even if it works favourably on the child labour problem but at the cost of welfare of the poor families that supply child labour. An ideal policy should be the one that is able to work on both counts.

9.2 Overview and policy implications of results

In general equilibrium models, child labour is treated as an input whose aggregate supply is endogenously determined. Hence, the aggregate supply function of child labour in an economy should have a microeconomic foundation and should be determined from the maximizing behaviour of the working families that supply child labour. Our first task would be to identify the working families from which the supply of child labour comes. If we consider poverty to be the primary factor behind child labour and, believe the luxury axiom of Basu and Van (1998) to be valid, there should be a group of poor adult workers who consider themselves as poor and decide to send many of their children to the job market to supplement low family incomes although they are altruistically concerned about the well-being of their children. Because of these two reasons, the supply function of child labour by a family should come out as a negative function of the family income from nonchild sources and as a positive function of the child wage, suggesting that the income and price effects are positive and negative, respectively. We have exactly found such a supply function of child labour proceeding with a Cobb-Douglas type of family utility function.

Then, comes the question of production technology. Because adult labour and child labour are two inputs of production, a relevant question is what the relationship between these two inputs is. Are they complementary to each other or substitutes? Empirical evidence rules out the possibility of complementarity between these two inputs. No production activities can be cited where child labour cannot be substituted by adult labour, refuting the so-called nimble fingers argument. Hence, these two factors are substitutes. The degree of substitutability, however, varies from one activity to the other. In the simplest possible case where these two are perfect substitutes, the family supply of child labour becomes constant, suggesting that the income effect and the price effect are equally strong, thus cancelling out each other's effects. On the other hand, when the two types of labour are imperfect substitutes, the family supply function comes out as a decreasing function of the ratio between adult wage and child wage. The child wage is the opportunity cost of children's leisure. If given the child wage (adult wage), the adult wage (child wage) rises, the supply of child labour falls (rises) due to a positive income effect (negative price effect). In such a static optimization exercise of the household, the aspect of skill formation and its role on its supply decision regarding child labour have not been considered.

Subsequently, however, we have considered an intertemporal decision-making problem of the household where there is provision for skill formation on the part of some of the children in the household. The guardian is endowed with a given child labour time that he allocates in the current period between work and schooling. Children who work in the current period grow as unskilled workers in the future, although they immediately contribute to family income. On the contrary, children attending school in the current period do not immediately contribute anything to the family income, although they become skilled workers in the future and earn the skilled wage, which is higher than the unskilled wage. An interior solution is attained at the point where the marginal loss in current family income equals the discounted marginal future benefit. The supply function of child labour derived in the process is a positive function of the current income of the household from nonchild sources due to the positive income effect and a negative function of the child wage because of the negative price effect. On the other hand, the supply of child labour decreases with an increase in the return to education because it makes schooling more attractive.

These are some of the supply functions of child labour by a family under different circumstances, which we have used in the preceding chapters.

Trade sanction against the products that the developing countries export and that contain child labour in certain stages of production is a highly controversial issue. It is held that the WTO has advocated this instrument in order to rob the developing nations of their comparative advantages in certain labour-intensive commodities, citing humanitarian reasons. However, the Bangladeshi experience showed that such a policy would make the child workers and their families severely worse off.[2] Besides, according to UNICEF (1997), only 5 per cent of child workers in the developing world are engaged in the exports sector. Hence, trade sanction is not the right approach to the problem of child labour in the developing world. In terms of a three-sector, full-employment general equilibrium model with a nontraded final agricultural commodity, it has been shown that trade sanction on the internationally traded agricultural commodity that uses child labour only to an insignificant extent not only unequivocally aggravates the child labour problem in the society but also makes the poor child labour–supplying families worse off. Then, a three-sector Harris and Todaro (1970) type of dynamic general equilibrium model has been built up where there is provision for skill formation and child labour is used only in the rural sector in order to show that, although trade sanction on the agricultural commodity might lower the gravity of the child labour problem, the policy unambiguously raises the urban unemployment problem of adult unskilled labour and lowers the welfare of the families that supply child labour. Thus, the results of both of these models demonstrate that the advocacy by the WTO and certain developed nations like the U.S. in favour of imposing trade sanctions on exports by the developing world in order to fight against child labour may not have any sound theoretical basis.

The developing nations are plagued with problems. Some of the most significant of them are low rates of economic growth, poverty and inequality, involuntary unemployment problem and incidence of child labour and the like. If one scrutinizes the nature of market interventions by the governments in the developing countries like India one would come across diverse economic policies that are being pursued to address these problems. Often two or more policies are simultaneously undertaken by the authority to mitigate a single problem. The policies designed to alleviate a specific problem may also indirectly affect other problems because different sectors of an economy are interlinked with one another in different ways. Hence, it quite possible that different policies undertaken concurrently to take care of varied problems may nullify each other's effects, thereby producing very little or no impact on the extent of a particular problem. To show how this is at least theoretically possible, a three-sector, full-employment general equilibrium model has been developed where child labour and adult labour are assumed perfect substitutes. There are two informal sectors, with one of them producing a nontraded input for the formal manufacturing sector. In this setting, the net outcome of four different policies – an education subsidy scheme providing short-term pecuniary benefits to the guardians of the schoolgoing children, an agricultural price subsidy, trade liberalization in the form of tariff reduction and an liberalized investment policy resulting in higher FDI flow – are examined in light of the aggregate supply of child labour in the economy. The analysis has found that these policies always produce mutually opposite effects on the child labour problem. Therefore, if all of them are simultaneously adopted, the net effect could go either way depending on the values of different parameters of the system.

As mentioned at several earlier places, abject poverty has been the single largest factor behind the incidence of child labour in the developing countries. Hence, it follows that the eradication of poverty is a necessity for alleviating child labour. A two-period, three-sector full-employment general equilibrium model with provision for skill formation for children through schooling has been developed with an eye to identifying the different possible channels through which economic liberalism (e.g. FDI flow) or a domestic policy designed to address the problem of child labour works. The supply function of child labour has been derived from the intertemporal family welfare-maximizing behaviour of the households. The analysis has identified three such channels: an increase in the initial income of the household from no-child sources (eradication of poverty), a decrease in earning opportunities for children (reduction in child wage) and the increase in the return to education. Hence, even if the first factor does not work favourably the incidence of child labour in the society can indeed fall only if the combined favourable effect of the remaining two factors can dominate the first effect. Therefore, the analysis shows that the reduction of poverty is not a prerequisite for the child labour problem to ameliorate. The policy implications of this analysis are that the regulatory authority should not only make use of poverty eradication programs but also should give sufficient emphasis on improving the return to education through improving the quality of the education system and on resorting to different incentive schemes to keep children in school.[3]

The government of a developing country often resorts to different agricultural subsidy policies with an eye to mitigating poverty. Because more than 50 per cent of the working population, directly or indirectly, still heavily relies on agriculture to earn their livelihoods, it is expected that such subsidy programs would ultimately benefit the poorer segment of the working class.[4] If the economic conditions of this class improve, it would lead to less poverty and hence less poverty-induced child labour. On the other hand, agricultural dualism is an important feature of the developing nations where backward agriculture and modern (advanced) agriculture coexist in a rural economy. In backward agriculture, child labour is intensively used in many of the stages of production. On the contrary, in advanced agriculture, because of modern methods of cultivation, child labour is hardly ever used. Using a three-sector full-employment model with agricultural dualism, it has been found that a price subsidy policy to backward agriculture aggravates the incidence of child labour, although it improves the welfare of the families that supply child labour, whereas a price and/or a credit subsidy policy to advanced agriculture produces exactly the opposite effects. These results question the desirability of agricultural subsidy policies from the perspective of mitigating both child labour and poverty. Besides, subsidy policies produce distortions in both commodity and factor markets that lower social welfare. In this backdrop, it has been shown that a scheme of direct cash transfer to poor households that may be financed by lump-sum taxes on the richer segment of the society not only succeeds to fight against child labour but also improves the welfare of the poor working families.

Next, it has been shown that the midday meal program and other incentive programs providing short-term pecuniary benefits to the households that send at least some of their children to school so that human capital formation takes place over time may fail to deliver the goods. Although these schemes are very popular and widely applied in different developing countries to fight against child labour, the analysis theoretically establishes that the desirable outcome may not always be guaranteed. A three-sector, full-employment general equilibrium model has been built up for the analytical purpose where there is scope for the acquisition of skills on the part of the children attending school in the current period. The basic result of the model is that an incentive program like midday meals, designed to keep children in school, may backfire and increase the incidence of child labour in the society by decreasing both unskilled wage and the return to education under suitable parametric restrictions.

A peculiar and new dimension of the child labour problem in recent times is the one of the increasing use of child labour, both in absolute and relative terms, in providing domestic services to the richer segment of the population of the society. This problem is peculiar because even though the overall incidence has decreased over the last few years (ILO 2013), the use of children in such activities, which are hazardous and highly exploitative in nature, has been increasing. This aspect has been theoretically analyzed in terms of a four-sector, full-employment general equilibrium model where, apart from agriculture, child labour is also used to provide nontraded services to the richer segment of the population. The richer segment of the population is comprised of the capitalists, skilled workers and the highly paid adult unskilled workers employed in the unionized low-skill manufacturing sector. FDI-led economic growth raises the aggregate income of the rich people, thereby increasing the demand for the nontraded services. The analysis has found that even if the policy mitigates the problem of child labour in aggregative sense, it drives child workers to the services sector in an increased proportion. The analysis has then explained the necessity of a composite policy that should accompany the liberalized investment policy so that the undesirable effect of FDI-led growth on domestic child labour can be taken care of. One such supplementary composite policy could be imposition of lump-sum taxes on rich people and the redistribution of the tax proceeds in favour of the poor unskilled workers through the direct cash transfer program. It has been verbally explained why such a supplementary policy is likely to be successful, especially when economic growth alone fails to address the problem of domestic child labour.

Thus, our theoretical analyses of many of the facets of the problem of child labour in the developing world conducted through several general equilibrium models that capture different real-life situations reveal that the existing policies designed to fight against the menace of child labour are not indeed unmixed blessings. Some of them help to mitigate the problem but worsen the welfare of the poor families that supply child labour, while some others produce exactly the opposite effects. The existing policies ranging from trade sanctions, liberalized trade and investment policies to domestic policies like education subsidies providing immediate monetary benefits, agricultural subsidy programs and so on have their own shortcomings and may fail to fulfill their objective(s) under different situations. While establishing the possibilities of failure of the existing instruments in a few chapters, it has been analytically shown or verbally argued that a redistribution of income from rich to the poor is expected to be more effective in addressing the problem. However, the existing mechanisms of redistribution, such as through conventional subsidies designed to uplift the poor people above the poverty line, might lead to paradoxical situations where the child labour problem goes up while the impoverished people experience deterioration in their welfare. Besides, price and input subsidies distort both factor and commodity markets and lead to the misallocation of economic resources thereby lowering national welfare. Moreover, due to bureaucratic formalities and rampant corruption in the delivery mechanism, subsidies in many of the cases do not reach the target group. We have shown that the redistribution of income should take place through the route of imposing lump-sum taxes on the rich and the redistribution of the tax proceeds via direct cash transfer to the poor. It is gleefully noted that India has already made it mandatory to transfer many of the subsidies directly to the bank accounts of the target group through the Aaadhar Card scheme.

9.3 Scope for future research

Globalization is a complex process with many facets. Some aspects of globalization may create difficulties for poor households with children, while there could be some other that may help in reducing the child labour problem. Consumerism, a natural by-product of globalization, might be a factor responsible for the increasing child labour incidence in the high growth–prone areas. Globalization perpetuates consumerism and encourages values based on individuals' freedom to pursue their own monetary interests, resulting in societies obsessed with consuming. It implies a trend towards commodification, which is manifested by an eagerness to acquire new goods and services. As the UN Commission on Sustainable Development, 7th Session (1999) points out, "[C]onsumption and production patterns in developed countries strongly influenced patterns in developing countries, particularly in the context of globalization and trade liberalization. This occurred not only through trade and investment, but also through communication, mass media, advertising and marketing". In this age of increasing influence of information technology and media, even the underprivileged segments of the developing world are lured by consumerism. As viewed by FAO (2005), the consumption pattern of even urban low-income groups is showing significant change towards noncereal consumption and more towards industrial items. Rao (2000) has pointed out that demonstration effect and the availability of a variety of foods could be some of the reasons behind the change in the consumption pattern in the case of India. Strong demonstration effects not only affected food consumption pattern, it also resulted in increased preference for disposables and nonessential luxury items. Using data from the National Home Sampling Survey, carried out in 2001 in Brazil, Sawaya et al. (2005) have shown how globalization influenced consumption and dietary pattern in Brazil. For example their study reveals that television ownership has permeated all layers of the society, from the upper and middle classes to less privileged areas. In the poorest urban areas such as Natal, in the state of Maranhão, the penetration of television sets was close to 86 per cent. Television is today the main source of entertainment, even for lower-income families, who spend five to eight hours a day in front of the television. As the developing economies are moving towards a world of homogeneous consumption, the poorer segments of the society are finding it difficult to maintain their relative consumption standard.

As mentioned on several occasions, poverty is believed to be the single largest force behind the problem of child labour. If we accept the luxury axiom of Basu and Van (1998),assume that poor households send out their children to work only when their family incomes from nonchild sources fall below a certain critical level. However, the critical level itself is not constant, and in the present consumerist society, the minimum acceptable income limit is indeed increasing. Hence, even if globalization raises the earning opportunities of the poor, it may be insufficient (given a modest trickle-down effect) for them to maintain the relative consumption standard. Consequently, they may use the only means in their possession, their hapless children, for higher earnings.[5] In this way, globalization may push the poor households to use their only wealth, their children, to support growing consumption needs in a consumerist society.[6]

Besides, in this book, we have not paid any attention to the role of credit market imperfection behind the problem of child labour. Some works in the literature, such as Ranjan (1999, 2001) and Jafarey and Lahiri (2002, 2005), have discussed different dimensions of the problem in the presence of credit market imperfection using either partial or general equilibrium structures. The contributions of these papers have been discussed in different places of this volume. However, there is further scope for future research in this area. An important dimension of the credit market imperfection is the interaction between formal and informal credit markets. In a developing country like India, there are two different sources of credit to the borrowers: a *formal* credit market comprised of commercial banks, regional rural banks, credit cooperatives and the like and an *informal* credit market consisting of professional moneylenders, traders, landlords and so on. The formal credit market is competitive and supplies credit to the organized production sectors of the economy at relatively low rates of interest. On the contrary, the informal credit market is characterized by high degrees of imperfection and is found to be the major source of credit to the unorganized production sectors like agriculture, urban informal sector and so on. Professional moneylenders, having local monopolistic power arising out of their intimate knowledge about borrowers, charge exorbitantly high rates of interest. In the presence of formal credit, a market for informal credit exists either because the supply of formal credit is inadequate or because there is a delay in the disbursement of formal credit. The interactions of the two credit markets are expected to play a crucial role in the determination of the informal interest rate and hence the incidence of child labour that arises out of credit market imperfection.[7]

Furthermore, in our analyses of different aspects of child labour, we have concentrated only on altruistic and mutually altruistic households. However, in the developing countries, we come across several cases where parents sell their children to human traffickers or engage them in prostitution and other illegal activities for the sake of their own interest. The behaviour of this type of selfish guardian has been analyzed by Gupta (2000) using a partial equilibrium framework. To a selfish guardian, a child is like an asset that can be leased for rental income. To the employer, a child worker is like a machine that can fetch a profit. Gupta (2000) has assumed the so-called consumption efficiency hypothesis (CEH) of Leibenstein (1957) to be valid so that the nutritional efficiency of child workers is a positive function of their level of consumption. The child wage consists of two components: a meal component and a cash component. The child worker consumes the meal component while the guardian appropriates the cash component for his own consumption. Nonetheless, the higher the level of consumption of child workers, the higher their physical efficiency and hence the higher would be the level of output produced by them. Quite naturally, the employer (selfish guardian) would like to increase the meal (cash) component to the extent possible. The employer and the guardian play a bargaining game jointly determining the child wage and its composition of meal and cash components. In the case of a selfish guardian, there would always occur a corner solution; that is, he will always send all of his children to the job market in order to maximize his own consumption/income. However, if some costs are associated with child-rearing at least up to age when the children can be sent out to work, an interior solution would have occurred. Such costs are met through borrowing from the credit market. The number of children that the guardian would like to have would come out from the condition of equality between the marginal cost of having an additional child and the marginal income that the additional child fetches. The cost function of child-rearing must satisfy some essential properties so that the second-order condition of maximization of the guardian's income is satisfied. The marginal cost must be rising at a nondecreasing rate with the number of children. Why this marginal cost is nondecreasing may be explained in terms credit market imperfection. Once the supply function of child labour is derived, it is to be fitted into a general equilibrium model to find out appropriate policies that can address the problem under this situation. It should, however, be emphasized that the aspect of child-rearing should ideally be studied in a dynamic set-up.

Another important dimension of the problem is the role of women empowerment. Traditionally, in the male-dominated society of a developing country like India, all household decisions, including children's schooling and labour supply, are unilaterally taken by the male member of a family. In many of the cases, it is seen that women are not allowed to work outside and add to family incomes. Women themselves tend to put more weight on the need to care for their children and dependents than to work outside. This choice is strengthened by social norms that place much emphasis on domestic tasks as a woman's primary responsibility. These norms are relatively much more stringent in the rural areas vis-à-vis cities. However, in the cases where women work outside and earn independently compared to men, they spend a significantly higher proportion of their income on purchases of goods and services that promote the nutrition, health and education of their children and general well-being of their families (Duncan 1997; Quisumbing et al. 1998; Kurz and Welch 2000). On the contrary, men tend to spend most of their income on nonfood items and their personal luxury articles, like alcohol and cigarettes, or reinvest it in their work or businesses (Guyer 1988; Hoddinott and Haddad 1995; Anderson and Baland 2002). Hence, it is quite likely that women empowerment leading to an increase in their bargaining power within the family would lower the supply of child labour by a working family.

Nonetheless, what would happen to the aggregate supply of child labour in the society requires systematic theoretical analysis using suitable general equilibrium models. This is because, even though the family supply of child labour decreases following an increase in the intrahousehold bargaining power of the women, the number of poor families that supply child labour might increase due the adult labour reallocation effect. The overall problem of child labour in the economy goes up if the second effect dominates over the former.

One of the other notable directions in which future research may be conducted is as follows. With globalization and easier access to higher education, especially for those who can afford the costs of higher education, women are increasingly becoming qualified for high-skill jobs. This is particularly the situation in and around the cities. Because these females are being increasingly engaged in outside jobs, they do not find enough time to do their household activities themselves. Consequently, they require domestic help for looking after their household jobs. This is also economical for these skilled female workers because the skilled wage is higher than the adult unskilled/child wage. This might be one of the reasons why the demand for child labour has significantly increased in recent times. The model that we have employed to analyze the problem of domestic child labour in chapter 8 cannot be used in this case. The reason is that, to capture the present scenario, one has to construct a suitable general equilibrium model, where the supply of aggregate skilled female labour is also endogenously determined.

Future policy-based theoretical research dealing with the aforesaid aspects of the child labour problem is highly welcome.

Notes

1　See ILO (2012).
2　See note 1 in chapter 3.
3　Some of these issues have been discussed in Jafarey and Lahiri (2005).
4　As per Indian Census 2011, about 54.6 per cent of the working population is engaged in agricultural activities in India.
5　Even though some developing countries like India and China have managed to grasp the opportunities of globalization in terms of higher rate of growth in GDP, due to little trickle-down, inequality is increasing. Strong economic growth has failed to translate into significant reductions in poverty in these countries. For others, the situation is even worse. One may go through Tendulkar et al. (1996), Khan (1998), Wade and Wolf (2002), Riskin (2004), Sen and Himanshu (2004), Wade (2004), Reddy and Minoiu (2005) and Basu (2006) for more details on this issue.
6　Some argue that consumerism in the north displaced the problem to other southern countries with lenient labour policies concerning child workers. Their desire for cheaper goods allows for the exploitation of vulnerable children in manufacturing and other industries. Based on this argument, they advocate policies like social labeling or even banning the importation of products produced by children, which will discourage consumption and weaken the pull effect. Nevertheless, given the fact that only 5 per cent of child workers in the developing world are engaged in the exports sector (UNICEF 1997), the strength of this pull effect is not expected to be very large. However, one cannot ignore the pull effect of the increase in domestic consumption of goods and services produced by child labour. See Chaudhuri and Dwibedi (2007) in this context.
7　Chaudhuri and Gupta (1996), Gupta and Chaudhuri (1997), Chaudhuri (2001) and Chaudhuri and Ghosh Dastidar (2011), among others, are some of the works

that provide a theory of interest rate determination in the informal credit market in the presence of formal credit using partial equilibrium structures. On the other hand, Chaudhuri and Gupta (2014) have provided such a theory in terms of a three-sector general equilibrium model, starting from the microeconomic behaviour of the informal sector lender in an imperfectly competitive credit market.

References

Anderson, S. and Baland, J.M. (2002): 'The economics of Roscas and intrahousehold resource allocation', *The Quarterly Journal of Economics*, 117(3): 963–995.

Anti-slavery Reporter. (1996): 'Child labour and the social clause', Series VIII, 2(4), November 6–7.

Basu, K. (2006): 'Globalisation, poverty and inequality: What is the relationship? What can be done?', *World Development*, 34(8), 1361–1373.

Basu, K. and Van, P.H. (1998): 'The economics of child labour', *American Economic Review*, 88(3), 412–427.

Chaudhuri, S. (2001): 'Interaction of formal and informal credit markets in backward agriculture: A theoretical note', *Indian Economic Review*, 36(2), 411–428.

Chaudhuri, S. and Dastidar, K.G. (2011): 'Corruption in a model of vertical linkage between formal and informal credit sources and credit subsidy policy', *Economic Modelling*, 28(6), 2596–2599.

Chaudhuri, S. and Dwibedi, J.K. (2007): 'Foreign capital inflow, fiscal policies and incidence of child labour in a developing economy', *The Manchester School*, 75(1), 17–46.

Chaudhuri, S. and Gupta, M.R. (1996): 'Delayed formal credit, bribing and the informal credit market in agriculture: A theoretical analysis', *Journal of Development Economics*, 51(2), 433–449.

Chaudhuri, S. and Gupta, M.R. (2014): 'International factor mobility, informal interest rate and capital market imperfection: A general equilibrium analysis', *Economic Modelling*, 37, 184–192.

Duncan, T. (1997): 'Incomes, expenditures and health outcomes: Evidence on intrahousehold resource allocation', in: L. Haddad, J. Hoddinott and H. Alderman (eds.), *Intrahousehold Resource Allocation in Developing Countries: Models, Methods and Policy*, Johns Hopkins University Press, Baltimore and London, 142–164.

FAO. (2005): 'Globalisation of food systems in developing countries: Impact on food security and nutrition', FAO Food and Nutrition Series 83. Available at: ftp://ftp.fao.org/docrep/fao/007/y5736e/y5736e02.pdf

Gupta, M.R. (2000): 'Wage determination of a child worker: A theoretical analysis', *Review of Development Economics*, 4(2), 219–228.

Gupta, M.R. and Chaudhuri, S. (1997): 'Formal credit, corruption and the informal credit market in agriculture: A theoretical analysis', *Economica*, 64, 331–343.

Guyer, J. (1988): 'Dynamic approaches to domestic budgeting: Cases and methods from Africa', in: D. Dwyer and J. Bruce (eds.), *A Home Divided: Women and Income in the Third World*, Stanford University Press, Palo Alto, CA, 155–172.

Harris, J.R. and Todaro, M.P. (1970): 'Migration, unemployment and development: A two-sector analysis', *American Economic Review*, 60, 126–142.

Hoddinott, J. and Haddad, L. (1995): 'Does female income share influence household expenditure? Evidence from Cote d'Ivoire', *Oxford Bulletin of Economics and Statistics*, LVII, 77–97.

ILO. (2012): *Making Progress Against Child Labour: Global Estimates and Trends 2000–2012*, International Labour Office, Geneva.

ILO. (2013): *Global Child Labour Trends 2008 to 2012*, International Labour Office, International Programme on the Elimination of Child Labour (IPEC), Geneva.

Jafarey, S. and Lahiri, S. (2002): 'Will trade sanctions reduce child labour? The role of credit markets', *Journal of Development Economics*, 68(1), 137–156.

Jafarey, S. and Lahiri, S. (2005): 'Food for education versus school quality: A comparison of policy options to reduce child labour', *Canadian Journal of Economics*, 38(2), 394–419.

Khan, A.R. (1998): 'The impact of globalization in South Asia', in: A.S. Bhalla (ed.), *Globalization, Growth and Marginalization*, Macmillan, London.

Kurz, K.M. and Welch, C.J. (2000): 'Enhancing nutrition results: The case for a women's resources approach', International Center for Research on Women.

Leibenstein, H. (1957): *Economic Backwardness and Economic Growth*, John Wiley, New York.

Quisumbing, A.R., Haddad, L., Meinzen-Dick, R. and Brown, L.R. (1998): 'Gender issues for food security in developing countries: Implications for project design and implementation', *Canadian Journal of Development Studies*, XIX (Special Issue), 185–208.

Ranjan, P. (1999): 'An economic analysis of child labour', *Economic Letters*, 64, 99–105.

Ranjan, P. (2001): 'Credit constraints and the phenomenon of child labour', *Journal of Development Economics*, 64, 81–102.

Rao, H.C. (2000): 'Declining demand for food grains in rural India: Implications', *Economic and Political Weekly*, 35(4), 201–206.

Reddy, S. and Minoiu, C. (2005): 'Chinese poverty: Assessing the impact of alternative assumptions', *Review of Income and Wealth*, 47(3), 283–300.

Riskin, C. (2004): 'The fall in Chinese poverty: Issues of measurement, incidence and cause', Columbia University Mimeograph. Available at: http://www.peri.umass.edu/fileadmin/pdf/conference_papers/Riskin_paperA.pdf

Sawaya, A.L., Martins, P.A. and Martins, V.J.B. (2005): 'Impact of globalization on food consumption, health and nutrition in urban areas: A case study of Brazil', FAO Food and Nutrition Series 83. Available at: ftp://ftp.fao.org/docrep/fao/007/y5736e/y5736e02.pdf

Sen, A. and Himanshu. (2004): 'Poverty and inequality in India: I', *Economic and Political Weekly*, 39(38), 4247–4263.

Tendulkar, S., Sundaram, D.K. and Jain, L.R. (1996): 'Macroeconomic policies and poverty in India 1966–67 to 1993–94', Monograph, ILO, New Delhi.

UN Commission on Sustainable Development. (1999): 'Consumption and production patterns – Decisions of the General Assembly and the Commission on Sustainable Development, The UN', 7th Session New York, 19–30 April 1999.

UNICEF. (1997): 'The state of the world's children', Oxford University, Oxford.

Wade, R.H. (2004): 'Is globalization reducing poverty and inequality?', *World Development*, 32(4), 567–589.

Wade, R.H. and Wolf, M. (2002): 'Are global poverty and inequality getting worse?', Exchange of Letters Published in Prospect Magazine, UK. Available at: http://www.prospectmagazine

Author index

Subject index

For Product Safety Concerns and Information please contact our EU
representative GPSR@taylorandfrancis.com
Taylor & Francis Verlag GmbH, Kaufingerstraße 24, 80331 München, Germany

www.ingramcontent.com/pod-product-compliance
Ingram Content Group UK Ltd.
Pitfield, Milton Keynes, MK11 3LW, UK
UKHW020951180425
457613UK00019B/628

* 9 7 8 0 3 6 7 3 7 4 6 5 5 *